# Teaching
## MotionDesign

**Course Offerings and Class Projects from the Leading Undergraduate and Graduate Programs**

Edited by **Steven Heller and Michael Dooley**

70123173

12   11   10   09   08                    5   4   3   2   1

Published by Allworth Press
An imprint of Allworth Communications, Inc.
10 East 23rd Street, New York, NY 10010

Cover and interior design by James Victore

Page composition/typography by Integra Software Services, Pvt., Ltd., Pondicherry, India

ISBN-13: 978-1-58115-504-4
ISBN-10: 1-58115-504-2

Library of Congress Cataloging-in-Publication Data

Teaching motion design: course offerings and class projects from the leading undergraduate and graduate programs / edited By Steven Heller and Michael Dooley.
    p. cm.
Includes index.
  ISBN-13: 978-1-58115-504-4 (pbk.)
  ISBN-10: 1-58115-504-2 (pbk.)
1. Computer animation—Study and teaching (Higher)—United States.   2. Computer graphics—Study and teaching (Higher)—United States.   3. Computer animation—Vocational guidance—United States.   4. Computer graphics—Vocational guidance—United States.   I. Heller, Steven.   II. Dooley, Michael (Michael Patrick), 1948–

  TR897.7.T43 2008
  006.6'9602373—dc22

                                                                                2007040588

Printed in the United States of America.

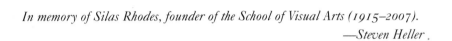

*In memory of Silas Rhodes, founder of the School of Visual Arts (1915–2007).*
*—Steven Heller .*

*To my son, Christopher Dooley, with admiration and respect for all you've put in motion.*
*—Michael Dooley*

*contents*

## Section 1: Freshman

## Section 2: Sophomores

## Section 4: Seniors

# Section 5: Graduate

# To Move or Not to Move:
# It's No Longer a Question

When I am asked—as is often the case—"What has been the most significant change in graphic design practice over the past decade?" one, two-syllable word comes to mind: motion.

Owing to the desktop-accessibility and user-friendliness of such programs as After Effects, Final Cut Pro, and Flash (to name the most popular software, though there are others), motion is no longer a complicated or even novel add-on to design; it's a requisite for almost all media, even print. In fact, otherwise conventional newspapers and magazines are now relying heavily on produced video segments for the Web or as podcasts, not simply to augment conventional news and feature coverage but to provide alternative means of storytelling. The role of the graphic designer is, therefore, no longer limited to moving type around on the printed page (or screen) but has expanded to injecting kinetic assets into presentations. Graphic designers are migrating into fields that were once exotic, but now are endemic.

So when addressing how graphic designers—if that is even the best term for the new breed of twenty-first century visual communicators—should be educated now and in the near future, while training in typography and composition are still formidable, motion literacy is essential. Moreover, it is largely integral to the ways in which the new generation of design scholars is thinking anyway. Static is out, movement is in.

Most high schools have been less than enthusiastic about teaching graphic design (and typography) as part of a well-rounded arts education curriculum, but with the widespread availability of video and animation software, and low-cost hardware—as well as a the boom in YouTube and other video sharing Web sites— videography is currently almost as routine as the three R's and just as essential to visual literacy. Many art schools, not to mention media arts programs in universities, require at least a basic understanding of the tools and aesthetics of motion design. Soon, if not already, motion will be viewed as a language skill, every bit as necessary as writing. In high school my son, who is now in film school, was encouraged to write scripts for videos he would present as veritable "essays" in subject areas like English, history, and even science.

Linking the word "design" to motion is not new; there have been motion design pioneers going back to the early days of film and television. Yet it will surely become more common as greater needs for motion on TV, the Web, and numerous hand-held devices now available expand in the marketplace. And the integration of type, picture, and sound (sound design is another huge growth area) has already made its impact known throughout school and industry. My coeditor's son, Chris (see page 241), for example, went from studying traditional graphic design to founding a firm devoted to making graphics for television and the Web. But those graphics are not simply the special effects that are sewn into another director's overall work but rather integral motion pieces, often with their own beginnings, middles, and ends. With advanced motion capabilities (literacy *and* expertise) designers have become producers, directors, and overall creators of everything from motion shorts to features, destined for anything from the Internet to the silver screen, from television shows to games.

This Allworth Press "Teaching" series of syllabi has already covered graphic design and illustration, two component parts of the visual communications matrix. Typography logically folded into graphic design, and writing folded into illustration (what with the surge in graphic novels). Each collection of syllabi includes a few courses in motion as well, but these were viewed as more ancillary than primary. *Teaching Motion Design* is a consequence of the increased integration of these essential disciplines with kinetics. Where once the skill set of a film or television title-sequence designer, for instance, was some kind of hybrid within the graphic design and film industries (although among the former it was a kind of exalted or romantic pursuit), now it is the norm. For a graphic designer not to know how to make type move, or for a filmmaker not to have competency with animated type and other graphic effects, suggests an anomaly. With motion as the glue, combining graphics, typography, and narrative storytelling is the new inclusive commercial art.

But it is not necessary to convince the reader that this field has erupted into one of the largest of the commercial arts or that to be skilled in its practice is indispensable for anyone engaged in graphic, film, video typography, game, Web, and future design areas. *Teaching Motion Design* is a response to the changing world of graphic design and design education and, if you like, an interim report on the various methods currently being taught. There is not one graphic design program we have surveyed that does not include motion in its curriculum. Although some are quite rudimentary approaches, the range is wide and the expected outcomes vast—from introduction to motion theory to creating professional music videos. This is the first compilation to make these respective course offerings available so that some educators can begin to build motion offshoots or departments, while others can see what is missing in the burgeoning field of study.

*Steven Heller*

# Genesis of the Book

In the beginning was the image.

And the image was chiseled into the dark cave walls of the earth. And the image evolved from carvings on stone to paint on papyrus and multiplied and begat sequences. And invention begat the Phenakistoscope and Zoetrope, and lo, the images moved. And the brothers Lumière said, "Let there be celluloid projections," and screens were populated with living creatures and graphic images for the world to behold.

And Winsor McCay re-created caves and dinosaurs, and Georges Méliès re-created the moon and the heavens, and both took the actions of humans and melded them with the graphics of motion. And many forms blossomed and became abundant, and blessed were Émile Cohl, Richard Williams, and John and Faith Hubley.

And shadow puppetry begat Lotte Reininger, Jiri Trnka, and the brothers Quay. And Léopold Survage created motion abstraction, which brought forth Oskar Fischinger, Mary Ellen Bute, Ed Emshwiller, and Norman McLaren. And Raoul Barré created the motion studio, which produced Disney, Fleischer, Zagreb, and UPA. And the cinema produced Saul Bass, Pablo Ferro, and Kyle Cooper.

And technology created the computer, which brought forth John Whitney, Stan VanDerBeek, and Pixar. And ink was transfigured into pixels and Bezier curves and wire frame modeling.

And there were many wise and gifted instructors from venerable institutions of wisdom and learning who preached the gospels of motion graphics.

And their words were made text, rich with a multiplicity of voices and visions.

Thus Chris Perry, Graham Elliott, and others spoke unto their disciples of interfaces, interactivity, digital video, 3-D modeling, music video, multimedia, and many other varieties of motion. And Christian Hill, Karen Zimmermann, and others spoke of historical processes and contemporary productions.

And thus Laurie Burruss, Matt Normand, and others spoke of theories, practices, and principles. And Heather Shaw, Sarah Lowe, Jeff Miller, Brian Lucid, and others spoke of space, sound, storyboards, and structural organization. And Isabel Meirelles, Martin Venezky, Peter Byrne, Tony Brock, and others spoke of time-based text and typography.

And thus Tracy Colby, Liisa Salonen, John Canemaker, Mike Nguyen, Chad Reichert, and others spoke of content, characterization, emotional engagement, storytelling, and nonnarrative expression.

And Jay Chapman proclaimed unto the disciples, "Your images move yet your bodies are like stones; lay down your pens and stylus pads, arise from your desks and workstations, and move in time and space, and dance."

And the disciples created, and they beheld what they made, and saw that it was good.

And as a unity the instructors commanded, "You have partaken of the fruits of our knowledge and nourished yourselves. Now by your actions you will be known, so go forth and evolve, and multiply."

Thus it was done, and the earth marveled and rejoiced.

xvi

*Michael Dooley*

# section 1

### freshman

COURSE TITLE: Fundamentals of Usability
TEACHERS: Amy Smith and John Barton
FREQUENCY: One Semester
LEVEL: Undergraduate
CREDITS: 3
DEGREE: Bachelor of Fine Arts
SCHOOL: College of Visual Arts, St. Paul, MN

## summary and goals

This class focuses on the fundamentals of user-centered design and usability issues surrounding Web-based interfaces (Internet, PDA, cell, etc.). We examine information architecture models, content/design relationships, user behaviors, and user testing scenarios. The goal is ultimately to develop awareness of the pitfalls of poor design and usability while honing good design habits.

Outcomes:

- Analyze the usability of the Web (content and navigation).
- Examine content hierarchy.
- Emphasize content/design relationships.
- Capitalize on user conventions and discuss what they are.
- Examine users' mental and conceptual models of the Web.
- Analyze "Hunter vs. Gatherer" psychology.
- Research content digestion and retention.
- Examine project workflow and find or develop efficiencies.

Technology: Students use the following development tools: Photoshop, ImageReady, Microsoft Word, and Dreamweaver. Final testing is typically done with a variety of Web browsers: Firefox, Safari, Internet Explorer.

## assignments and projects

### 1. Online Journal and Staging Web Site (on-going assignment)

Maintain a personal and individual online production journal throughout the entire semester. This journal will primarily act as a practice/staging area for the coding and testing of interface ideas. In addition to uploading coursework, the journal may also contain links to favorite Web sites, personal writings, portfolios, etc.

## 2. Writing for the Web (2 class periods: discussion and assignment)

Review and discuss online writing techniques. Students will select a short body of text to rewrite based upon the studies of writing for the Web.

## 3. Homepage Redesign (2 weeks)

Select a homepage that suffers from usability issues and put together a "design action plan," execute the design, conduct user testing, and do revisions as necessary.

## 4. Task-Based Design 1: Media Player (4 weeks)

With a group, research and create a "media player" that will support video, audio, and photos. Students are expected to analyze the specific TASKS of viewing those various types of media from within one interface, formulate a redesign plan, and execute the design process: creation of overall layout, cutting up of graphics, and coding the final pages. A round of user testing and further design tweaks will follow the initial design phase. The final step in this assignment is for students to UPLOAD all of the functioning HTML pages to their personal Web spaces.

## 5. Task-Based Design 2: Companion Web Site to Media Player (5 weeks)

With a group, analyze the specific TASKS of completing a transaction or discrete set of tasks (e.g., purchase, registration, post to a bulletin board, etc.), formulate a redesign plan for the Web site, and execute the actual redesign process: creation of overall layout, cutting up of graphics, and coding the final pages. A round of user testing and further design tweaks will follow the initial design phase. The final step in this assignment is for students to UPLOAD all of the functioning HTML pages to their personal Web spaces.

# recommended readings

Krug, Steven, *Don't Make Me Think*, New Riders Press, 2005.

McCracken, Daniel, and Rosalee Wolfe, *User-Centered Website Development: A Human-Computer Interaction Approach*, Prentice Hall, 2003.

COURSE TITLE: Introduction to Time-Based Media

TEACHER: Chad Reichert

FREQUENCY: Fall and Spring Semesters

LEVEL: Freshmen

CREDITS: 3

DEGREE: Bachelor of Fine Arts

SCHOOL: College for Creative Studies, Detroit, MI

## course summary

Projects introduce students to time-based visual communication environments. Unique conditions influencing the roles of typography, image, symbolic systems, narrative, and sound and time systems are assessed in the resolution of assigned projects. Students are exposed to the tools, theories, aesthetics, and techniques used in time-based message building.

## course objectives

- To introduce students to the basic concepts of creating messages in time
- To utilize sound, image, and type as basic components of time-based communications
- To provide students with a historical overview of time-based media
- To utilize storyboarding as a means of visual and verbal articulation
- To demonstrate an introductory understanding and manipulation of digital and analog techniques that pertain to time-based communications
- To develop a working knowledge of software appropriate to introductory concepts in time-based media

The course is intended to assist the student in developing:

- A design methodology that evolves thematic concepts through a series of assessment stages. Each stage will consider component elements and the integration of elements used in the development of time-based communication.
- A design methodology that is open to changing conditions

# requirements

- Attendance is required. Three unexcused absences will reduce your grade by one full letter.
- Grades will adhere to the standard scale used by this college. Late projects will be down graded one letter grade for each class period they are overdue. Projects over two class periods late will not be accepted.
- Portfolio: The final portfolio and final project are due on the last regular class day.

# project 1—reverse storyboard

Visual communicators use a variety of sketching techniques as aids in translating concepts/ideas into meaningful communications. Sketching, using whatever tools are appropriate, translates abstract thoughts into tangible realities. Furthermore, the process of sketching refines the communicator's selection, improving the potential of the message to reach the intended audience. Time-based communication introduces new sets of conditions that fundamentally change the nature of sketching. The method used to sketch a temporal idea is a storyboard. The storyboard outlines the narrative and develops compositional models for type, images, image frames, transitions, and sound.

**ASSIGNMENT: WEEK 1.** For this project select a QuickTime movie piece from the discussed Web sites. Develop a well-organized storyboard on a single panel of mat board. Use still images and text to model and articulate what is occurring in the piece.

# project 2—experience overdrive

An experience can be defined as knowledge and skill in something gained through being involved in it, or exposed to it, over a period of time. To remember an experience we must rely on the act of storytelling. A story mirrors the surrounding world and constructs a reality of its own, meeting the cognitive, psychological, and emotional needs of a person. A compelling story allows us a playlike experience where we identify with its characters and actively participate in all of its events. The experience that storytelling offers is not only a personal experience, it is a universal experience that encompasses world cultures. It's because of this cultural divide that we must be aware that experiences can be irrelevant to others who don't share our ideologies, philosophies, or geographic location. Universal themes can transcend boundaries such as race or language only if the content and delivery are carefully considered.

**ASSIGNMENT.** The assignment is for students to document an experience that they participate in during the course of a given day. Each student will begin by analyzing the kind of experience it is, discussing its significance, and learning how to tell a compelling story. We will explore the relationships between first- and second-hand observations and see how their experiences can be resequenced and possibly reinterpreted to modify the stories and their intended messages. For each phase of the project, students will be responsible for handing in a storyboard and process movie.

The objectives for this assignment are:

- To understand the role of narrative in time-based media
- To examine relationships between imagery, type, and sound
- To develop a proficiency in appropriate time-based software and hardware
- To establish a vocabulary and discourse in time-based media

**PHOTOGRAPHY: WEEKS 2–3.** In the first phase of the project, you will take a sequence of forty digital photographs that encapsulate and represent the significant moments of the experience. Within the sequence you must tell a story that reveals a narrative that considers a beginning, middle, and end. Do NOT edit your initial sequence. Keep the shots in the order in which you reacted. Be sure to document the experience thoroughly, including the condition of the environment and secondary observations. Your sequence and shot selection will be the only visual clues the viewer may react to. Pay attention to how and what you are photographing.

**TYPOGRAPHIC: WEEKS 3–6.** In the second phase you will write about the experience you just participated in. You can use either found or original text that will give insight into your story. Either way, it should not be just an explanation of the exact sequence of activities but words and sentences that give us verbal clues as to what your thoughts, actions, and intentions were. You will then reconstruct your experience using the assembled text. Built in Photoshop and Illustrator, you will examine the relationship between type and photos and develop a storyboard based on your verbal interpretation.

**SOUND: WEEKS 7–8.** In the third phase you will re-create your experience using only sound. Please refer to both your photographs and writing to help guide you through the selection process. Just like visual stimuli, audio can explore depth, scale, and emotion. What happens when sound becomes a verb, noun, or adjective? What happens when sound replaces image? With your lens cap ON, you will pick out themes, emotions, and ideas addressed through your imagery and text, and record sounds that compliment, supplement, and contradict your ideas.

**INTEGRATION: WEEKS 8–11.** By embracing the strange and seemingly unnatural, you will compose a sequence that is twenty-five seconds in length and combines all phases into a final QuickTime video. During this assembly phase be aware of how individual elements work in isolation and as part of a greater whole.

# project 3—recontextualization

**ASSIGNMENT.** Everyone comprehends and interprets information differently. Multiple audiences translate to multiple levels of understanding. In *Flatland*, Edwin Abbott creates a fictional world that deals with topics ranging from politics and culture to science and math. Some concepts are easier to understand than others. Although he is concise in his explanations, naturally some ideas will be lost on the reader. Based on the novel, each student will determine the subject matter and content, and recontextualize it to achieve a new level of understanding as it pertains to a chosen and specific audience and/or environment. Each project should be forty seconds in length and include video, sound, illustration, and type. Careful integration of elements and a cohesive execution are vital to the success of the project. The final project can take the form of a public service announcement, exhibition, lecture event, or Web or commercial broadcast.

The objectives for this assignment are:

- To understand the role of rhetorical and narrative devices in graphic storytelling
- To develop an ability to manipulate sound, type, and moving image
- To effectively contextualize an idea and recognize the importance of audience in graphic storytelling

**READING AND ANALYSIS: WEEK 11.** Having already read the book earlier in the semester, each of you should now revisit the text, identifying ideas, themes, and issues that you can exploit. In class we will discuss your ideas and help determine which are worth pursuing.

**VISUALIZATION AND STORYBOARDING: WEEKS 11–12.** Two rounds of storyboards will be due. The first will be a black and white draft that articulates the main visual and verbal directions you would like to pursue. In class we will discuss the appropriateness of your idea, who your audience is, and the practical nature of producing your project.

**ASSEMBLY AND PRODUCTION: WEEK 12–13.** Now that your storyboard has been refined, you have a road map to follow as you start your production.

Schedule out the next two weeks to determine the who, what, where, and when of your project.

**REFINEMENT AND FINAL PRESENTATION: WEEK 14.** The class critiques a draft and a final project.

# recommended reading

Abbott, Edwin, *Flatland: A Romance of Many Dimensions*, Dover Publications, 2007.

Ades, Dawn, *Photomontage*, Thames & Hudson, 1986.

Berger, John, *Ways of Seeing*, Penguin, 1990.

Cage, John, *Empty Words*, Wesleyan University Press, 1981.

McCloud, Scott, *Understanding Comics*, Harper, 1994.

Miller, Paul D., *Rhythm Science*, MIT Press, 2004.

Nyman, Michael, *Experimental Music: Cage and Beyond*, Cambridge University Press, 1999.

7

COURSE TITLE: Introduction to Time-Based Media
TEACHER: Doug Kisor
FREQUENCY: Fall and Winter Semesters
LEVEL: Freshman, required course
CREDITS: 3
DEGREE: Bachelor of Fine Arts
SCHOOL: College for Creative Studies, Detroit, MI

## course description

We are in the midst of a communication transformation brought about by digital tools and digital environments. Information is moving away from the domain of a static, dominantly linguistic model, toward the multisensory, dynamic, audiovisual confluence that is the nature of digital media. Digital multimedia has a potential to express the hybrid nature of information. Projects will assess the components and domain of multisensory models in motion/time sequences. An understanding of time-based structures is considered the foundation for a more broad understanding of "new media" communication using the Web, interactive models, and other channels.

The critical analysis of students' work will focus on the understanding of the cognitive and perceptional conditions that affect messages conceived to function in time. Formal analysis will be based on applying principles developed in the Typography I and II courses, including the use of image, typography, color, space, sign, format, and the associated cognitive relationship of the communication components. Students are expected to master elements of the software relevant to the development of assigned projects.

## project 1

For this project select a time-based piece from the Web sites discussed in class. Develop a well-organized storyboard on a single panel of mat board. Use still images and text to model and articulate what is occurring in the piece. Your assessment needs to include notes articulating the connotation of movement, sound, image, symbol, camera view, typographic gesture, and pacing:

STRUCTURES AND COMPOSITION (How is the screen space being used?)
IMAGE AND IMAGE TYPE (What is the nature of the image? What is implied?)
SYMBOLS AND SYMBOL TYPES (What symbolic forms are being used? Why?)
TIME (Analyze carefully the use of time, note the time break for each change/cut/transition.)

SOUND (What are the roles of voice, music, and rhetorical sound?)

INTENT (What is the collective intent of all the visual, sound, and pacing elements?)

MEANING (What is the collective meaning of all the visual, sound, and pacing elements?)

Include a descriptive text next to each image selected. Selected images should represent definitive changes: a cut, transition, or some other obvious change occurring on screen. Include an additional narrative articulating other key points listed above. Organize the project on black core mat board, aligning the sequence horizontally. Use an aspect ratio for image size of 3 by 4.5 inches (approximate).

Discussion: Week 1

Project Due: Week 2

Software Introduction: Week 2

# project 2a: temporal experience/narrative structure

This project is about visual narrative temporal translation, context, intent, and interpretation.

- Temporal: of, pertaining to, or limited by time
- Narrative: an account; a tale; a story
- Content: verbal/visual

The quality of words consists in their abstract, alphabetic, and symbolic character. The verbal is more cerebral, more linear, and more predictably sequential than the visual. The visual is based on the eye and sense of place and viewpoint in the objective world.

I would like you to organize a one-hour experience. This needs to be something you have not done before in a place you have not been.

Go bowling, visit a location, say a Laundromat in Dearborn, or go to a building in downtown Detroit and take the elevator to the sixth floor, ride the people mover, do something—don't worry, just try something. Whatever it is that you do, it must be new and in a new location, a place you haven't been. Take a journal and a digital camera or video camera. In the journal, at the moment you leave, indicate the time of day, the temperature, and your mood.

The journal will act as a guide outlining the narrative/temporal experience.

1. Assess the environment: look at the street, at signs, at changes in the architecture or scale of space. Examine the color, surface, topography, decorative elements, etc.

2. Observe activities: people walking their dogs, workmen, people on benches, etc.

3. Consider the nature of activities: daily rituals, games, projects, whims, etc. Who are these people: man/woman, old/young, student/worker, etc.?

**4.** Record language, what people say, record the language in your head, the internal voice that is always talking—seek meaning!

**5.** Note conditions: active areas, quite areas, commercial areas, residential areas. What differentiates one from the other, what are the visual codes that signify difference?

Use a time code to establish the temporal relationship of events and experiences (basically a graph or timeline).

Indicate in your journal when you take a photo and why. Use images not only to capture large scale or broad areas but also as a method to help understand small spaces and your impressions. The images should be visual representations of the particular conditions that are discussed and observed in your narrative.

At the end of your walk, when you have reached your destination, indicate what is there, why you made this selection, and relevant observations defining your mood and the significance of closure.

Number of images: sixty to eighty

Organize the material in a three-ring notebook with the narrative integrated with your image studies. Images should be actual. Meaning, directly derived from the environment. Images can include found objects and rubbings that aid in translating the environment into visual form.

Complete the walk and have the material for week 3.

# project 2b: narrative storyboard

Different than print, time-based communication creates an environment that alludes to our perception of the natural world. In it we are able to use value, scale, and motion to create the illusion of dimensional space.

The static nature of print limits its ability to approximate that illusion of dimensional space at the same convincing level.

The goals of this project are:

- To create communication that explores the possibilities of space, taking into account how we see
- To use typography as a primary communicator
- To consider how we read and organize type communication
- To explore zones that communicate to the user areas where events happen

*Cognition: The process of knowing in the broadest sense, including perception, memory, and judgment*

*Perception: The mental grasp of objects, qualities, by means of the senses; awareness; comprehension, insight, or intuition or the faculty for these*

*Comprehension: The act of grasping with the mind, the capacity for understanding ideas, facts, etc.*

Develop three storyboards, each representing a different segment of your experience. Your initial exercise is typographically based. To begin you need to develop defining language for each of the three stories. Use time-based communication as a channel through which your message will be developed. That is, letters can join to create words, words to create statements. The movement of words in the sequence can alter meaning, shifting the read as the message changes over time.

Write a statement of intent for each of the three storyboards. Consider beginning, middle, and end.

Consider: the conceptual role of language, meaning of movement, movement, cognition, zones, transitions, time, mutation, and scale.

Each narrative should be twenty seconds long.

Use accordion-fold storyboards with image windows based on a 3:4 aspect ratio. Include annotations for what is occurring in each sequence. Begin with a quick pencil study. Use Photoshop and Illustrator to image final storyboards.

Review: Week 4

Due: Week 5

# project 3: sound/image

Sound is temporal, understood within a specific tempo. Sounds are learned; meaning is based on culture, context, and experience.

Develop two storyboards based on your initial narrative.

Reshoot images when necessary; keep in mind the concepts discussed regarding image narrative, the ability to translate an idea into a sequence of related images.

Use the following types of sounds:

1. Translation of environmental sounds
2. Selection of tempo/music that supports the conceptual theme

Duration for each storyboard: twenty or thirty seconds (This does not mean twenty-four or twenty-eight seconds; it means twenty or thirty seconds.)

Project 3 runs from week 6 to week 9.

# project 4: beauty/mythologies video

**Beauty:** A pleasing quality, associated with harmony of form or color, excellence of craftsmanship, truthfulness, originality, or another, often unspecifiable, property. A quality or feature that is most effective, gratifying, or telling.

**Myth:** A real or fictional story, recurring theme, or character type that appeals to the consciousness of a people by embodying its cultural ideals or by giving expression to deep, commonly felt emotions.

Read the essays from *Beauty* by Diane Ackerman and John Miller and *Good Looking: Essays on the Virtue of Images* by Barbara Maria Stafford. Consider the meaning and myth of beauty in a broad sense. Select four people, each a different age and gender, consider ethnicity, seek people from different backgrounds. Ask these people about beauty. Use issues from the essays as aids in framing different types of questions. Keep the interviews short, from five to ten minutes. Seek concise answers. Videotape the interviews. Be sensitive to light, shadow, composition, and details in the environment. Build on your experience in developing still-image solutions. Look for essential meaning in gestures.

Consider hands, eyes, mouth, and body language as key contributors to meaning. Project 5 runs from week 11 to 15, and the assignments break down as follows:

**Week 11:** Discuss Final Cut Pro.

**Week 12:** Review videos.

**Week 13:** Create two storyboards, each dealing with a separate theme for thirty to sixty seconds. Studies. Work in class, discuss and refine concepts.

**Week 14:** Review working prototypes. Work in class, discuss and refine studies.

**Week 15:** Work to make very beautiful things. Major event! Final project due.

## readings

### New Media/Hypermedia

Bolter, Jay David, *Writing Space: The Computer, Hypertext, and the History of Writing*, Lawrence Erlbaum Associates, 1991.

Bolter examines the new interactive role of the reader and writer in the hypertext-authoring format of computer technology. Bolter divides his study into visual and conceptual "writing spaces," with a chapter devoted to the intersection of critical theory and the hypertext format.

Cotton, Bob, *Understanding Hypermedia from Multimedia to Virtual Reality*, Phaidon Press, 1993.

Delany, Paul, and George P. Landow, *Hypermedia and Literary Studies*, MIT Press, 1994.

Goux, Melanie, and James A. Houff, *On Screen In Time: Transitions in Motion Graphic Design for Film, Television and New Media*, Rotovision, 2003.

The book provides a practical tutorial and examples from sixteen motion graphics design offices with accompanying interviews.

Landow, George P., *Hypertext: The Convergence of Contemporary Critical Theory and Technology*, John Hopkins University Press, 1992.

Drawing heavily on both Derrida and Barthes, Landow assesses the impact of electronic text, or hypertext. Landow offers chapters on the relationship between critical theory and hypertext, the new roles of writers and readers, and the impact hypertexts will have on education and literature.

## Theory/Critical Thinking

Barthes, Roland, *Image/Music/Text*, Hill and Wang, 1977.

A collection of important essays by the French literary critic. Particularly relevant to graphic design are the essays about photography and the text, including "The Photographic Message," "Rhetoric of the Image," "Death of the Author," and "From Work to Text."

Barthes, Roland, *Mythologies*, Noonday Press,1972.

One of Barthes' earliest (1957) and most accessible works, *Mythologies* analyzes popular culture in the form of very brief essays on a variety of topics. Included is the essay "Myth Today," a summary of Barthes' framework defining his concept of "mythology."

Berger, John et al., *Ways of Seeing*, Penguin, 1972.

Berger's important and accessible Marxist analysis of the relationship between Western painting and the ideology of advertising.

Blonsky, Marshall, ed., *On Signs*, John Hopkins University Press, 1985.

An extensive collection of essays on semiology from some of the major figures such as Barthes, Derrida, Lacan, and Eco, *On Signs* reflects the application of semiotics to a wide range of topics and to nonspecialist audiences. Included is "I Listen to the Market," Milton Glaser's thoughts on his program for Grand Union supermarkets.

13

Glauber, Barbara, ed., *Lift and Separate: Graphic Design and the Vernacular*, The Cooper Union for the Advancement of Science and Art, 1993.

This exhibition catalogue explores the role of vernacular culture as an influence on graphic design practices. A wide range of essays cover topics such as skateboarding culture, the anonymity and naiveté of the commercial artist, an analysis of New York City graffiti, and the recontextualization of signs. Among the contributors are Jeffery Keedy, Lorraine Wild, Steven Heller, and Mike Mills.

McLuhan, Marshall, *The Gutenberg Galaxy: The Making of Typographic Man*, University of Toronto Press, 1962.

An important social and cultural analysis of the impact of print culture on civilization by this maverick thinker who gained great popularity in the 1960s. McLuhan's aphoristic writing style is rendered typographically in pull-quotes with an index of these "glosses."

## Information Structures/Methodologies

Friedman, Mildred, *Graphic Design in America: A Visual Language History*, Harry Abrahms, 1989.

Harmon, Katherine, *You are Here: Personal Geographies and other Maps of the Imagination*, Princeton Architectural Press, 2004.

Hollis, Richard, *Graphic Design: A Concise History*, Thames & Hudson, 2002.

Johnson, Paul, and Martin Eidelberg, *Design 1935–1965: What Modern Was*, Harry Abrahms, 2001.

Kerbs, Manuel, and Dimitri Bruni, *Norm: The Things*, Gestalten Verlag, 2002.

Meggs, Philip B., and Alston W. Purvis, *Meggs' History of Graphic Design*, 4th ed., John Wiley & Sons, 2005.

Roberts, Lucienne, and Julia Thrift, *The Designer and the Grid*, Rotovision, 2002.

Tufte, Edward, *Envisioning Information*, Graphics Press, 1990.

Tufte, Edward, *The Visual Display of Quantitative Information*, Graphics Press, 2001.

## Anthologies

Ackerman, Diane, and John Miller, *Beauty*, Chronicle Books, 1997.

Beirut, Michael, William Drenttel, and Steven Heller eds., *Looking Closer: Critical Writings on Graphic Design*, Allworth Press, 2006.

Beirut, Michael, William Drenttel, and Steven Heller eds., *Looking Closer 2: Critical Writings on Graphic Design*, Allworth Press, 1997.

Beirut, Michael, Jessica Helfand, and Steven Heller eds., *Looking Closer 3: Critical Writings on Graphic Design*, Allworth Press, 1999.

Heller, Steven, *Design Literacy: Understanding Graphic Design*, Allworth Press, 2004.

Jury, David, ed., *TypoGraphic Writing: Selected Writing from Thirty Years of TypoGraphic, the Journal of the International Society of Typographic Designers*, with an introduction by Wim Crouwel, ISTD, 2001.

Lupton, Ellen, *Mixing Messages: Graphic Design in Contemporary Culture*, Princeton Architectural Press, 1997.

Stafford, Barbara Maria, *Good Looking: Essays on the Virtue of Images*, MIT Press, 1988.

## Design Periodicals

*Artforum*, United States

*Blueprint*, United Kingdom

*Communication Arts*, United States

*Dot Dot Dot*, Netherlands

*Design*, United Kingdom

*Eye*, United Kingdom

*Graphis*, Switzerland/United States

*Idea*, Japan

*ID Magazine*, United States

*Metropolis*, United States

*Print*, United States

*Wired*, United States

COURSE TITLE: Computer Animation 1

TEACHER: Chris Perry

FREQUENCY: One Semester

LEVEL: Introductory

CREDITS: 4

DEGREE: Bachelor of Arts

SCHOOL: Hampshire College, Amherst, MA

## summary and goal of class

This course introduces students to the production of animated short films with the tools and techniques of three-dimensional (3-D) computer graphics. Readings and lectures cover the theoretical foundations of the field, and the homework assignments provide hands-on, project-based experience with production. The topics covered include modeling (the building of 3-D objects), shading (assignment of surface reflectance properties), animation (moving the objects over time), and lighting (placing and setting the properties of virtual light sources).

This class is designed to be the first of a two-class series that, as a whole, provides students with a solid introduction to all facets of 3-D production. As you will learn from the week-by-week summaries, character animation is emphasized a great deal more than modeling, shading, and lighting. The reason I've structured the class this way is because I've found students take much more quickly to animating (that is, actually moving objects around over time) than to the generally more technical, mathematical, and programming-heavy areas of production. Once hooked by animation, however, students seem much more willing to work outside of their comfort zones in order to build upon their motion in one way or another. Note that the second course in the sequence rectifies this imbalance, so that by the end of the two-course sequence students will have had a balanced exposure to all parts of production.

## week by week

Note: the course was designed to fit snugly into twenty-four, bi-weekly class meetings, and that is the syllabus presented here. However, it can stretch comfortably into at least twenty-eight meetings, particularly by providing more breathing room between the final project milestones (see below).

**WEEK 1.** In this week I motivate the course, arguing why 3-D computer graphics is a unique approach (compared to the studio arts and photography, in particular) to generating images. I introduce the ray-tracing algorithm as a good way to understand, practically, how a 3-D artist's creative decisions impact the final quality (and the render time) of his or her work. I also cover basic transformations (translate, rotate, scale), both in the abstract and in the software package being used. I do the same for orthographic and perspective projections.

The first assignment (see below) is given at the end of week 1 and is due at the next class meeting.

**WEEK 2.** This week introduces animation as the varying of numerical data over time. Terms such as *keyframes* and *interpolation* are defined, and methods for controlling interpolation (ease in, ease out, etc.) are explored. Two principles of animation (timing, and squash and stretch, in particular) are introduced with a number of video examples. Students read about all of the principles in John Lasseter's SIGGRAPH article (see readings below).

The second assignment is given at the end of week 2 and is due a week after it is assigned.

**WEEK 3.** This week introduces the transformation hierarchy and more principles of animation (anticipation, follow-through/overlapping action, and secondary action). Once again, students encounter these ideas first on the whiteboard and in video examples during class, and then revisit them in practice through an assignment.

The third assignment is given at the beginning of week 3 and is due a week after it is assigned.

**WEEK 4.** This week covers more principles of animation (staging, exaggeration, slow in/slow out, and arcs) and, in assignment four, gets students to put together everything they've learned so far about staging, composition, and animation.

The fourth assignment is given right after the third is handed in, and students have a week and a half to complete it.

**WEEK 5.** Although all assignments to date have been viewed in class, significantly more class time is devoted to viewing and critiquing assignment four. The remaining time is spent first discussing what some call the "layered" approach to hierarchical animation (animating from the root of a hierarchy to the leaves). The rest is spent introducing lighting. I draw heavily from Sharon Calahan's chapter in *Advanced RenderMan* (see readings).

Assignment five is given at the end of week 5 and is due in a week.

**WEEK 6.** The discussion of lighting continues this week, but this time from a mathematical perspective. I cover basic models such as Lambert and Phong, introduce the idea of a surface normal, and essentially quantify lighting in the most basic of ways in order to give students enough control to duplicate a reasonably complex lighting rig (see assignment five).

Assignment five is due in the middle of this week; and after it is reviewed in class, the remaining time is spent introducing the final project. Each student works on his or her final project for the remainder of the term and is expected to present material to the class during seven "milestone" reviews. The first milestone is due at the start of week 7.

**WEEK 7.** This week begins with storyboarding, breaking down shots, and other skills necessary to help students complete the second milestone. The rest of the week is filled with the very basics of polygonal modeling. In particular, I discuss applying the earlier, simple transformations to subcomponents of an object instead of to the entire object at once (vertices, faces, edges). Students learn how to bring 2-D images into the software so they can model to a reference.

The second final project milestone is due at the end of this week.

**WEEK 8.** This week covers more modeling concepts. We discuss building more complex shapes out of modified geometric primitives and discuss some of the tools that allow for polygon creation from scratch (such as lathe-like tools). Some time is also spent discussing rigging hierarchical characters. In particular, we cover the material necessary to allow a student to rig, say, a bouncing ball with a rigid, nonde-forming appendage attached to it. This requires "breaking" the transformation hier-archy so that the scales of the parent object don't completely apply to the child object.

The third milestone is assigned at the beginning of this week and is due in a week.

**WEEK 9.** Both class meetings this week focus on critiquing in-progress work. The first is a review of milestone three (the students' models). After that review is com-pleted, I spend a little time talking about the process of "blocking" (i.e., putting in the basic timing and poses to communicate where one is going with an animated scene). Milestone four is assigned and is due at the start of the very next class. That class is dedicated entirely to reviewing student work in milestone four.

Milestone five is assigned at the end of this week and is due in a week.

NOTE: This week's deadlines have traditionally been very difficult for stu-dents. If you are teaching this material and have extra time, I suggest allowing breathing room between milestones three and four.

**WEEK 10.** This week is devoted to animation. The first class is focused on meth-ods for completing animation of complex characters. We move beyond the layered approach and explore pose-to-pose, "pop-thru," and others.

The second class is the final animation dailies review where we go over mile-stone five.

Milestone six is assigned and is due in a week.

Traditionally, students don't quite have their animations complete for milestone five as expected. Here is another area where some breathing room in the schedule could help.

**WEEK 11.** This week is devoted to shading and lighting. The first class covers making simple patterns, using basic textures, and other tricks (both in lighting and shading) to add visual complexity to the students' films. The second class is a review of the work for milestone six (lighting), where still images from each student's film are seen and critiqued.

Milestone seven is assigned at the end of this week and is due in a week.

**WEEK 12.** At this point, students are very busy outside of class trying to polish their motion, tweak their shading and lighting, and render their films. So I devote significant class time in the first class period to fielding whatever questions they might have. I then show clips from films, commercials, and from various online sources in an effort to entice them to continue their studies in the next term. These clips feature tools and techniques that they now are able to recognize as "special" (such as muscle systems for rigging, 3-D paint for texturing, subsurface scattering and other advanced shading methods, etc.).

The final class is devoted entirely to screening the students' films. There is generally not enough time to critique, which at this point in the term is just as well.

# assignments/projects

### Assignment 1: The Camera

This assignment is intended to give students experience with:

- Running the 3-D software package and loading an existing scene file
- Setting the camera position, orientation, and focal length to achieve a particular composition
- Rendering the camera view using the software package's renderer
- Handing in homework

The specific task is to load a preexisting scene file and create three different images from the file by moving, orienting, and configuring the virtual camera.

### Assignment 2: 2-D Bouncing Ball

This assignment is intended to give students experience with:

- Using the graph editor
- The animation principles of squash and stretch, and timing
- Making a draft render (Maya "playblast") to preview (and hand in) your motion

The student's goal in this assignment is to animate one cycle of a bouncing ball in front of a static orthographic camera (one cycle means that the ball starts up high, bounces off the ground, and goes back up). The students are to make use of the animation principle of squash and stretch to enhance their ball's motion and concentrate closely on timing to make the ball bounce naturalistically.

The scene file they start with has a ball ready to go in the "side" view. They need to keep the ball on-screen through the entire animation and not animate the camera. The ball has two translation channels for moving it around and one scaling control to squash and stretch it. It also has a rotation control if needed, but I encourage them to start by using just translation and scaling.

## Assignment 3: Bouncing Ball with Tail

This assignment is intended to give students experience with:

- Animating hierarchies
- The principles of anticipation, follow-through/overlapping action, and secondary action

Each student has to animate a bouncing ball with a tail starting at rest on the ground, jumping up in the air, and coming back to rest after landing.

Like the last assignment, the scene file they are starting with has the ball ready to go in the "side" view again. They need to keep the ball on screen through the entire animation and not animate the camera. The ball has two translation channels for moving it around and one scaling control to squash and stretch it, as before. It also has a single rotation channel. Each of the three tail nodes has a single rotation channel only.

19

## Assignment 4: 3-D Bouncing Balls

This assignment is intended to give students experience with:

- Building their own shot
- All of the animation principles they've studied so far, with particular emphasis on staging and timing

Their goal is to animate a single shot (no more than five seconds) containing two distinctly different bouncing balls. One could be heavy like a bowling ball and the other could be squishy and bouncy, for instance. They should not animate the camera, though, of course, they will need to position the camera, orient it, and set its focal length appropriately for the shot they envision.

Once they have a clear idea of how they want to present their two bouncing balls, they are to build their own scene files using the two objects in the project folder ("assignment_04"). It is fine to import the same object multiple times to do this, but they are not allowed to use other objects. The idea here is for them to come up with a shot that is interesting because of the placement of the camera and the motion of the objects ONLY, not because they stuck some fancy geometry in there.

## Assignment 5: Lighting the Head

This assignment is intended to give students experience with:

- Creating, positioning, aiming, and setting the properties of lights
- Rendering a high-quality, antialiased image

The project folder contains a scene file and two images. Their goal is to re-create the target image to the best of their abilities by adding lights to the scene file that's provided. Once they have accomplished this, they are to render an antialiased, full-resolution image and hand in both the image and their final scene files.

## Final Project General Description

For the final project in this class students will create a short, character-driven film from the ground up. They must work within the following constraints:

- The final film must showcase the interaction between a single character and an object.
- Students must build both the character model and the object model themselves.
- So as not to detract from the interaction, they should create a minimalist environment (like those used in assignments 4 or 5). They are free to get these models from other sources.
- The character should be hierarchical (like the ball with a tail), but should have no more than FIVE visible nodes in the hierarchy. Eyes are not included in this limit.
- Students' films should be made up of no more than four shots.
- Students' films should run no longer than ten seconds.

While the movie is the ultimate goal, over the next seven weeks students will hand in a number of assignments that act as stepping stones to get them there. These "milestones" are required just like the previous assignments even though they all fall under the domain of a single final project.

### Final Project Milestone 1: Preproposals

The goal of milestone 1 is to get students thinking about different project ideas.

They hand in three final project "preproposals." Each preproposal should contain a short written treatment (one paragraph) of the final movie the student is envisioning (in the present tense). They are to include a simple sketch of both the character and the object with each treatment so as to identify the complexity of the models they're considering. They number the preproposals in order of preference (#1 being their favorite, and so on).

### Final Project Milestone 2: Full Proposal

The goal of milestone 2 is to get students to work out as much as possible on paper before diving into production.

To complete milestone 2, students must hand in a hardcopy proposal containing the following information:

- The title of the project
- The approximate duration of the movie in seconds
- The frame rate, aspect ratio, and spatial resolution of the film
- A written treatment
- A storyboard
- One or two lighting reference images
- A model list
- A model packet for every model

### Final Project Milestone 3: Models

The goal of milestone 3 is for each student to build all of the models for their films. It is expected that they will be simple, polygonal objects, probably built by jamming modified polygonal primitives together. The emphasis is on design, not complexity. It is critical that the models that need to be rigged are rigged for this milestone.

Each student is asked to hand in a folder containing all of his film's models, and the contents of this folder are reviewed in class.

### Final Project Milestone 4: Layout/Blocking Dailies

The goal of milestone 4 is for the student to lay out each of the film's shots and present basic blocking animation so that the overall flow of the scenes is understood. Students are asked to hand in digital movie files, one for each shot. These are reviewed in class.

### Final Project Milestone 5: Animation Dailies

The goal of milestone 5 is for the students to complete most or all of the motion for their films. The emphasis is on performance and clear communication of the film's intended story. Once again, they are asked to hand in digital movie files to be reviewed in class.

### Final Project Milestone 6: Lighting Dailies

The goal of milestone 6 is for the students to add lights to each of their shots and render a representative still image (for each shot) to be reviewed in class. The critique is focused, as are all the milestone reviews, toward helping the students accomplish what they wanted to accomplish in their original final project proposals. In this case, it is commenting on how the lighting decisions they've made (or not made) are translating into the final frames.

### Final Project Milestone 7: Final Films!

The goal of this milestone is for students to complete their films. They are asked to hand in a single digital movie file that is viewed in class. They are also asked to hand in their project folders so that the instructor can look more closely at their work as necessary.

## outcome/conclusion

Students who complete this class successfully will have attained a good, low-level understanding of 3-D computer graphics that is independent of a particular software implementation. This is perhaps the most important goal of the course and will serve them well no matter what software they end up using later on.

They will also have produced a short, animation-driven film in a particular software package and will thus leave the course with practical, functional experience.

Finally, they will have had their hands held through an intensive production process, showing them that they are capable of substantial production work while also demonstrating how important it is to maintain a strict schedule while doing that work.

## readings

In the past I have used Isaac Kerlow's *The Art of 3-D Computer Animation and Imaging* as a course text; however, the readings I assign each week jump all over the book because its approach to teaching the material differs from my own.

The aforementioned Lasseter article from SIGGRAPH has the following full citation:

> Lasseter, John, "Principles of Traditional Animation Applied to 3D Computer Animation," in Proceedings of the 14th Annual Conference on Computer Graphics and Interactive Techniques, ed. M. C. Stone, ACM Press, 1987: 35–44. http://doi.acm.org/10.1145/37401.37407

The aforementioned Calahan chapter comes from the text *Advanced RenderMan: Creating CGI for Motion Pictures* by A. Apodaca and L. Gritz (Morgan Kaufmann, 1999).

COURSE TITLE: Beginning Character Animation
TEACHER: Mike Nguyen
FREQUENCY: Two Semesters
LEVEL: Freshman, required course
CREDITS: 3 per semester
DEGREE: Bachelor of Fine Arts
SCHOOL: California Institute of the Arts, Valencia, CA

## summary and goal

The objective of the class is to build a firm foundation in character animation based on the understanding of what gives rise to the life beneath animated movements, how life forces affect applications and approaches to the basic principles of animation. The aim is also to explore the unique possibility of animation as a form of expression, in particular, the traditional animation medium and its relation to the larger context of filmmaking language. Visual examples through various film clips as well as class demonstrations are to be used.

## week by week

### First Semester

**WEEK 1.** Why animate? An overview looks at fundamental thinking toward bringing the animated character to life and its relation to film language.

**WEEK 2.** The importance of studying life and the ability to apply the knowledge gained to the animated work.

Different ways of using life's references.

A general look at the physics of the real world and how they translate into the various animated worlds dictated by their respective styles and designs.

Understanding the physical makeup of the character, identifying the movable masses within the structure, from skeletal to the feel of mass and mobility.

Communicating gestures in physical terms through:

- Clear silhouette
- Balance
- Angle and tilt
- Twist and turn

Thoughts on applying life-drawing knowledge to animation.

**WEEK 3.** Understanding life forces, both physical and emotional, and their effects on forms. The ability to FEEL, to describe the intended intensity of force from a single pose, through motion.

The element of time in animation—the textures of one's, two's and three's.

Animating approaches—staying loose, visualizing forms in motion, building blocks, thumb nailing process, straight-ahead, pose-to-pose, etc.

Exaggeration in animation.

Arcs—gravitational and physical forces affecting arc projection.

**WEEK 4.** Anticipation.

Squash and stretch—keeping the animated forms organic.

The importance of delayed parts—follow-through and overlapping.

Rhythm in movements—contrast in speed, patterns, accents.

The importance of timing.

**WEEK 5.** Understanding the spirits behind the animated forms.

Spirit affects mannerisms.

The communicating of gestures in emotional terms—communicating gestures in motion.

Animation performance—design affecting performance texture, broad vs. subtle.

Clarity in movements.

Full body pantomime vs. facial communication.

The interest in poses vs. the unfolding between poses.

The relation between head, shoulders, and hands.

Sincerity.

Performance types—realistic, stylized, theatrical.

**WEEK 6.** Elements in graphic composition, contrast and arrangement of graphic elements within a working space.

Animation designs—contrast of graphic elements in various screen aspect ratios.

The feel from a composition.

Styles and art directions.

The importance of atmospheres.

Design reflecting personality.

Clarity in character designs.

**WEEK 7.** Film language and its relation to various approaches to animation.

Composing in film—relating compositions.

Directional flow of a composition from scene to scene.

Placement of main elements relating from scene to scene.

The static shot and camera moves.

General thoughts on film editing.

**WEEK 8.** Storyboarding process—the various stages.

Choices of long, medium, or close-up shots.

Story reel and animatics.

Work books.

**WEEK 9.** The layout stage for animation—scene staging.

    Layout in relation to animating.

    Choosing field sizes.

    From rough to clean-up layouts.

**WEEK 10.** Thoughts in approaching a scene—scene length and intent.

    Understanding the relation of scenes within a sequence.

    Visualizing scenes before animating.

    Feel the force, accents, and rhythms.

    Thumb-nailing process.

    Thoughts on animating a scene—finding the leading force.

    Keep forms loose, staying rough in drawing.

    Static pose and pose suggesting lead in motion.

    Delay parts.

**WEEK 11.** An overview of music and sound effects in film.

    Voice performance.

    General thoughts on approaching dialogue scenes.

**WEEK 12.** Ideas and materials for the animated medium.

    The canvas of film—short, series, and feature length.

**WEEKS 13–14.** Reviews and workshops.

## Second Semester

Students work on a nondialogue short film project up to one minute, thirty seconds in length, due at end of the school year.

    Class time is converted to workshops with more time for addressing particular creative issues on a one-on-one basis. This course puts first semester thoughts into practice, constantly reinforcing the fundamentals of animation.

## Class Projects

### Project 1: Adapting a Pose

Students are to design a character of themselves when they were five or six years old.

    Look for twenty live-action poses with interesting gestures from photographs to study, borrow, and adapt these poses for the character.

    Make silhouettes of these final poses to accompany this presentation.

### Project 2: Rolling Assignment

Transfer, by means of cut and paste, and register a series of preanimated drawings to animation papers. Make up to five drawings. Students are to learn how to roll and see the animation drawings in motion on the animation disc (for more information on animation disc go to *www.alangordon.com/s_animation.html*).

### Project 3: Bouncing Can in One Place

A cylinder shaped object made of rubber is to be bounced up and down. Timing, anticipation, and exaggeration principles are to be explored.

### Project 4: Roller Coaster

Design a long shot of a roller coaster track. Animate a train of up to five cars rolling about the track. A look at how weight in relation to gravitational force affects arcs.

### Project 5: Bouncing Ball

Animate a bouncing ball across the field. Students are to convey a specific type of mass through motion, such as a beach ball or a rubber ball. Squash and stretch is to be examined.

### Project 6: A Fox Waving its Tail

Design a fox sitting on a fence, put the body on one level as a held cel, and animate the tail waving back and forth. Follow-through and overlapping are to be explored.

### Project 7: A Flour Sack Hops

Design a flour sack character with three distinct movable parts and animate the character hopping across the field. This assignment is to reinforce the basic animation principles covered in earlier assignments. Rhythms and pacing of the scene are also to be examined.

### Project 8: A Character Walk

Design a character and make a walk that would describe an emotional thought.

### Project 9: One-Shot Scene

Create a complete one-shot scene of a character in a pantomime situation up to fifteen seconds in length with full layout.

### Project 10: Compositional Exercise

Give assorted compositional assignments for students to explore the various screen aspect ratios. The exercises should involve composing a set of predetermined graphic elements within a specific working space and describing a phrase of music.

### Project 11: A Ninety-Second Short Film

Create a short film up to ninety seconds in length with no dialogue. This assignment occupies the entire length of the second semester and is the major final project of the class.

## conclusion

To create an illustration of a movement is simple, but to give life to a movement requires much sensibility, inquisitiveness, hard work, and perseverance. This class does not aim toward teaching specific techniques but acts as a springboard to further explorations, to inspire students to have broad and solid fundamental views, encouraging the individuals to find their way to creative expression through the medium of animation.

## recommended readings

Thomas, Frank, and Ollie Johnston, *The Illusion of Life: Disney Animation*, Hyperion, 1981.

Williams, Richard, *The Animator's Survival Kit: A Manual of Methods, Principles, and Formulas for Classical, Computer, Games, Stop Motion, and Internet Animators*, Faber & Faber, 2001.

# section2
## sophomores

**COURSE TITLE:** Advanced Motion Graphics

**TEACHER:** Joel Lava

**FREQUENCY:** One Semester, twelve weeks

**LEVEL:** Student's year in school is less important than his experience, so the instructor must see previous work or know the individual's skill level.

**CREDITS:** 3

**DEGREE:** Bachelor of Fine Arts

**SCHOOL:** California Institute of the Arts, Valencia, CA

## summary and goal of class

The goal of this class is to recognize mograph genres and transition techniques, and to understand quick-read communication. By the end of the class, students should have animated, and gained valuable experience with, a ten-second show open/logo resolve.

## week by week

**WEEK 1. INTRODUCTION.** Six major mograph categories will be covered . . . they can all overlap and combine, but this is a good approach:

1. Fluid—This is animation that flows smoothly from shot to shot, from design frame to design frame. It's as though morphs are going on when, in reality, it's just seamless graphic elements moving from one scene to the next. Psyop is king of this style.

2. Organic—This genre feels real, though still artistic. Often the frame is dark and moody with hints of photo-real textures and many exaggerated lens flares. Visual effects are becoming more prevalent in motion graphics and could be listed here. Imaginary Forces is known for this genre.

3. Vector—This is based out of Illustrator or other vector programs. Dealing mostly with silhouettes and solid colors, using vector images allows for massive scaling of elements without loss of detail. Brand New School did this genre well.

4. Hand-Drawn—This genre got popular as a rebellion from clean vector and typically employs paint drips, rough paper, or a jittery stop motion feel. Eyeball's rebrand of Comedy Central is a good example.

5. Collage—Also known as "Kitchen sink" style, collage may involve throwing in everything to the kitchen sink. Just like the collages of cut out magazine images we make in second grade, this style has the same feel, an often frenetic, rapid animation style. Stardust does this well.

6. Film—This style is seen in film titles and trailers. There is a pacing common to trailer graphics and they have a heavy focus on typography. Picture Mill does good stuff here.

**WEEK 2. ART OF THE ENDTAG.** An endtag is the mainstay of motion graphics—there's always a need for them and they pay well. An endtag is the five-second graphics presentation of the company logo that comes at the end of a twenty-five-second commercial. The class will discuss the ways an endtag comes together, its purpose artistically, and the role it plays as the bread and butter for a company. This discussion includes logo resolves (How does the logo form from different shapes into the final presentation?). Logo resolves are also important for show opens, such as the formation of titles for MTV shows or regular drama TV shows that require a signature title page that moves but is still easy to read.

**WEEK 3. COPYING AND CONCEPTING IN MOGRAPH.** Discuss how originality plays out in design. Film medium is more original, while design lifts more from itself and everywhere else. Still, the best design has an inviting concept and an engaging idea behind the bells and whistles. Show many examples, such as the Psyop Lugz spot compared to the Logan iPod spot with Eminem.

**WEEK 4. DESIGN STORYBOARDS.** Discuss method and approach to creating boards. How many? How big? And how do you show motion in still frames? One must convey concepts clearly, while leaving ambiguity to play in the mind of the client. For a commercial presentation, it's best to do at least six frames for a board. It is now common to post boards online as opposed to printing the boards out and pasting them on blackboard. Instead of doing several 4:3 frames, another method is to do wide panoramic frames that are more majestic and imply horizontal movement.

**WEEK 5. POPULAR TECHNIQUE.** After Effects 3D (AE 3D) is more limited then regular 3D because it only allows for animating with planes, though these planes can be precomps of footage or other 3-D shapes made from assembled planes. AE 3D can be a quick way to add depth and dynamism to a normally flat and boring animation. Give a demonstration of how to properly set up a 3-D camera (parent the Rotation and Position nulls to camera instead of animating the camera itself) and some tricks to get it to work or make cool stuff.

**WEEK 6. LIVE ACTION.** Demonstrate different ways live action can be incorporated into motion graphics. This includes green screen. It would help to have green screen footage to demonstrate how to key.

**WEEK 7. LIVE ACTION CONTINUED.** Discuss how to animate different live-action clips together. Show how to storyboard for a shoot and how to do a rough cut with green screen footage.

**WEEK 8. INTRO TO 3-D.** Show how simple and complicated 3-D visual effects are incorporated. Explain what a beginner can do, and how to work with an experienced 3-D vendor and incorporate its elements. Possibly demonstrate CINEMA 4D and Maya, and discuss the pros and cons of each application.

**WEEKS 9–12.** Mostly criticism and technical help.

## class projects

Endtag (animation due week 3)
Logo Resolve (boards due week 3, animation due week 6)
Final project (boards due week 7, animation due at the end of the course)

## recommended readings

*Adobe After Effects Classroom in a Book*, Adobe Press, 2006.
Meyer Trish, and Chris Meyer, *Creating Motion Graphics with After Effects*, CMP Books, 2004.

COURSE TITLE: Media in Motion 1 and 2

TEACHER: Tracy Colby

FREQUENCY: Two Semesters, fifteen weeks each

LEVEL: Sophomore, required course

CREDITS: 3 per semester

DEGREE: Bachelor of Fine Arts

SCHOOL: Otis College of Art and Design, Los Angeles, CA

## summary

At the start of Media in Motion 1, students focus on finding and telling stories while they acquire skills in Photoshop, Illustrator, and Final Cut Pro. Students are introduced to concepting, production, and postproduction processes through creating individual and group projects. As part of this process, students learn professional practices in project management and presentation. About two-thirds of the way through the semester, motion graphics concepts and principles are introduced, and the students begin to design for motion while learning how to use After Effects.

In Media in Motion 2, the primary focus is on motion graphics concept development, design, and production. Students are introduced to the principles of animation through exercises and projects. Motion concepts are explored for assigned problems, and files are created using Photoshop, Illustrator, and Final Cut Pro. They are then integrated with audio in After Effects to produce design and storytelling solutions. More advanced aspects of After Effects, such as perspective space, lighting, and expressions, are also explored. Concept, narrative, design principles, and color theory are emphasized to increase the emotional impact on the audience. Students work on both individual and group projects.

**Goal.** The goal of this yearlong class is for the students to learn how to tell stories that create maximum emotional involvement in an audience. Students also learn to use hardware, software, and other analog and digital tools in their work and to understand what professionalism means in the context of motion design.

## media in motion 1

**WEEK 1.** Students begin the year with a storytelling project using postcards. The images need to be collaged and seamlessly integrated. Visual and intellectual dissonances are presented as one successful design strategy for the postcards. Students are introduced to technical issues and professional practices, and they begin to work in Photoshop with scanned images.

**Project: The Travel is Broadening postcard series.** Students create three postcards that present us with intellectually and visually dissonant events on a journey. These visual situations must amuse, amaze, inform, and otherwise involve us. The address side of the card is also required. It must include a stamp that emphasizes the essence of the card, plus a message to the recipient. Examples from previous years are shown.

**WEEK 2.** Postcards are discussed, and students receive suggestions for the improvement of their postcards. Help with revisions is given to prepare for a graded critique the following week. More Photoshop tools are presented and experimented with.

**WEEK 3.** After the graded critique, students begin their first time-based assignment, the slate. A three- to five-second slate presents information about the movie that follows it. The slate should also visually relate to the movie that follows it. The concept of a countdown is presented with examples and discussion.

**Project: Slate and Countdown.** For this project, a countdown is defined as that time and those experiences that precede an important event. For a child this might mean counting down to Christmas. For astronauts there are many countdowns that lead up to the launch of the spaceship. The students must present a well-organized, linear countdown to an event in eleven Photoshop images with audio appropriate to the countdown. Numbers are optional, although they can help to increase the tension of the preevent sequence. The total duration of the piece is up to thirty seconds, including slate and credits.

**WEEKS 4–5.** Students bring the required Countdown assets to class to make their first movie. Final Cut Pro is introduced to the students via lecture and demonstration, after which the students work with their Countdown files in Final Cut. The instructor and teaching assistant help students solve problems during the class. Issues of levels, color, image quality, file management, render, formats, and codec are discussed as they arise. All movies are due near the end of class so that we can all view and comment on them. Students choose an affinity group of three to five people for the fifth week's One Day Movie project, must buy a thirty- to sixty-minute DV tape, and must arrange for digital video camera and tripod. While this is a group project, each student is responsible for creating an initial story line that will be voted on in the group.

**Projects: Countdown revision and One Day Movie.** During the week students will revise their Countdowns per the comments of the instructor and the teaching assistant. The One Day Movie project groups meet and agree on a story. Each student should have his own vision for the agreed upon story so that an adequate number of shots can be made for editing purposes. Individual storyboards are required. Groups must have a tripod and digital video camera, both of which are available from our video lab.

**WEEKS 6–9.** During these weeks additional Photoshop and Final Cut information including green screen techniques are presented. A new project topic, How I/We Got Here, is presented to the class. Students explore possibilities for this individual project through Web and library research. Students are encouraged to develop a metaphor for their particular take on the meaning of this phrase. This project is open to their own points of view and pieces have ranged from how they came to Otis to cultural creation myths, interpretations of adventures, epic novels, and poetry.

**Project: How I/We Got Here Movie.** The project includes metaphor/concept development, storyboards, presentation of boards in class, creation of elements, taping, capture, editing, and, at the end, a presentation of the piece in class. Students must demonstrate progress with the project each class day. The final movie is due at the beginning of class in the ninth week.

**WEEK 10.** This week students are introduced to type creation in Illustrator. They are presented with the possibilities of using type as word and/or as image. Basic typographic terminology is introduced and, via type selection, students create an expressive visual "voice" for two poetic forms that are opposite in mood and feel.

**WEEKS 11–12.** The students begin to use type in After Effects. They import type outlines from Illustrator and begin to animate them by setting keyframes for changes in the Position and Rotation Transforms over time. The students learn about animation assistants and move to animating anchor points, time stretching, reversing, layer, and blending. Motion blur and useful effects are introduced. Students begin a series of exercises that help them to design for motion, such as picking a font and using it to expressively animate a word that describes a mood or emotion. Students must include audio and a slate, and make a fifteen-second QuickTime movie.

**WEEKS 13–14.** Students pick a haiku and animate it with audio to emphasize its emotional experience. They then begin to work with aspects of masking, track mattes, and transparency when using type. Precomposing and blend modes are also introduced.

**WEEK 15.** The final exam is a practical one. It is called The Book—The Movie. Students are given a book and asked to create a fifteen-second piece that, through motion, color, type, and image, gives us the essence of the book. Students have used auto repair manuals, dictionaries, collections of photographs, how-to books, and literary works to make these final movies.

# media in motion 2

**WEEK 1.** There is a brief review of the After Effects topics covered in the previous semester plus new information on parenting, precomposing, nesting comps, and collapsing transforms. The first project is a one-week intensive called The Animated Road Sign. Students design informational road signs for nontraditional places and animate them in such a way that we experience them. They must have either audio or music or both in an animation of twenty seconds or less.

**WEEK 2. Project: Effects-O-Rama.** Students take a series of still images, or use a number of different pieces of footage, apply one to four effects to each of them, and then render them as a movie. This lets the students see what the effects do to their files and how they can work in combination. Movie duration is to be one minute, and it should have music or some other form of audio as part of the piece.

**WEEKS 3–6.** Introduction of perspective space, lights, and cameras in After Effects. Begin Print to Motion project.

**Project: Print to Motion.** The premise of this project is that by taking a well-designed print piece and creating an animation that is not a literal interpretation of it, the students will:

- Choose something that appeals to them emotionally, visually, and intellectually
- Be deeply involved in understanding the concept and visual construction of the piece
- Become more aware of how type is used effectively
- Have a bit of distance from the creation of the still image
- Feel freer to experiment

35

Research is required, including a presentation of information about the designer and the client. Also required are style frames that give us the look and the feel of the piece without being a formal sequential storyboard. Duration will be thirty to sixty seconds. Audio and/or music are required. Credits must include the designer's and client's names and the name of the publication in which the print piece appeared.

**WEEKS 7–8.** After Effects topics include more arcane tools such as vector paint, path text, continuous rasterization, more Photoshop for After Effects, and the dreaded Expressions in After Effects. We now begin the Nursery Rhyme project.

**Project: The Nursery Rhyme.** Students take a traditional English-language nursery rhyme and translate it into a film genre, such as horror, musical, screwball comedy, etc. They build characters and backgrounds by parenting unlikely objects or body parts together and animate the rhyme.

**WEEKS 9–13/14. Project: The Otis Scholarship Benefit.** Each year the Media in Motion 2 classes create motion graphics for our Otis Scholarship Benefit. The Benefit is a gala evening for Otis's benefactors and features a runway show of the outstanding work that the fashion-design juniors and seniors have done under the direction of fashion-industry mentors such as Bob Mackie and Todd Oldham.

The Media in Motion 2 students take direction from the head of our School of Fashion Design. They then choose one of the ten or more fashion-designer mentors, research the scene direction the mentors have given the fashion students, and create a motion graphics piece to open the scene at the show. They also extend or create another piece to act as a visual background for models. Students create a brief opening motion graphic for the entire benefit and credits to end the show as well. Our sophomores deliver the work according to contract specifications on an agreed-upon date. Professionalism is emphasized along with storytelling skills.

**WEEK 15.** Students build a DVD of their work for both semesters and reflect on their experiences over the past year.

COURSE TITLE: Interactive Media

TEACHER: Al Wasco

FREQUENCY: One Semester

LEVEL: Sophomore

CREDITS: 3

DEGREE: Associate of Applied Business Degree in Visual Communication and Design with a concentration in Interactive Media

SCHOOL: Cuyahoga Community College, Cleveland, OH

## summary

This course is about:

- Using the capabilities of the computer to create an experience that engages the eyes, ears, and mind
- Storytelling, words, music, conversation, work, and games
- Creating compelling and informative computer-based multimedia presentations

We will explore the possibilities and limitations of digital media, working primarily with Macromedia Director and incorporating photography, audio, and video.

**Objectives.** If you successfully complete this course, you will be able to:

- Explain the similarities and differences between print and electronic media and how these affect the design process
- Use flowcharts, storyboards, and other methods of visualizing your idea and presenting it to an audience
- Use sequencing and pacing effectively to create and sustain interest
- Choose and use sound for mood, emphasis, and information
- Understand the primary capabilities of Macromedia Director software
- Use Macromedia Director to create an interactive narrative presentation incorporating sound, visuals, and interactivity
- Use simple testing methods to evaluate user response to your work

**Technology.** Macromedia Director and/or Flash, Photoshop, sound-editing software (e.g., Audacity, Soundtrack, GarageBand)

**Student Requirements.** Second year status (of two-year program), digital imaging competency

# week by week

**WEEK 1.** Introductions . . . what to expect in this class. What is interactive multimedia? Why Macromedia Director? A look at some interactive work.

Macromedia Director (DIR): Overall interface; score window; paint window; timing in frame-based media; creating visual elements; importing visuals and sound. Create a simple linear movie; simple tempo channel control.

**WEEK 2.** Interaction. Types of interaction, history, recent developments.

DIR: Tempo channel, wait for mouseclick; transition channel; simple behaviors; pause/continue, hold on frame. Toolbar buttons; better buttons via exchange cast member. Transition movie; pause/continue controls.

**WEEK 3.** Planning. Putting ideas on paper: concept paper, storyboards, paper prototypes.

DIR: User controls: tool palette buttons; using prebuilt behaviors; writing your own behaviors; creating a projector to show your movie on any Macintosh.

**WEEK 4.** Navigation and user experience. How do I get there? Where am I? How do I get back? Role of feedback, visual and auditory; user expectations.

DIR: Cursor change behavior; puppetsounds; visual feedback.

**WEEK 5.** Sound. Uses (background, narration, SFX), sources, technical issues.

DIR: Capturing sound from CD; importing; recording in Director; using sound channels; multiple channels; syncing sound to action.

**WEEK 6.** More sound: creating and controlling. Overall look and feel; use of metaphor, etc.

Introduction of Director Tricks Jukebox (midterm project, due Week 8)

DIR: Sound channel vs. puppetsounds; multiple channels; stopping sound. Simple sound editing with SoundEdit. Creating musical backgrounds with SmartSound. Recording and importing.

**WEEK 7.** Director Tricks Jukebox: sketches and storyboards due.
Animation!

DIR: Tweening; real-time animation; step animation; tweaking animation: ease-in/ease-out; tweening size, blend, etc.

**WEEK 8.** Director Tricks Jukebox due.
Introduction of final project (due Week 16 )

**WEEK 9.** BREAK—NO CLASS

**WEEK 10.** Developing a larger project. Scheduling, priorities, sources. Naming and organizing source material; archiving; production notes.

DIR: Using MouseEnter/MouseLeave; sprite as cursor; animated cursors.

**WEEK 11.** Visuals, sound, interaction, and emotion.

DIR: Visual effects: on/off, fades, cycling, etc; ink effects. Importing and controlling QuickTime and Flash.

**WEEK 12.** Director and the Internet. Go to URL from movie; planning for Shockwave format; Shockwave, Flash, and QuickTime

DIR: Typographic concerns: text cast member vs. graphic text; choosing fonts; embedding fonts.

**WEEK 13.** Workday.

DIR: Shockwave: delivering on the Web.

**WEEK 14.** Final Project user testing. Each student arranges for two people to come to class and look at projects.

DIR: Special topics as needed.

**WEEK 15.** Final revisions. Make changes based on user input; other improvements and modifications.

DIR: Special topics as needed.

**WEEK 16.** Final project due and critique.

**WEEK 17.** Portfolio, production and beyond. Creating a "shell" to play multiple movies; adapting for the Web; burning a cross-platform CD. We'll burn a CD of class projects for everyone.

# assignment: intimate portrait

Create a multilayered portrait of a person (other than yourself), a place, or a thing. Show three separate and distinct views or layers:

1. SURFACE: This refers to the outside, which anyone can see at a glance or at first encounter. Think about your impression of someone you meet briefly at a party, your view of a place the first time you visit, or your feeling in a car the first time you drive it. What emotion best describes your first reaction?

2. BELOW THE SURFACE: This involves those aspects of the subject that you learn after you've spent some time with him/her/it. Think about a co-worker you know casually, a cousin you see once in a while, a vacation spot you've been to a couple of times, or a tool you've used for a while but haven't really mastered. What emotion best describes your understanding of the subject at this level?

3. CORE: This delves into that which you know, see, or understand only because you are extremely close to the subject. Think about your closest friend, a place you go to because you feel at your best when you're there, or a beloved object that you'd risk your life to save in a fire. What emotion expresses your intimate knowledge of the subject?

Develop a way of showing each layer: you can use any combination of visuals, sounds, and/or words (text). Choose an approach that fits the subject and the layer you're portraying. Some things are best shown with images, others work better as sounds, still others as words, spoken or written. Of course you can combine two or more of these.

Create each layer as a separate Director movie. Try to work on all of them more or less at the same time, so all three develop together and play off of each other. Think about how you can provide ways to explore all layers, allowing the user/viewer to go back and forth among them, rather than creating a strict first-second-third linear structure.

A successful project will:

- Show three distinct layers of your subject,
- Provide an engaging way for the user/viewer to move between and among the layers, and
- Have a strong emotional impact: the user/viewer should come away feeling your deep connection to this subject.

## recommended readings

Crawford, Chris, *On Interactive Storytelling*, New Riders, 2005.
    More oriented toward game design than other books, technical and specific.

Dawes, Brenda, *Analog In, Digital Out*, New Riders, 2007.
    Takes a "big picture" view of interactivity, from snow globes to processing movies digitally in order to covert them to abstract typographic patterns.

Kirstof, Ray, and Amy Satran, *Interactivity by Design*, Hayden Books, 1995.
    A cookbook for planning and developing multimedia, getting a bit long in the tooth.

Laurel, Brenda, *Computers As Theatre*, Addison-Wesley, 1993.
    A classic that includes the significant "rule": Think of the computer not as a tool, but as a medium.

McAdams, Mindy, *Flash Journalism*, Focal Press, 2005.
    Practical applications of Flash to create interactive narratives. Written for Flash MX 2004, making it in need of technical revision.

Pearce, Celia, *The Interactive Book*, Macmillan Technical Publishing, 1997.
    This book focuses on the inspiration for, and explanation of, interactivity.

Saffer, Dan, *Designing for Interaction*, New Riders/AIGA Voices That Matter, 2007.
    Concepts, practices, and methods of connecting people with the products they use.

COURSE TITLE: 3-D Computer Animation Workshop 1

TEACHER: Phil McNagny

FREQUENCY: One Semester, once a week

LEVEL: Undergraduate

CREDITS: 3

DEGREE: Bachelor of Fine Arts

SCHOOL: New York University, Tisch School of the Arts, Kanbar
Institute of Film and Television, Animation Studies, New York, NY

## objectives

My main goal in this class is to equip you with a firm beginner's understanding of Maya, one of the leading 3-D packages in the industry. Not only will you learn about Maya, you will leave the class with a better grasp of what creating in 3-D entails, regardless of the program (i.e., tool) you use.

While we will cover animation principles in this class, it is important you understand that in order to achieve your best potential, all the groundwork must be in place. After all, as a 3-D creator you will be wearing many hats! This means that without a good model, the animation can't be at its best; and if the lighting or texturing is wrong, your piece won't look its best. All this is to warn you that we won't be jumping into any involved character animation at first. Rather, we will start off with modeling and then work our way through other facets of the process, so that when our class concludes, you'll be ready to take on bigger projects of your own.

One thing to note: Because of the amount of information we have to cover in fourteen classes, if time permits, it is very likely I will cover territory from other parts of our syllabus just to be sure we get it all!

## assignments

These will be announced in class but will include readings and lessons from the textbook, some short animations I assign, and evaluations of animation I have you watch, etc. I will not expect a final thirty-second piece, but instead, shorter, more focused studies.

# evaluations

Each student will be graded based on the following:

- Attendance and class participation/contribution: 20%
- Assignments (their completion, timely submission, and quality): 80%

# week by week

**WEEK 1.** Attendance policy: DON'T MISS!!! Basic concepts of 3-D creation, from inception to final product. An introduction to the Maya interface and the main toolset. A few very simple tasks to perform during class, including a look at common scene elements. The concept of translation (X, Y, Z). Importance of using the help files. No homework.

**WEEK 2.** Review of week 1 material. Nodes (the building blocks of the program) and channels. The importance of history to your workflow. Introduction to surface creation and an explanation of the different modeling methods used. Polygons and components of a polygonal surface. Modeling techniques (booleans, smoothing operations, splitting faces, duplicating, mirroring, etc). Homework.

**WEEK 3.** Further work with polygons. Proper layout of faces determined by the object's final use. Flipping normals, quad vs. triangular tessellation, duplicating and extracting faces, extruding along a curve, etc. Homework.

**WEEK 4.** In-class demo of building a simple face using the poly proxy method and image planes. Importance of edge loops and point placement. Homework.

**WEEK 5.** Diving in deeper—using the attribute editor, outliner, hypergraph, and hypershade to affect various nodes of the objects you've created. First attempt at animating (bouncing ball) using nonlinear deformers. Students will also gain a basic understanding of keyframing and the timeline, and the graph and trax editors. Overview of animation principles. Homework.

**WEEK 6.** NURBS overview and components of a NURBS's surface—the curve, importance of tangency and isoparm placement (very quick demonstration with surface skinned to a set of bones), creating curves with EP and CV tool. Rebuilding curves, making surfaces by revolving or lofting curves, curve-on-surface (duplicate surface curve). Snapping objects and CVs to other CVs, curve and centers of objects. Extruding a curve along another, conversion of NURBS's surfaces into polygonal surfaces. Quick introduction to patch modeling (and why anyone even thought of it). In-class lesson (if time allows) and homework assignment.

**WEEK 7.** Modeling with subdivision surfaces and their popularity in the industry. Screening of Pixar's *Geri's Game*. Switching between hierarchy and proxy mode, creasing, joining edges and vertices; levels to work at; texturing and animating using a poly proxy. Introduction to (or review of) deformers; lattices, sculpt deformers, clusters, Artisan (how these work at the surface and subsurface levels). Homework.

**WEEK 8.** Animation (yeah!) topics. Building your models so as to optimize "animatibility." Building a good skeleton (adding joints, rerooting). Different options for skinning and how to choose which is best. FK/IK. Various IK handles and which to use. Using the connection editor, channel editor, and adding/removing/locking attributes. Bring aspirin! Homework.

**WEEK 9.** More animation topics. Further work with IK systems and the IK spline handle. Homework.

**WEEK 10.** Discuss animation principles and how they can be implemented in Maya (and when are they appropriate). I will show examples and hold class discussion on this. How to animate using Maya. Setting keyframes, breaking connections (using channel editor), setting playback range, fps, playblasting, f-curves, dope sheet, key tangency and how it affects timing and movement. Homework.

**WEEK 11.** Setting up a scene. Which lights to use for a desired effect. Cameras—when to move the camera and when to zoom/adjust f-stop. Importance of camera movement in storytelling, how to avoid jerky camera moves (nothing yells "amateur" like sloppy camera).

**WEEK 12.** Texturing. Using multilister vs. hypershade. What a shader does (defines the appearance of the geometry in your scene, going so far as to alter the topology of your surface). Creating shading networks and how to achieve certain looks. Differences between shaders and utilities in Maya. Homework.

**WEEK 13.** Texturing. Examples of some useful shading networks. Using utility nodes to help with animation. Homework.

**WEEK 14.** Further texturing and shading work. Rendering topics, using hardware renderer, mental ray, IPR, and the various settings within render globals. Final class wrap up.

## required reading

Derakhshani, Dariush, *Introducing Maya 7: 3D for Beginners*, Sybex, 2005.

**COURSE TITLE:** 3-D Computer Animation Workshop 2

**TEACHER:** Phil McNagny

**FREQUENCY:** One Semester, once a week

**LEVEL:** Sophomore

**CREDITS:** 3

**DEGREE:** Bachelor of Fine Arts

**SCHOOL:** New York University, Tisch School of the Arts, Kanbar Institute
of Film and Television, Animation Studies, New York, NY

## objectives

In this class I want to get you to the next level in your understanding of Maya, to expand on what you've learned in your introductory courses, and to start you off working on your first personal projects. This means we'll take a closer look at modeling, build more complex (and functional) rigs, do some simple scripting to speed up our workflow, dig deeper into texturing and UV mapping, and even explore some of Maya's dynamics capabilities. You'll also try your hand at some animation exercises from the course text, *Stop Staring: Facial Modeling and Animation Done Right*.

## assignments

I will announce assignments in class, but they will include readings and lessons from the textbook, some short animations I assign, evaluations of animation I have you watch, etc. I will expect a final project from this class, whether it's an animated character or some beautifully lit scenes.

## evaluations

Each student will be graded based on the following:

- Attendance and class participation/contribution (which includes your presence and participation in the forum): 20%
- Assignments (their completion, timely submission, and quality): 80%

# week by week

**WEEK 1.** Attendance policy: DON'T MISS!!! Overview of program commands, creating one's own hotkeys and marking menus, etc.

**WEEK 2.** Delving deeper into polygons and sub-d's; flipping and averaging normals; using the bevel tool, cut faces tool, and quad vs. triangular tessellation; possibly an overview of the Bonus Tools and MJ Poly tools (installing MEL scripts may have to be covered!). Homework. Develop project further.

**WEEK 3.** Demonstration of building a simple face based on chapters from *Stop Staring* with examples of poly layouts from the pros. Homework (projects should be close to finalization).

**WEEK 4.** NURBS modeling in more detail. Examples of animating a loft or extrude, trims and birails, projecting curves on a surface, animated sweeps and their use, introduction to patch modeling (if students are not familiar with this technique). Homework. Projects should be finalized by this point.

**WEEKS 5–6.** Building more user-friendly rigs. Joint layout, IK handles, constraints, iconic representation, SDKs, IK spline handles, mixing soft and rigid binding for best effect. Homework. Check up on project progress.

**WEEK 7.** Other animation techniques: animating along a path and achieving more predictable behavior, using dynamics to solve simple animation tasks and then animating to match, baking keys.

45

**WEEK 8.** Creating character sets and using the trax editor and clips to move animation from one scene to another. We'll also cover the AnimExport/Import plugin. Homework. Check up on project progress.

**WEEKS 9–10.** Texturing NURBS, poly and sub-d objects and the different approaches one would use. Texture optimizations (baking shadows and textures), displacement and bump mapping, shading networks and utility nodes. If time permits, more in-depth exploration of lighting.

**WEEKS 11–12.** Exploration of particle and soft/rigid body dynamics and their requisite fields. A possible look at cloth, but no promises! Check up on project progress.

**WEEK 13.** Lighting and camera work. Make up for whatever didn't get covered or what needs repeating.

**WEEK 14.** Viewing of final projects, milk and cookies. Final class wrap up.

# required reading

Osipa, Jason. *Stop Staring: Facial Modeling and Animation Done Right*, Sybex, 2007.

**COURSE TITLE:** Time-Based Communication: Grammar and Syntax

**TEACHER:** Wojtek E. Janczak

**FREQUENCY:** One Semester, thirteen weeks for four hours per week

**LEVEL:** Undergraduate

**CREDITS:** 3

**DEGREE:** Honours Bachelor of Design

**SCHOOL:** York University, York/Sheridan Honours Bachelor of Design
Program, Toronto, Ontario

## summary and goals

The course focuses on the visual grammar and language syntax of time-based communication and motion graphics and explores concepts and techniques involved in the integration of images, typography, digital video, and audio into vibrant and persuasive communication environments. (For more information, see the course Web site at *www.yorku.ca/janczak/courses/time2006*.)

46

**Outcomes.** Upon completion of this course, students should be able to:

- Critically review and demonstrate a contextual understanding of issues related to the time-based communication and motion graphics visual culture
- Investigate the visual grammar and creative strategies of the time-based communication and motion graphics
- Appreciate the creative and conceptual aspects, as well as technical issues, of the subject matter
- Produce creative time-based communication and motion graphics projects using standard computer software
- Demonstrate independence and self-initiation in learning
- Continue to pursue any research interests in time-based communication and motion graphics visual culture or production in the industry
- Establish an individual vision and creative thinking philosophy

**Technology.** Software: Final Cut Pro, After Effects, Flash. Hardware: digital camcorders, digital decks, computers.

**Student Requirements.** Third-year level of the program

# week by week

**WEEK 1.** Project introduction

**WEEK 2.** DUE: Preliminary project definition and research

    1. Creative Brief—Written proposal. This includes:

       1.1  Project title

       1.2  Project overview

       1.3  Project goals and objectives
- Who is the client?
- What does the client/organization want this project to accomplish?

       1.4  Audience study (primary and secondary)
- Who is the audience?
- What are their needs and expectations?
- What do we want the message to accomplish for the selected audience?

       1.5  Content requirements. Content requirements are defined in order to determine what forms of information need to be included in the product: text, images, audio, video, etc.
- General content description
- List of categories and subcategories

       1.6  Content sources: text, images, video, sound, music
- Where do you acquire the content? Did you write your own text? Take photos? Hire professionals?
- Did you use existing sources? Where did they exist? In what format?

       1.7  Delivery environment (technical and functional requirements) for the screen-based information. Technical and functional requirements are defined in order to determine the project functionality.

       1.8  Production tools (software and hardware)

       1.9  Schedule

       1.10  Research. Information sources: books, articles, Web sites, etc.

       1.11  Comparative study. Visual/conceptual references: URLs for online examples, movies on CDs, DVDs, videotapes, etc.

    2. Narrative: sixty-second narrative presented in a print format

    3. Storyboard: Storyboard and script in a print format

**WEEK 3.** DUE: Refined Creative Brief, Narrative, and Storyboard
For the next class:

**1.** Final Creative Brief presented in hard copy and online

**2.** Final Narrative presented on hard copy, and voice-recorded version presented in digital format online

3. Final Storyboard due in hard copy and in QuickTime digital format online

**WEEK 4.** DUE for grading (worth 30% of the final grade):

1. Final Creative Brief presented on paper and online
2. Final Narrative due on paper, and recorded and presented in digital format online
3. Final Storyboard due on paper and QuickTime format online

For the next class:
Preliminary prototype (digital storyboard): full length sixty seconds
Start shooting video and include it in the prototype

**WEEK 5.** Production and postproduction
DUE: Preliminary prototype online (movie 1)

**WEEK 6.** Production and postproduction
DUE: Refined prototype online (movie 2)
Introduction to project 2 as project 1 concludes
For the next class: Project definition and research: analysis of project requirements, research, planning
Preliminary Creative Brief, preliminary flow chart (project map), and preliminary storyboard for project 2 are to be presented during the week 8 class.

**WEEK 7.** Reading week
Continue postproduction and complete the Final Movie.

**WEEK 8.** Presentation (worth 20% of the final grade): Final Movie
DUE: Preliminary Creative Brief, flow chart (project map), and storyboard for project 2
For the next class, revise and complete the Creative Brief, the flow chart (project map), and the storyboard.
The final written/visual proposal will be presented online and in printed format. Start creating and collecting contents: text, images, multimedia files

**WEEK 9.** DUE: Final Creative Brief presented online and in printed format; final flow chart (project map); and final storyboard presented online and in printed format
For the next class: Digital Prototype 1

**WEEK 10.** DUE: Prototype 1 online
For the next class: Prototype 2

**WEEK 11.** DUE: Prototype 2 online
For the next class: Prototype 3

**WEEK 12.** DUE: Prototype 3 online

    For the next class: complete the project

**WEEK 13.** DUE: Presentation of the Final Project online and on a CD/DVD

# assignments and projects

## Project 1: Time-Based Communication

The outcome of this project has a form of a time-based message expressed as a digital video. It consists of a sixty-second movie focused on one of the following topics: social issues, environmental problems, human relations, media, sexuality, violence, information technology, education, design, art, government, poverty, health.

    Students select a topic, develop a verbal and visual proposal, and produce a movie in a QuickTime format for a CD/DVD and World Wide Web distribution.

## Project 2: Narrative/Interactive/Experimental

Keywords: narrative, interactive, digital video, animation, navigation, interface, communication and information design, rich media.

    This can be an individual OR group project.

    Four alternatives:

1. Narrative/interactive/digital video/animation/navigation/information design

    A project combining digital video (Final Cut Pro, After Effects) in an interactive environment (Flash, ActionScript). The project can also include Flash animation.

2. Narrative/interactive/animation/navigation/information design

    An opening main screen with links to informative instructions in the form of time-based animations.

    It can be a collaborative project. Students work initially in groups consisting of three or more people to select a topic for the project. Each student designs a main screen and an instructional animation. Once all three (or more) instructional animations are completed individually, they should be exchanged between students and linked to the individual main screens. The project will be presented and graded individually.

3. Narrative/interactive/animation

    A Flash animation that introduces multiple options/choices to the audience. It gives the viewer an opportunity to branch off and select a sequence of narrative parts. This option is similar to alternative two, but it is an individual project.

4. Narrative/digital video/animation/communication and information

    A QuickTime movie or Flash animation time-based narrative.

# recommended readings

Curran, Steve, *Motion Graphics: Graphic Design for Broadcast and Film*, Rockport Publishers, 2001.

Curtis, Hillman, *MTIV: Process, Inspiration and Practice for the New Media Designer*, New Riders, 2002.

Davis, Joshua, *Flash to the Core: An Interactive Sketchbook by Joshua Davis*, New Riders, 2002.

Dick, Bernard F., *Anatomy of Film*, 4th ed., St. Martin's Press, 2002.

Galore, Janet, and Todd Kelsey, *Flash MX Design for TV and Video*, John Wiley & Sons, 2002.

Gremmler, Tobias, and Tanja Diezmann, *Grids for the Dynamic Image*, AVA Publishing, 2003.

Krasner, Jon, *Motion Graphic Design and Fine Art Animation: Principles and Practice*, Focal Press, 2004.

Meyer, Trish, and Chris Meyer, *Creating Motion Graphics with After Effects*, CMP Books, 2004.

Seol, Euna, *Flash MX Motion Graphics*, Sybex, 2002.

Woolman, Matt, *Moving Type: Designing for Time and Space*, RotoVision, 2000.

Ziegler, Kathleen, Nick Greco, and Tamye Riggs eds., *Motion Graphics: Film & TV*, Watson-Guptill, 2002.

## summary and goals

Understanding Visual Narrative is a sophomore-level course that reexamines foundational design education via the integration of time-based media for communication. A "primer" toward understanding narrative sequencing, it is a rigorous approach to the fundamentals of visual communication within motion design.

The course edifies theory and practice related to time-based media—motion, sound, sequencing, and narrative—integrated with traditional typographic and design pedagogies.

Ideation methods for storytelling are introduced—brainstorming, mind mapping, writing, storyboarding, and diagramming—whereby students learn specific processes toward narrative communication vis-a-vis a visual design context. Course goals:

- Merging traditional studies in form and communication with vocabularies and guiding principles specific to screen-based media
- Indoctrinating time-based media in tandem with foundational design curricula
- Integrating motion literacy in an informed manner, rather than adding motion for motion's sake
- Arming students with theory, practice, and vocabularies for narrative in communication design

## outcomes

1. Students revisit a time-honored design assignment, "The Black Square Problem" (Wilde, Judith, and Richard Wilde, "Part 1: Graphic Design Exercises," *Visual Literacy: A Conceptual Approach to Graphic Problem Solving*, Watson-Guptill, 1991: 16–27.) via the use of typography, color, animation, and four black squares to communicate the following concepts: order, increase, bold, congestion, tension, and playful (Wilde 17).

2. Students produce a three-minute typographic animation comparing and contrasting the history and form of three type classifications.

3. Students write and produce a one-minute animation based on the concept of "Cause and Effect," by writing a short story, breaking it down to a twelve-step storyboard, and translating it to motion with sound/music.

## assignment one—the black square problem revisited: text, color, motion

Technology: Macromedia Flash

Synopsis: "The Black Square Problem" is a classic assignment used by design educators to teach fundamentals of form and communication. Using four black squares, students create six compositions each illustrating the following concepts:

*order, increase, bold, congested, tension, playful (Wilde 17)*

"The intention of this problem is to develop a geometric idiom through the discovery of the various two-dimensional design principles needed to extend a limited graphic vocabulary." (Wilde 17) By working through the contrast of negative/positive within a limited space, students experiment by creating meaning from abstract forms.

The Black Square Problem Revisited: Text, Color, Motion reinterprets the students' original 8 × 8 inch solutions (created in gouache) from "The Black Square Problem" by applying typography, color, sequencing, and motion. Students learn the basics of storyboarding and the visual dynamics necessary to express the concept of an existing composition via time.

First, students apply the following attributes:

1. Addition of typography to original black and white gouache compositions (using the word the composition represents)
2. Addition of color
3. Storyboard one composition (that has the addition of text and color) for animation
4. Use of motion to signify the composition

### Part One: Text

Choose four original gouache compositions and integrate the word that corresponds to each layout. (For instance, if the composition represents "bold," then incorporate that word into your original composition.) How does the typography fit the layout? Can the word be broken up? How does the addition of typography affect the existing composition?

Pursue no less than three varying typographic treatments per composition. Limit font choices to the following: Helvetica, Univers, Futura, Gill Sans, Frutiger, Bodoni, Baskerville. (Use one font per composition, however, a combination of weights, sizes, and/or italics within a single composition is acceptable.)

## *Process*

Choose four existing "favorite" gouache compositions. Cut letterforms of varying sizes and arrange (by hand) within your original black square solutions (work from photocopies of original gouache compositions). Once you have four existing compositions resolved with the addition of type, convert your "analog" layouts to Illustrator.

## Part Two: Color

Next, apply the following color methods for each of your four black square and text compositions in an 8 × 8 inch square:

> **1.** One composition uses complementary colors.
>
> **2.** One composition uses monochromatic colors.
>
> **3.** One composition uses analogous colors.
>
> **4.** One composition may use four (or less) colors of your choice.

53

## *Process*

Begin by sketching in colored pencil, cut paper, or tissue overlay. Lecture on color (Itten, Johannes, *The Elements of Color*, Van Nostrand Reinhold, 1970) and color for print and screen. Explanation of CMYK, RGB, and Pantone. Translate final sketched color compositions to Illustrator.

## Part Three: Motion

Choose one of the four—final squares, color, and text compositions—to develop a storyboard showing the concept conveyed via motion. For instance, how does the concept of "bold" animate? How can your composition, with the addition of time, reinforce the concept? The last frame of the storyboard is the finished "static" composition. Remember:

> • Properties: shape, color, surface, size, dimension
> • Transformation: direction, gesture, displacement; kinetics/physics and velocity
> • Space: location, position, framing, focus, point of view, and depth of field
> • Time: sequence, tempo, and transitions

## *Process*

Storyboard frames can be sketched by hand or created digitally. Use expressive arrows to imply direction and speed. There is no limit to the number of storyboard frames—concept dictates content. However, final animations cannot exceed fifteen seconds.

    Animate storyboards in Flash. (Beginner Flash tutorial in class.) Students are limited to working within their existing compositional elements: four squares, text, and color. (Do not add supplemental graphics/photography, music, or sound to the existing composition.)

## Objectives

The intent of this assignment is to apply principle concepts in form and composition, typography, color, and time-based media to convey a message via the use of a simple, graphical, and dynamic composition.

## Deliverables

1. Four static compositions finished at 8 × 8 inches, completed in Illustrator, and printed out in color, mounted to Bristol board

    2. One animation finished at 6 × 6 inches (432 pixels × 432 pixels) and completed in Flash (.swf) at 15 frames per second (fps)

## Schedule

### Part One: Text and Color

**WEEK 1.** Project assigned. Lecture on typography.

**WEEK 2.** Come to class with original black square compositions, glue sticks, scissors, and additional cutting materials. Work in class to incorporate text into original black square compositions. Lecture on color.

**WEEK 3.** Using Illustrator, have several iterations each of the four compositions using the addition of text and color. Have work printed to hang for critique.

### Part Two: Motion

**WEEK 4.** Have finished color and text compositions mounted to present in class. Have storyboard sketches for animations for critique. Flash tutorial in class, work in class on animation.

**WEEK 5.** Have rough animations ready for critique.

**WEEK 6.** Have finished animations (.swfs) ready to present in class.

# assignment two—typographic evolution: classifications in motion

Technology: After Effects

Create a series of three animations that work together as a single time-based piece, visually examining the structural and historical differences between your choice of three typefaces.

Animations should be sequential (oldest typeface to the most recent), and each should capture and express the distinct visual qualities and personalities of each font.

## Process

1. Choose three different typefaces, each from different periods of history that reflect their time of origin. At least two choices must be part of the following classifications:

*Old Style, Italic, Transitional, Modern, Egyptian, Sans Serif*

2. Be certain the three choices span a fair range of time. (For example, not all fonts can be from the 1960s.) Refer to *Typographic Design: Form and Communication* by Rob Carter, Ben Day, and Philip Meggs (John Wiley & Sons, 2002: 34, 35) as a reference for typographic classifications.

3. Choose a piece of writing—seventy-five words or less—from the time period of each font. Content can be a short paragraph from literature, a poem, a quotation, a news story, or an important text from history. How does the content relate when strung together? Create interesting juxtapositions in meaning via the content, such as news information or poetry. How can an older poem be contrasted with a modern one?

4. Choose sound/music—not necessarily from the time period of the font—that reflects the personality and weight of the typeface and content. What kinds of sounds merge with an old style font? Or with a sans serif? Sound and/or music is used to synch animations and set the tone for the content.

5. Animations should visually explore how each of these typefaces are distinct, and explore comparisons of these differences (and/or similarities.) How are these characteristics exploited? Focus on a single aspect of each typeface that makes it unique—what are the advantages of using time-based media to show this?

Characteristics such as ascenders, descenders, strokes, stems, terminals, serifs, loops, eyes, crossbars, etc., are aspects to hone in on. Refer to *Typographic Design: Form and Communication* as a reference for detailed descriptions of type anatomy (Carter 28, 29).

55

6. Lastly, the end plate (last frame of the animation) contains the credits: typeface, date, designer, writing, author, sound/music, and artist.

## Objectives

This assignment uses time-based media to identify, classify, and highlight the differences and similarities in typographic classifications and anatomy. Via the use of shape, space, tempo, sequence, and movement connections can be implied, created, and interpreted in new ways. Students are encouraged to be as creative as possible with this assignment, to inspire a sense of play, while clearly communicating an underlying message via their choice of content via dynamic expressive typography.

Think about:

- Which comes first, the fonts or the content? Are fonts chosen first and then content to suit them? Or vice versa?
- What is the content? How is the concept driven by the content? What fonts best suit that content?
- Is new meaning derived from the combination of content?
- How can animation benefit the communication?

## Technical Specifications

1. Work in After Effects
2. Animations must be three minutes or less.
3. Work at 30 fps
4. Edit Specs:

- DV/DVCPRO–NTSC (Avoid "animation" setting—the files are too large and have a tendency to skip)
- Quality Best
- No Stretch
- Audio Output: 22.050 kHz, 16 bit, Stereo

## Notes

Be critical of font choices. Avoid novelty fonts, system fonts, (such as Courier, Verdana, Arial, Monaco, etc.), and any fonts that have a "city" name.

This assignment exploits the subtleties (and possibly not-so-subtle characteristics) in type design. This is a type-based assignment—keep imagery to a minimum.

## Schedule

**WEEK 7.** Introduction of assignment. Lecture on screen literacy and dynamic typography.

**WEEK 8.** Have all fonts, content, and sound/music chosen, and a rough storyboard for all animations. (Storyboards sketched by hand.)

**WEEK 9.** Tight storyboards in digital form. Rough cut for first animation—sets tone, style of editing, and introduces the content and concept.

**WEEK 10.** Rough cut of all animations for critique.

**WEEK 11.** Refinement of all animations for critique.

**WEEK 12.** Final cut of all animations (viewed as one complete animation) ready to present.

### Resources/Inspiration

Anonymous Content: *www.anonymouscontent.com*
Imaginary Forces: *www.imaginaryforces.com*

# assignment three—cause and effect:
# a twelve-step visual narrative

Technology: Students may choose iMovie or After Effects.
    Students are required to produce the following:

> **1.** A short story/narrative based on the concept of "Cause and Effect"
> **2.** A twelve-paneled accordion fold book, photography only, serving as a tight storyboard of the narrative
> **3.** A one-minute video using the photography stills from the storyboard, animated together with sound and transitions

### Part One: Twelve-Panel Accordion Fold Book

Develop a twelve-step visual narrative to express an event that involves the concept of cause and effect. All narratives have key elements that need consideration:

- All narratives have a beginning, a middle, and an end.
- Use a limited cast of characters (three or less).
- The "problem" is revealed in the first paragraph, setting up the "solution" for the ending. The narrative must come full circle and have conflict/resolution.
- There's clearly a "cause" and an "effect."

### Process

1. Develop a narrative in writing, three paragraphs, three hundred words or less. It needs to have something involving a "cause and effect" scenario that uses no dialogue

2. Sketch a visual storyboard for the narrative. The initial storyboard can be more than twelve steps. Storyboards will be condensed during class critique.

3. Using the storyboard as a guide, shoot digital (still) photographs of the narrative. Take twenty-four to thirty-six shots, possibly more, to insure all the various events of the narrative are captured at multiple angles. This allows you to determine which angle best describes the action that is taking place. Remember:

> **Crossing the line:** *keep the camera on the same side of actors' bodies for a conversation. For instance, if two characters are seated at a table, keep the camera on one side of the table in getting separate shots of each. If the camera position moves to the other side of the table, thus reversing the location of each character, this confuses the viewer as to the characters' positions in space.*
>
> **Get plenty of coverage.** *This gives clarity in storytelling. For example, an object of importance needs several close-ups. "Coverage" also means covering the scene, being certain to include all the information needed to set the stage. This is accomplished by taking several shots (twenty-four to thirty-six) early on in the process before narrowing the storyboard down to twelve.*

4. In class, photographs will be distilled to the essentials, making the storyboard as concise as possible.

5. Have twelve definitive photographs to express the narrative, bound sequentially as an accordion fold book.

## Part Two: Animated Video

Part one of this assignment develops a twelve-step visual narrative to express an event that involves a cause and effect scenario. Next, create a short video utilizing the twelve photographs from your accordion fold book as your storyboard.

### Guidelines

1. **No dialogue.** How can conversation be conveyed via gesture and/or sound? Be creative in the approach.

2. **Video must be one minute or less.** Three acts, each twenty seconds or less.

3. **Transitions.** What are the transitions between frames? In the accordion fold book, the viewer moves from image to image by flipping the page. How does this translate to time-based media? For instance, a radial wipe implies the passage of time; while a hard cut implies the present. Be aware of your choices in applying transitions between your frames.

4. **Sound.** Sound sets the tone, tempo, and "dialogue" of the film. What are the choices? Be certain use of music doesn't interfere with the story. It might be wise to use music with no lyrics. (Remember, this is not a music video.) Does the video need different styles of sound to set the tone for different scenes?

## Objectives

This assignment moves the concept from a tight, print storyboard into the realm of time-based media. How does the same narrative translate to motion? As designer and author of the narrative, define the approach toward translating static media to dynamic media.

## Technical Specifications

1. Work in iMovie or After Effects.
2. Videos are one minute or less; three acts (twenty seconds each)
3. To show videos in class, export as:

   - Go to "File" » "export"
   - Choose "QuickTime"
   - Format: CD-ROM

## Schedule

### Part One: Twelve-Panel Accordion Fold Book

**WEEK 13.** Project Assigned. Lecture on Hollywood narrative 30–60–90 device. View film examples of montage technique in class (Eisenstein, Sergei, *Battleship Potemkin*, Goskino, 1925) and use of sound (Hitchcock, Alfred, *North by Northwest*, Metro-Goldwyn-Mayer, 1959).

**WEEK 14.** Have written story, storyboard sketches, and all thirty-six (possibly more) photographs to present in class. Photographs will be distilled to twelve keyframes during class critique.

**WEEK 15.** Have twelve-step accordion fold book completed for critique. Hand in for grading.

### Part Two. Animated Video

**WEEK 16.** Have all stills animated in iMovie or After Effects. Bring a rough edit of your video to class. Have sound/music choices made.

**WEEK 17.** Rough cut videos due to screen in class for critique.

**WEEK 18.** Film screening: Final edit of QuickTime narratives due.

COURSE TITLE: Sequence, Time + Space

TEACHER: James Pannafino

FREQUENCY: Fall Semester, twice a week for three hours

LEVEL: Sophomore, required Course

CREDITS: 3

DEGREE: Bachelor of Fine Arts

SCHOOL: Mercy College, Computer Arts and Design Program, Manhattan
and White Plains, NY

## summary of class

This course is an introduction to time-based computer arts and design. Through an investigation of narrative structures, spatial compositions, and sound, students will explore the fundamental techniques and aesthetics of the moving image utilizing storyboarding, two-dimensional animation, and motion design as means of communication. Research, critical analysis, and concept development will be emphasized.

Upon completion of the course, the student will be able to:

- Apply principles of narrative structure to the creation of time-based media
- Create concept storyboards
- Create visual scores
- Understand properties of sequence and series
- Understand the technical requirements of moving images
- Critically analyze kinetic forms
- Communicate and formally present concepts

## grading

Projects: 70%

Class participation and project presentation: 10%

Final test: 10%

Attendance and professionalism: 10%

## week by week

### WEEK 1

SESSION 1. Class Introduction.
Syllabus review: Class structure, expectations, and grading.

Presentation: Review various types of animations and motion graphics. Medium: claymation, stop motion, digital, cell, etc. Designers: Saul Bass, Kyle Cooper, etc. (show lots of examples!). Followed by class discussion.

**SESSION 2.** Presentation: Persistence of vision, suspension of disbelief, presence.

Studio work time: Have students develop a thaumatrope and zoetrope in class. Using these simple handmade toys will allow students to better understand and discuss persistence of vision without getting caught up with the techniques of computer programs.

## WEEK 2

**SESSION 1.** Presentation: Narrative and sequence.

1. Sequence structure: linear, nonlinear, multilinear
2. Dynamic juxtaposition: layered, sequential, simultaneous
3. Narrative connections: temporal, spatial, logical
4. Question and answer
5. Meaning: connotative (paradigmatic/syntagmatic) and denotative (Pudovkin/Eisenstein: montage/juxtaposition theories)

Have students (in teams of four) watch an animation and study narrative. It is key they understand the narrative and sequence terminology presented at the beginning of class.

**SESSION 2.** Have students break down the narrative structure of the movie they watched (last session) to better understand how it was built. Students will use the following framework to break down narrative structure:

1. Context
2. Beginning
3. Catalyst
4. Turning point
5. Middle
6. Climax
7. Closure
8. End

## WEEK 3

**SESSION 1.** Introduce Storyboarding Project 1: Part 1—Narrative Development.

**SESSION 2.** Studio work time: Narrative Development project.

# WEEK 4

**SESSION 1.** Presentation: Storyboarding—Camera in the Mind's Eye, distance, long shots, medium shots, close-up shots, camera angles, eye-level shots, low-angle shots (worms eye view), and high-angle shots. Show lots of examples!

Introduce Storyboarding Project 1: Part 2—Traditional Storyboard.

**SESSION 2.** Studio work time: Storyboard development (focus on camera angles and telling the story, not finished drawings).

# WEEK 5

**SESSION 1.** Storyboarding Project 1: Part 2—Traditional Storyboard progress due: class critique.

**SESSION 2.** Studio work time: Development of finished storyboard, panels mounted on black board.

# WEEK 6

**SESSION 1.** Final storyboards due: class critique, student presentation.

Presentation formats: video/film/CPU (digital), keyframes, frame rate, display resolutions, frame aspect ratios, open/closed framing, time code, title and action safe, duration and pause.

Introduce Storyboarding Project 1: Part 3—Animatic. Students will add motion, duration, and pause to enhance the narrative.

**SESSION 2.** Studio work time: Animatic project.

# WEEK 7

**SESSION 1.** Animatic project due: class critique.

Presentation: Editing basics: timing, foreshadow and recall, rhythm and pace; basic principles of audio (theory/technical).

Introduce Project 2—Rhythm project. Show examples of rhythm (both visual and audio).

**SESSION 2.** Studio work time: Rhythm project.

# WEEK 8

**SESSION 1.** Rhythm project due: class critique.

Presentation: Frames per second/timing, in-betweens, easing in/easing out, and duration vs. speed. Discuss the usefulness of a grid in motion graphics and reinforce basic typography principles.

Introduce Project 3—Moving Type. Show examples in static format, Web-based and television graphics.

**SESSION 2.** Studio work time: Moving Type project.

## WEEK 9

**SESSION 1.** Moving Type project due: class critique.
Introduce Project 4—Motion Graphic. Show examples in static format, Web-based and television graphics.

**SESSION 2.** Studio work time: Motion Graphic project.

## WEEK 10

Studio work time: Motion Graphic project.

## WEEK 11

**SESSION 1.** Motion Graphic project due: class critique, student presentation.
Presentation: Game design interaction: component framework, temporal events, structural, rules, modes of play, and game design patterns.
Introduce Project 5—Game Design project. Review simple game play and interaction. Have students create a game list and discuss why the interactions of the games work.

**SESSION 2.** Review game concepts.
Studio work time: Game Design project.

## WEEK 12

**SESSION 1.** Class critique of game design ideation.
Presentation: Simple graphics within games and sprite interaction. Discuss basic function of game design.

**SESSION 2.** Studio work time: Game Design project.

## WEEK 13

**SESSION 1.** Review game development: progress and realization are key.

**SESSION 2.** Studio work time: Game Design project.

## WEEK 14

**SESSION 1.** Review game development: testing stage, working out bugs of the game.

**SESSION 2.** Studio work time: Game Design project.

## WEEK 15

**SESSION 1.** Game Design project due: class critique, student presentation. Stress on interaction of game play and less on technical aspects.

Review information that will be on the final.

**SESSION 2.** Final test on terminology and principles used throughout the semester.

# projects

Projects for this course will involve short-term, in-class projects, longer multiweek projects, and written assignments (topic and evaluations of projects). While most of these projects are used to teach particular theories, principles, and skills, a focus on the content and message (or narrative) should always be present.

## Multiweek Projects

1. Storyboarding Project: Understanding Narrative and Sequence.

Part 1—Narrative Development. Students will develop a sequel to the movie they watched using the same narrative structure they used to break it down. Have students work in groups and write out each part of the narrative structure.

Part 2—Traditional Storyboard. The major part of this project is investigating narrative structures. This project can incorporate found imagery as well as self generated photos or drawings. Students will use the narrative they developed in class and create a visual sequence of drawings to communicate the story.

Part 3—Animatic. This third phase of the project will introduce After Effects (AE) and allow the storyboard to become an animatic. Students will bring the panels of the board into AE and use the techniques introduced: duration of shots, transitions, and camera movements and zooms. If the length of a sequence is an issue, students can animate only one or two scenes.

2. Rhythm Project. Take the word "rhythm" and communicate it through visual repetition. Stress the meaning of the word through the animation on its parts (the six letters that make up the word).

3. Moving Type Project. Options include: word transition of opposites project (metamorphosis of one word to another, capturing the definition and emotion); or animating a word or phrase to reflect meaning.

4. Motion Graphic Project. Using minimum imagery (still photos or drawings as backgrounds) and utilizing typography, line, color, and shape, create a sequence in AE or Flash. The length of the animation should be limited to ensure the focus is on the sequence. The topic is "Social Advocacy." Students will choose a point of advocacy that they maintain as their own. From there, they are to think of how the time-based features of AE can empower their message. The project should: A) educate the viewer, B) advocate a specific position, and C) be representative of the student's personal "voice." The goal is not to inspire political correctness as much as it is to say something with conviction and poignancy.

5. Game Design Project. This should be a simple game concept, not an involved, story-based game. Students will work in teams and build a 2-D side scrolling game to better understand game design interaction. Using simple game design programs like Power Game Factory (Mac) or Game Maker (PC) will allow students to focus on basic game theories such as component framework, temporal events, modes of play, and game design patterns.

## outcome or conclusion

This class gives students a timeless set of skills in the area of narrative structure and time-based design. Students will be able to apply these skills to animation development, motion graphics design, and game design interaction.

## required readings

Bellantoni, Jeff, and Matt Woolman, *Type in Motion*, Rizzoli, 1999.
McCloud, Scott, *Understanding Comics: The Invisible Art*, Harper, 1994.
Woolman, Matt, *Motion Design: Moving Graphics for Television, Music Video, Cinema, and Digital Interfaces*, RotoVision, 2004.
Woolman, Matt, *Moving Type: Designing for Time and Space*, RotoVision, 2000.

## recommended readings (for game project)

Salen, Katie, and Eric Zimmerman, *Rules of Play*, MIT Press, 2003.

# section 3

## juniors

COURSE TITLE: Animation Action Analysis 1

TEACHER: John Canemaker

FREQUENCY: One Semester, once a week for thirteen weeks

LEVEL: Sophomore/Junior

CREDITS: 3

DEGREE: Bachelor of Fine Arts in Film

SCHOOL: New York University, Tisch School of the Arts, Kanbar Institute
of Film and Television, Animation Studies, New York, NY

## objective

This is a workshop in the application of basic principles of motion and animation
that aims to sharpen students' skills in observation of simple actions and develop
their ability to caricature movements for animation. (Techniques are applicable to
traditional and computer animation.)

## format

The class: The workshop is divided between lectures/demonstrations and student
presentations of homework assignments (exercises in animation videotaped as a
pencil test). Students are expected to take notes during class and devote substantial
time to homework. In part of each class students will prepare assignments with
one-on-one advisement from the teacher.

Facilities: Each student will become proficient in using the pencil-test video
camera stands ("Lunch Box") to shoot assignments.

## evaluation

Each student will be given a grade based on the following criteria:

- Attendance and class participation: 50%
- Homework assignments on video: 50%

## week by week

Following is the content of the weekly schedule for thirteen classes.

Lectures/screenings/guests are subject to change; but the seven student test
scenes are due during the classes indicated. Corrections of test scenes are due the
following week.

**WEEK 1.** Orientation. Demonstrate/discuss principles of animation, for example: squash and stretch, anticipation, staging, straight-ahead vs. pose-to-pose, follow-through and overlapping action, arcs, slow in and slow out, secondary action, timing, exaggeration, solid drawing, appeal. Analyze *Fantasia*'s "Sorcerer's Apprentice" to reiterate principles. Pencil test tech. Discuss the required student video tests. Demonstrate how to plan animation scenes.

**WEEK 2.** Student test #1. A character tosses a tennis ball and hits it with a racket.

**WEEK 3.** Motion principles in the live-action human figure: analysis of Fred Astaire/Ginger Rogers in *Swingtime*; Astaire split screen in *That's Entertainment III* ("Wanna Be a Dancin' Man"); Astaire in *Funny Face* ("Let's Kiss and Make Up"); compare Mickey Mouse dance in *Thru the Mirror*. Test corrections.

**WEEK 4.** Student video test #2: A bird (or a man/woman) flaps wings (or arms) and eventually flies off the ground. Scene planning, clarity/simplicity: Felix the Cat; early Mickey Mouse.

**WEEK 5.** Weight analysis: *Gertie the Dinosaur*; hippos in "Dance Of The Hours" from *Fantasia*. Staging: "Limehouse Blues" from *The Great Ziegfeld*. Test corrections.

**WEEK 6.** Student video test #3. A figure picks up a boulder. Caricature and staging: staging "Over the Rainbow"; the witch's "Who Killed my Sister?" scene; and the introductions of Scarecrow, Tin Man, and Lion in an analysis of *The Wizard of Oz*; Madam Medusa mirror scene from *The Rescuers*; Charlotte Greenwood in *The Gang's All Here*.

**WEEK 7.** Sketching from the live model. Bring large size sketchpads. Screen *Walking* by Ryan Larkin. Test corrections.

**WEEK 8.** Student video test #4. A character walks, comes to a puddle, and jumps over it. Simple walks/runs: humans in *Modern Times*; animals in *National Zoo*; simple cartoon figures run/walk.

**WEEK 9.** Guest animator. Test Corrections.

**WEEK 10.** Student video test #5. A character walks against the wind, which shifts to behind. Analyze *The Little Whirlwind*; "Pastoral Symphony" winds; *The Band Concert*.

**WEEK 11.** Simplifying everyday activities/motions: Jiminy Cricket dresses on the run from *Pinocchio*; Medusa puts on a coat from *The Rescuers*; mime in *Children of Paradise*; Snow White cleans the house; *Peter Pan* bedroom sequence. Test corrections.

**WEEK 12.** Student test #6. Character puts on a coat and exits. Stylized designs/ limited animation: *The Street*; *Moonbird*; United Productions of America's (UPA) *Gerald McBoing Boing*; *Mr. Magoo*; Ward Kimball's *Melody*; *Toot Whistle Plunk and Boom*.

**WEEK 13.** Final class. Student test #7. Man/woman hears a dog inside a suitcase, opens it, and lets the animal out.

# recommended readings

Canemaker, John, *Walt Disney's Nine Old Men and the Art of Animation*, Disney Editions, 2001.

Thomas, Frank, and Ollie Johnston, *The Illusion of Life: Disney Animation*, Hyperion, 1981.

Williams, Richard, *The Animator's Survival Kit: A Manual of Methods, Principles, and Formulas for Classical, Computer, Games, Stop Motion, and Internet Animators*, Faber & Faber, 2001.

**COURSE TITLE:** Design Studio II

**TEACHER:** Ferris Werbin Crane

**FREQUENCY:** One Semester, once a week

**LEVEL:** Junior (after completion of preliminary courses)

**CREDITS:** 3

**DEGREE:** Bachelor of Fine Arts or Bachelor of Arts

**SCHOOL:** Robert Morris University, Pittsburgh, PA

## summary

**Catalogue Description:** Through a further series of integrated assignments, this course continues the refinement of the design process to a more advanced level. Emphasis as before is on individual learning, and by continuing the study of the design process, students begin to specialize in a focus area. By increasing the opportunities to initiate and negotiate their own assignments, the course will ensure that students are fully involved and committed to their own learning. The use of frequent team and student assessment and criticism, tutorial review, and group working will support the process. Technical and craft skills are further developed through active participation in solving specific design problems and the need to communicate ideas through skilled manipulation of various materials and processes. The course will be taught in the computer design lab.

**Instructor Additions:** This course continues developing skills used to create effective visual communications. As the department offers classes to all Media Arts students in television, documentary making, graphic design, motion graphics, and Web design/interactive after traditional foundation studies, all students will find the emphases on concept development, visual hierarchy, and movement to be helpful in their creative work. According to the quantitative study "The Impact of Digital Technology on Typographic Aesthetics" by Ferris Crane, as design students are exposed to more digital technology, elements originally seen in print, such as detail in forms, use of edges, shapes created by negative space, etc., diminish while the eye is attracted to movement and color. This class will provide connectivity of all these aesthetic elements, especially movement, in different environments and surfaces. After a review of visual hierarchy, there will be an assignment that will be applied to a round object (continuous movement), a flat surface with distinct edges, and then to a digital environment requiring sequencing. The final assignment will apply the student's choice of movement principles and aesthetic elements to a static surface.

# goals

Students will understand and employ the following:

- How to enhance visual communication through the use of motion
- Visual hierarchy
- The influence of aesthetics on motion
- How different objects and surfaces afford motion
- The use of the continuation theory (how one graphic element is related to another) to facilitate the flow of movement
- Gestalt or the lack of gestalt in facilitating movement
- The role of color, uniform shapes, alignment, randomness, contrast, and spatial relationships in connectedness (how one graphic element is related to another in movement)
- Sequencing and continuity within sequencing
- Constraint inherent in specific objects, surfaces, and environments and how to introduce movement within design parameters
- Interconnectedness between print and digital surfaces, objects and environment
- Edges and detail (often lost when motion is introduced)
- Historical influences of movements, people, technology, and culture on movement and visual hierarchy

# assessment

**Grading.** All work will be self-evaluated and professor evaluated using the same quantitative rubric.

**Critiques.** All students are expected to participate in individual and team critiques.

**Objective Feedback.** Each student will take one project to another department or office building, other than media arts, to have at least one person give objective feedback with the same quantitative rubric used in grading.

# lesson plan

### Weeks 1–2: Project I—Visual Hierarchy

**In teams.** Compare how Giotto di Bondone, Jan van Eyck, Jacqueline Casey, Warren Lehrer, or Fernando Gutierrez controlled the basic elements to develop visual hierarchy.

**Lecture.** How we now see. Comparing aesthetic preferences from the predigital era to our current digital environment as related to visual hierarchy, particularly movement.

**Assignment.** Scan three dry foods found in an Italian grocery or toys from a store such as pick-up sticks, jacks, marbles, etc., and design with a strong visual hierarchy. Reverse. See if the hierarchy remains. If not, adjust. Class critiques will occur at the end of each period.

## Weeks 3–6: Project II—Objects and Environments that Afford Movement

**In Teams.** Each student brings three round objects with graphics on them. How do these objects function? Which ones function the best and why? What are the design parameters? Given the movement of the objects, which designs enhance the functioning and why?

**Lecture.** How objects and specific environments contribute to motion in graphics as much as the actual graphics. Concepts of continuation (including the use of color, shape, alignment, and contrast), sequencing, and closure to create a gestalt are included.

**Assignment.** Design a drinking cup to be used at an Olympic event. During week three, ideas are to be sketched on tracing paper before computer use. Prototypes are due at the end of week five. Final projects are due at the end of week six. *Teacher note*: Prototypes are very important because they help students understand that on a round object, there is a design continuum.

## Weeks 7–9: Project III—Movement on a Static Surface with Edges

**Individual Research.** Research technology, people, and movements contributing to organized movement and random movement.

**Lectures.** "The Ancients' Rock" will discuss ancient attempts to order movement and space and "On the Edge" will involve contemporary movement explorations through order, lack of order, and edges.

**Assignment.** Design an Olympic poster for an event using the same elements as on the cup (round surface). Be sure to consider the role of edges in movement. Do they constrain or enhance movement?

## Weeks 10–12: Movement in a Digital Environment

**Lectures.** Continuity and gestalt in the sequencing of graphic elements. Historical and contemporary sequencing including but not limited to Eadweard

Muybridge, Harold "Doc" Edgerton, Marcel Duchamp, Karel Martens, Why Not Associates, etc. How digital aesthetics have unconsciously added constraints to design work.

**Assignment.** Using Flash, After Effects, or ImageReady, sequence the elements in the Olympic poster. The first class will be dedicated to storyboard development. Please put three rows of newspaper type on the top and bottom of your storyboard squares to remain aware of edges. Critiques will occur at the end of every class.

### Weeks 13–15: Melding Digital Aesthetics with Print Aesthetics Through the use of Movement

**Assignment.** Design for an event, institution, or person on a flat surface melding print aesthetics with the dynamics of the digital environment. Antiordering approaches will be accepted.

# recommended readings

Fiel, Charlotte, and Peter Fiel, *Graphic Design Now*, Taschen, 2005.

Gordon, Stephen, and Jenifer Wyman, *Primer of Perception*, Reinhold, 1967.

Hastreiter, Kim, and David Hershkovits, *From Ab Fab to Zen*, with an introduction by John Waters, Paper Publishing, 1999.

Kepes, Gyorgy, *Education of Vision*, George Brazillier, 1965. (This book is still available in used bookstores.)

Lidwell, William, Kritina Holden, and Jill Butler, *Universal Principles of Design*, Rockport, 2003.

Meggs, Philip, and Alston W. Purvis, *Meggs' History of Graphic Design*, 4th ed., John Wiley & Sons, 2005.

White, Alexander, *The Elements of Graphic Design*, Allworth Press, 2002.

## summary and goal of class

This is a survey course introducing the basic principles and practices of motion graphics as used in the film and television industries. In addition, you will learn to originate your own moving imagery using digital video cameras. The importance of sound recording and lighting also will be introduced. You will be shown the onramp of a basic motion graphics software application of Apple computers—iMovie, iDVD, and, if desired, Final Cut Express or Final Cut HD. With these software applications, you will learn the fundamentals of digital video imaging, sound recording, and editing, as well as how to utilize special effects and typography, which move in space and time. These elements are the basis for creating motion graphics.

The goal of this class is to create an "industry standard" portfolio for a student, entry-level position in the motion graphics industry. The final requirements, to be included in an interactive DVD portfolio, should demonstrate your developmental process, that is, a design brief, storyboard development, final frame grabs, and a finished motion-graphics film or television opening.

## grading

Class projects: 60 points

   Project 1: Video Group Portrait: 20 points

   Project 2: Film or Television Opening: 40 points

Ongoing work: 40 points

   **1.** The principles—discussions and written reading responses (RR): 20 points

   **2.** The practice—developing storyboards: thumbnails, roughs, comps, and finishes: 10 points

   **3.** The portfolio—packaging and presentation: 10 points

# calendar

*Weeks 1–4: Discover through direct experience what you can do in this field. Experiment and play with motion graphics. Become familiar with equipment, software, and interplay between group members in your crew.*

**WEEK 1.** Explain to students the class goals, outcomes, and expectations. Stress the importance of collaboration and creating a community of learners in an ever-changing technological environment. Emphasize readings, writings, and participation in discussions as ways of maintaining interest as well as longevity in graphic design—that is, become self-learners.

**CLASS 1.** Handout survey to students, make introductions all around, and go over the syllabus.

**CLASS 2.** Introduce Project 1: Video Group Portrait. Create a thirty-second video on a secret you've never told anyone—real or fictitious.

Show portraits done by students in the previous class. Divide students up into groups; have them exchange contact information and hand in group lists.

Studio: Brainstorm on video portraits.

**WEEK 2.** Begin parallel learning—reading as well as discussing principles alongside hands-on experiences with hardware and software.

All students must videotape another student and be taped themselves to get comfortable with being behind the camera as well as in front of it. They must create original footage, sound, and typographical design. This first project is primarily positioned as a learning experience, that is, to make mistakes and play.

**CLASS 1.** Discussion and RR forms due for *Becoming a Graphic Designer* by Heller and Fernandes; read the section called "Motion Graphics" and review the entry-level student portfolio.

Demonstration: Introduce the use of digital video cameras, audio recording, lighting, and tripod.

Studio: Begin shooting video portraits.

**CLASS 2.** Field work: Continue shooting group portraits.

Read *Final Cut Express* (*FCE*): "Old & New" on pages 6–9 and "Setup and Capture" on pages 25–42.

**WEEK 3.** Evaluate footage. Begin to examine aesthetics, technique, and technical aspects of creating a piece of motion graphics. Begin processing video.

**CLASS 1.** Critique: video portrait shoots

Demonstration: FireWire, use of camera as playback and backup

Studio: Feed in and begin editing video portraits.

Read *FCE*: "Sorting Through Your Footage" on pages 43–54 and "The Cutting Room" on pages 55–97.

**CLASS 2.** Studio: Demonstration of Final Cut Express tutorial; continue editing group portraits.

Read *FCE*: "Effects" on pages 99–128 and "Working with Audio" on pages 129–138.

**WEEK 4.** Continue by adding complexity to the visual narrative of Video Group Portrait. Learn technical aspects of output, archiving, and creating interactive DVDs. Begin to explore through readings different methods of creating motion graphic pieces—on and off the computer.

**CLASS 1.** Studio: Continue editing portraits; add text, audio, soundtrack, and special effects.

Read *FCE*: "Output" on pages 139–146.

**CLASS 2.** Critique: Bring in group portraits on DVD format for playback and hand in.

Read: *The Animation Book* by Kit Laybourne, "Basic Skills" on pages 3–17; "Storyboarding and Animatics" on pages 100–113.

Read: *The Animation Book*; pick ONE technique from pages 47–233 and write an RR form.

*Weeks 5–8: Visualize. Having become familiarized with the hardware and software, begin designing a visual narrative by drawing up major sequences and scenes through storyboarding the imagery, text, motion, sound, lighting, and timings of events.*

**WEEK 5.** Show overview of the history of filmmaking in the United States from Saul Bass and Robert Brownjohn to Kyle Cooper and MTV. Introduce practices of storyboard development through visual narrative concepts. Also, begin to discuss elements, not as evident in still graphic design, that is, the roles of time, motion, sound, and editing, in motion graphics and how these impact the making of motion graphics.

**CLASS 1.** Introduce Project 2: Film or Television Opening. Create an original motion graphics piece that is a minimum of thirty seconds for a film or television opening.

Show "Imaginary Forces" presentation by Karen Fong at Alliance Graphique Internationale, San Francisco conference.

Show examples of past student projects of motion graphics portfolios—storyboards and openings.

Studio: Brainstorm on project 2 in groups; begin thumbnails sketches.

**CLASS 2.** Discussion and RR forms due for *Sight Sound Motion* (*SSM*), chapter 12: "Time"

Studio: Project 2: Complete three storyboard thumbnail sketches by hand.

**WEEK 6.** Continue introducing elements and the impact designing with motion can make within the television or film "frame." Continue refinement of storyboards and visualization of moving type and imagery.

**CLASS 1.** Discussion and RR forms due for *SSM*, chapter 14: "Motion"
Critique: Project 2: Three hand-drawn storyboard thumbnail sketches are due.

**CLASS 2.** Studio: Project 2: Complete one storyboard rough by any technique.

**WEEK 7.** Move forward with designing within "the frame" and the visual narrative through consideration of additional elements such as music, natural sound, timing, synchronicity, etc.

Carry on with clearer visualization of storyboards, considering the impact that time, motion, and sound can contribute.

**CLASS 1.** Discussion and RR forms due for *SSM*, chapter 17: "Sound"
Critique: Project 2: One storyboard rough created by any technique is due.

**CLASS 2.** Studio: Project 2: Create one storyboard color comp by any technique.

**WEEK 8.** Investigate the role editing can perform in changing the visual narrative and typography by adding, eliminating, or heightening the action, sound, or text through this process. Finish up storyboards by adding timings for each scene, music, sound effects, typographical elements, transitions, and special effects. Group members choose or are assigned a role in the filmmaking process of project 2.

**CLASS 1.** Discussion and RR forms due for *SSM*, chapter 15: "Editing"
Critique: Project 2: One storyboard color comp created by any technique.
Optional: Create animatics.

**CLASS 2.** Project 2: One storyboard color comp created by any technique due; hand in an extra copy for grading.

Production planning session based on work groups and storyboard. Assign tasks based on skill, comfort or interest level, or group assignment—videography, natural sound, music, lighting, editing, special effects and text, and production oversight.

*Weeks 9–16. Actualize. Make, put together, and further refine project 2. Create an interactive DVD packaged portfolio.*

**WEEK 9.** Based on finished storyboards, go out and begin making the motion graphics film or television opening.

**CLASS 1.** Field work: Do a video shoot as a work group based on the storyboard.

**WEEK 10.** Review field shoots with storyboards. Based on critique, go back and reshoot or retake visuals, natural sound, cutaways, or angles to enhance the final opening.

**CLASS 1.** Critique: Video shoots

**CLASS 2.** Field work: Reshoot video

**WEEK 11.** Last chance to reshoot videos. Begin editing video footage together based on storyboards. Sound and music: Introduce as well as refine.

**CLASS 1.** Critique: Video reshoots

**CLASS 2.** Critique: Rough edits of group videos
Studio: Reedits of group videos

**WEEK 12.** Reedit videos. Start adding special effects and text in opening.

**CLASS 1.** Critique: Reedits of group videos

**CLASS 2.** Studio: Add special effects and text in the work group based on the storyboard.

**WEEK 13.** Fine-tune special effects and text with sound and music in opening.

**CLASS 1.** Studio: refine special effects and text with sound and music in the work group based on the storyboard.

**CLASS 2.** Critique: Special effects and text with sound and music
Studio: Redo special effects and text with sound and music.

**WEEK 14.** Last reiterations to make on opening.

**CLASS 1.** Critique: Redo of special effects and text with sound and music.

**CLASS 2.** Studio: Redo special effects and text. Prepare packaging of final version.

**WEEK 15.** Diagram branching system showing all the steps in project 2 to put into interactive DVD form. Add a "Design Brief" or explanation of your project 2.

**CLASS 1.** Critique: Prepared packaging of final version.

**CLASS 2.** Studio: Redo packaging of final version.

**FINALS WEEK.** Final group packaged presentations and critiques. Hand in finished and packaged DVD according to the entry-level portfolio in "Motion Design" from *Becoming a Graphic Designer*.

## required readings

Heller, Steven, and Teresa Fernandes, *Becoming a Graphic Designer: A Guide to Careers in Design*, Wiley, 2005. Section 2, "Motion Graphics."

Laybourne, Kit, *The Animation Book: A Complete Guide to Animated Filmmaking—From Flip-Books to Sound Cartoons to 3-D Animation*, Three Rivers Press, 1998.

Young, Rick, *Focal Easy Guide to Final Cut Express: For New Users and Professionals (The Focal Easy Guide)*, Focal Press, 2003.

Zettl, Herbert, *Sight, Sound, Motion: Applied Media Aesthetics*, Wadsworth Publishing, 2007. Chapters—"Time," "Sound," "Motion," "Editing."

# recommended readings

Codrington, Andrea, *Kyle Cooper*, Yale University Press, 2003.

Curran, Steve, *Motion Graphics: Graphic Design for Broadcast and Film*, Rockport Press, 2001.

Katz, Steven D., *Film Directing: Shot by Shot*, Michael Wiese Productions, 1991.

**COURSE TITLE:** Sound + Motion

**TEACHER:** Jeff Miller

**FREQUENCY:** Fall Semester

**LEVEL:** Junior, required course for both illustration and graphic
design majors

**CREDITS:** 3

**DEGREE:** Bachelor of Fine Arts

**SCHOOL:** Kansas City Art Institute, School of Design, Kansas City, MO

## summary of class

Sound + Motion is a convergence of foundational graphic-design vocabulary, sound, illustration, and animation that will result in the creation of narratives over time. We will create a dialogue between form and sound as they relate to motion. We will talk in depth about story forms. We will start our thinking by sketching and writing that will ultimately lead to sequential frame storyboarding, which will become the base for planning our animations. We will learn the basic principles of Flash animation to give life to our ideas. We will look at transition and how to manipulate and control conditions that pass from one motion to the next. We will learn to think critically and articulate those thoughts through both informal, in-class discussions and formal critiques. We will learn to use the element of time to speak as if it were a language. Above all, we will assault the senses with sight and sound.

## course goals

Create valuable connections between principles of graphic design, illustration, sound, and motion.

Continue the development of a strong conceptual 2-D framework.

Further skills that relate to illustration, design, and typography.

Learn the basics of Flash animation and digital sound design as well as continue growth of skills as relates to Illustrator and Photoshop.

Execute assignments/projects as they relate to conceptual, visual, and professional growth.

Learn the steps necessary to plan animations that encompass idea generation, storyboarding, writing, file management, editing, and presenting.

Further sharpen dialogue skills and critical thinking through class critiques.

Conduct simple research of existing new media examples and write a three hundred-word essay.

Develop presentation skills both verbally and visually as they relate to the presentation of motion and sound design.

## course content

Explore various aspects of sequencing that will lead to an understanding of storyboarding.

Conceptualize and execute a variety of storyboards.

Become critically aware of storyboard structures such as transitions, timing, and scale, and what movements over time suggest the intended tone and, most importantly, tell the story.

Learn basic Flash animation through in-class lessons.

Execute projects that are based on the learned lessons.

Learn how to record and edit sound digitally.

Apply the lessons of sound recording, digitizing, and editing to a variety of sound-design projects.

Use the processes of thinking, researching, storyboarding, animating, sound editing, experimenting, and testing to develop animations using Flash.

Understand the importance of collaboration as it relates to new media.

## week by week

**WEEK 1.** The first week consists of covering introductory information such as the course definition, course outline, syllabus review, and class expectations. The course content is supported with various professionally produced motion design examples from Digital Kitchen, Motion Theory, MK12, Psyop, Epoxy, and Kyle Cooper.

Recommend what version and where to purchase Flash software, the primary software tool that will be used throughout the course.

Provide a short lecture covering the principles of motion as theorized by Sir Isaac Newton: 1) Objects at rest will stay at rest and objects in motion will stay in motion in a straight line unless acted upon by an unbalanced force. 2) Force is equal to mass times acceleration. 3) For every action there is always an opposite and equal reaction.

In addition to Newton's laws of motion, various storyboarding terms and examples are introduced, which lead up to the first assignment: Project 1: Newton's Laws of Motion Storyboarding.

**WEEK 2.** Watch Digital Kitchen's "The Making of Six Feet Under," which covers how a main title is created from concept to post. Includes an excellent section on storyboards and time-based sequencing that is appropriate to project 1.

**WEEK 3.** Critique of project 1. Students present projects in groups of four to five. All work is analog, therefore the work is pinned up on walls for review.

Assign Project 2: Virus Storyboarding, which consists of three, nine-frame storyboards with storyboard script.

**WEEK 4.** Introduction to Flash software. To give students a framework of Flash, I show various professionally created Flash animations. Students then follow along as we cover the Flash interface, drawing tools, and animation basics, and keyframes are explained. Students are given a basic in-class assignment for me to measure their understanding of the lessons covered.

Formal critique of project 2.

**WEEK 5.** In-class Flash lesson. After reviewing the previous week's lesson, we move to new lessons, which cover aligning, arranging, testing, and publishing.

Assign Project 3: Square, Circle, Line Keyframe Motion Design, which consists of using simple keyframe animation as a way to start making basic motion designs based on the lessons learned up to this point.

**WEEK 6.** Formal critique of project 3.

In-class Flash lesson covering tweening, symbols, motion guide, importing .ai files, bit maps, shape tweening, shape hinting, what shape tweening can do, what shape tweening can't do, multiple shape tweening, symbols and instances, the symbol instance structure, time line vocabulary, creating a graphic symbol, motion tweening, shape tweening vs. motion tweening, basic motion tweening, tweening effects, editing multiple frames, and using a motion guide.

To give the students a framework of the next project assigned, I show relevant motion design references from Psyop, Picture Mill, and previous student work.

Assign Project 4: Swarm, a two-part assignment consisting of storyboarding and motion design.

Since this project spans multiple weeks, I lecture on the skill of time management. We discuss creating a calendar and selecting dates for when students need to reach certain parts of the motion design process. Example: Tuesday—roughs, Thursday—sketched out storyboards, etc.

**WEEK 7.** Project 4 storyboards due. Review storyboards on an individual basis.

**WEEK 8.** In-class Flash lesson reviewing tweening, symbols, motion guides, and importing .ai files, and covering animated graphic symbols, masking, mask reveal, organizing/beginning your project, duplicating/moving things around, and editing multiple frames, and a multiple layers demonstration.

**WEEK 9.** Show various professionally produced and previous student motion design examples prior to reviewing in-progress animations that are due. Project 4 in-progress animations due. Review in-progress animations on an individual basis.

**WEEK 10.** Project 4 formal critique. As a way to focus the students for the critique, I take a short amount of time and present simple guidelines on how to critique motion design. I ask students to consider the following when viewing the presented motion designs: Consider all aspects of the motion design such as what the motion is "communicating." Is the story complete and did the student use an effective point of view in regard to the story? Did the use of motion effectively convey the idea? How did the use of multiple shape and motion tweening, motion paths, layers, timing, speed/velocity, color, scale, and structure contribute to the intended motion of the piece?

**WEEK 11.** Sound is always enthusiastically received when introduced. This week consists of sound design and begins with a lecture covering basic audio terms such as: music, sound effects, voiceover, composition, sample, recording, cutting to sound, cutting to motion, levels, AIFF, WAV, MP3, etc.

The sound lecture is followed up with an in-class lesson on editing and designing sound.

Assign Project 5: Sound

**WEEK 12.** Review sound terms followed by critiquing project 5.

The following in-class Flash lesson will deal with sound and will cover importing sound, compressing sound, creating a new layer for sound, layer height, synchronizing sound, exporting to QuickTime, stopping sound, and using the stream setting.

Assign Project 6: Essay, as a way to have students look critically at a contemporary piece of motion design prior to their final motion design assignment.

**WEEK 13.** Project 6 is due.

Assign Project 7: My Robotic World, which consists of initial concepts, rough storyboards, rough animations, final presentation storyboard, and a final motion design. After discussing the project assignment, I show references from the following: Planet Propaganda, Modernista, MK12, various robotic videos, and previous student work.

In-class Flash lessons are taught covering bitmaps, types of bitmaps Flash can import, importing and compressing bitmaps, importing bitmap sequences, breaking apart bitmaps, stroking a bitmap, converting bitmaps to vectors, and combining bitmaps and vectors.

**WEEK 14.** Review various components of project 7 on an individual basis. Review various Flash lessons and answer any technical questions the students may have.

**WEEK 15.** The final week consists of a formal critique for project 7. The final critique is followed with a lecture on how to show motion design in a 2-D, non-time-based presentation.

# class projects

### Project 1: Newton's Laws of Motion Storyboarding

Basic storyboarding according to Newton's principles of motion

**Required:** Three, nine-frame storyboards using the 8.5 × 11 inch template provided. Include written descriptions. Any nondigital, black and white drawing media may be used (pencil, black pen, black marker, etc.).

**Due:** In progress sketches and notes. Three, nine-frame storyboards

**Sir Isaac Newton:** *Philosophiae Naturalis Principia Mathematica*, William Dawson & Sons, 1687 (also known as Newton's Laws of Motion).

1. Objects at rest will stay at rest and objects in motion will stay in motion in a straight line unless acted upon by an unbalanced force.
2. Force is equal to mass times acceleration.
3. For every action there is always an opposite and equal reaction.

## Process Guidelines for Project

**Step 1: Find Motion.** Find three examples of anything in motion that demonstrates at least one of Newton's three laws of motion. Motion must be uninitiated by the student. Students should "look" for motion and not create motion. For example, watching a ball being kicked back and forth instead of asking two people to kick a ball back and forth is an uninitiated motion. Studying the effects of curtains blowing in a window instead of twirling around fabric by hand is an uninitiated motion. The purpose for uninitiated motion is to challenge students to see motion in things that would otherwise go unnoticed.

**Step 2: Observe, Sketch, and Write about Motion.** After finding motion that represents Newton's laws of motion, begin by describing the motion with notes and sketching real-time drawings—drawings done on site that record the motion as it takes place. Students should produce a series of sequential drawings that tell the story clearly. After enough information about the motion has been recorded, students may redraw the event in nine frames that will make up the final storyboard. Final frames must be drawn with either pencil, black pen/marker, black ink, or black and white paint. No color or digital means will be used.

**Step 3: Edit Frames.** After you have made a sequence of drawings that tell the story, start editing the frames to exactly nine frames. Storyboards should tell the story of the motion in logical, sequential order—in other words, the events of the story should come right after each other in the order the story is being told. Students should look critically at how the sequence will begin, how the motion is conveyed, and how the story ends—all of which should be shown clearly in the final storyboard frames.

**Step 4: Transfer Final Frames to Storyboard.** Once each story is determined and communicates the motion in nine frames, transfer the drawings to the final template. This may be done by redrawing, photocopying, or tracing the selected frames. Add a brief, hand-written paragraph consisting of two to three sentences describing the motion for each storyboard below the frames.

## Materials Needed

Sketchbook, drawing paper, journal—whatever is comfortable for the student to sketch and take notes.

Three copies of the provided storyboard template. Black and white, nondigital media—pencil, black pen/marker, black ink, or black and white paint. No color or digital means will be used.

### Grading Out of 100

Concept: 60%. Student was able to visualize an appropriate, clear, well-organized, and memorable solution to the given problem.

Presentation/Craft: 30%. Level of finish achieved in final presentation.

Class Participation/Critique: 10%. Ability to articulate thoughts and ideas in a group setting and with the instructor about the project, in a professional and respectful manner that fosters and creates a learning environment.

## Project 2: Virus Storyboarding

**Required:** Three, nine-frame storyboards with storyboard script.

Virus: any of a large group of tiny infective agents causing various diseases, any harmful influence.

Biologically or electronically, we have all been infected with viruses. How do viruses infect? What do they look like and, most importantly to us in regard to motion, how do they move? Students should research what a virus is/can be as well as how it may move, morph, and infect. Is there such a thing as a good virus—what does that look like and how does that move and infect over time? How will students viruses move from host to host—will they split, divide, morph, mutate, kill, breed, multiply, etc.?

Students may use an existing virus or fictionally invent a virus based on the research of actual viruses. Is your virus friendly? Is your virus deadly? How does the virus survive? Is the virus a single celled organism or is it part of a billion-cell colony? Will your virus be electronic? Consider how to visually show the life span of the virus—from its inception to its successful infection, mutation, or death. Also consider the "tone" of your virus—will it be serious, playful, sad, empathetic, strong, cunning, etc.?

Use the storyboard process: writing, drawing, building/designing frames, and describing as outlined below.

**Step 1: Research Viruses.** Begin this project with simple research into the world of viruses. Attempt to become a brief virus expert to understand the subject matter.

**Step 2: Concept, Invent, Sketch, and Write.** After conducting simple research into the world of viruses, begin free writing and free sketching ideas that will lead to a narrative. Consider what the virus is composed of. Show how your virus moves. Show how the virus feeds, infects, and multiplies. What tone/personality will your virus communicate? Consider how you will be able to tell three different stories about your virus.

**Step 3: Build Final Frames in Sequential Order.** After you have made a sequence of drawings that tell the story, start editing and building the final nine frames for each story. Storyboards should clearly tell the story of the motion in logical, sequential order—in other words, the events of the story should come right after each other to make sense. Students should look critically at how the sequence will begin, how the motion is conveyed, and how the story ends. Give attention to how much information you need from frame to frame to tell the story.

Use the 17 × 11 inch template provided to place/mount final frames. Do not alter the template. Final frames must be black and white or gray scale. NO COLOR. You may use original art, or scanned or photocopied frames to place/mount to the final board.

**Step 4: Storyboard Script.** Include a brief paragraph consisting of three to five sentences describing the story for each storyboard. Place/mount these to the final board in the specified area on the provided template. Be sure to add your name and the title of the storyboard (*Backyard West Nile Virus*, for example).

### Materials Needed

Sketchbook, drawing paper, journal—whatever is comfortable for the student to sketch and take notes.

Black and white, nondigital media—pencil, black pen/marker, black ink, or black and white paint to name a few. No color or digital drawing means will be used for the execution of the storyboard frames. You may use digital means to scan in and print out final artwork.

### Grading Out of 100

Concept: 60%. Student was able to visualize an appropriate, clear, well-organized, and memorable solution to the given problem.

Presentation/Craft: 30%. Level of finish achieved in the final frames as well as the final presentation.

Class Participation/Critique: 10%. Ability to articulate thoughts and ideas in a group setting and with the instructor about the project, in a professional and respectful manner that fosters and creates a learning environment.

## Project 3: Square, Circle, Line Keyframe Motion Design

Using the Flash lessons learned in class, we will explore the principles of keyframe animation and continue to use the process of planning, storyboarding, and writing.

Begin by choosing three verbs and briefly define them. For example: *agitate— to stir up feelings; fade—to lose color, brilliance, etc.; multiply—to increase in number, degree, etc.* Using keyframe animation and the Flash tools learned in class, create three, five-second looping animated sequences that communicate the motion of the words. Use a square (or squares) for one word, the circle (or circles) for the other, and the line (or lines) for the third. You may use any combination of color. However, pay close attention to how color can support the visual communication of the word and motion. Use the process of free writing/sketching, storyboarding, and writing to plan your animations.

### Details

**Storyboards.** Three, nine-frame color storyboards using Illustrator. Use the template provided. Type your name, the chosen word, and sentences describing the intended motion below the storyboard frames. Using Acrobat, save a single PDF containing all three storyboards in addition to a black-and-white or color print out of each storyboard.

**Animations.** Three, five-second looping keyframe SWF animations.
Size: 320 pixels × 240 pixels
Speed: 12 frames per second (fps)
Name each animation by the chosen verb before the SWF extension (for example: agitate.swf).
Provide a storyboard PDF as well as three SWFs on a single CD. Label the CD as "Project 3: Square, Circle, Line Keyframe Motion Design" and include your first and last name.

### Grading Out of 100

Storyboards: 20%. Ability to visualize an appropriate, clear, well-organized, and memorable solution to the given problem in storyboard form as outlined above as well as how effectively the communication is executed in visual form. Level of finish and technical craft achieved.

Animations: 50%. Ability to visualize an appropriate, clear, well-organized, and memorable solution to the given problem as it relates to the use of color, form, and motion in regard to the choice of words used.

Animation Presentation/Technical Craft: 20%. Level of technical finish achieved in final presentation of the animations.

Class Participation/Critique: 10%. Ability to articulate thoughts and ideas in a group setting and with the instructor about the project, in a professional and respectful manner that fosters and creates a learning environment.

## Project 4: Swarm

Swarm is a two-part assignment: storyboarding and motion design.

Swarm: (1) a large number of bees, with a queen, leaving a hive to start a new colony, (2) a colony of bees in a hive, (3) a moving mass, crowd, or throng. It also means: (4) to fly off in a swarm, (5) to move, be present, etc., in large numbers, (6) to be crowded.

Throng: (1) a crowd, (2) any great number of things considered together, (3) to gather together, (4) to crowd into.

**Storyboard.** Begin by free writing what your swarm is composed of using any of the above definitions. You may certainly use bees, but it could be anything *moving en mass*. What is your mass and where, how and why is it moving? I want you to start seeing and visually communicating in terms of objects/forms moving in a mass. What is your swarm composed of? What is your swarm doing? Show us the motion of your swarm. After you have had a chance to start writing creatively, write at least three different, simple scenarios about your swarm while simultaneously sketching out storyboard frames that will become the visuals for the final animation. What will your swarm look like? Is it a swarm of something we recognize, a swarm of fictional forms or entirely abstract elements? Finally, choose one scenario and start creating your frames using Illustrator into one, nine-frame storyboard that shows the motion of your swarm. Use the space below the frames to describe the motion at that moment in time.

Since the storyboards will be used to generate ideas and as a guide for the final motion design animations, consider how you will incorporate the following in storyboard form: shape and motion tween animation, motion paths, and an effective use of point of view as it relates to the viewing area, timing, speed/velocity, and a limited two-color palette. You may only use two colors: for our purposes, white and black are each considered a color if you choose to use them.

I will provide you with a printed example of a template to use for final presentation. Follow this template exactly. I will also provide the template digitally for you to use since I would like these to be output with a printer in addition to as a PDF. Storyboards must be in color.

**Motion Design.** The second and final part of project 4 is a Flash animation. Using your research and storyboards as a guide, consider how to effectively design and animate your story to nine seconds *exactly*. Flash animations must effectively show the following: shape and motion tweening, motion paths, and use of layers, and an effective use of point of view as it relates to the viewing area, timing, speed/velocity, and a limited two-color palette. You may only use two colors: for our purposes, white and black are each considered a color if you choose to use them.

Consider how the use of scale, point of view, timing, velocity, color and transparency, illustration, multiple shape, and motion tweening will communicate your ideas clearly. How will the animation begin? How will you follow through with your idea to the end? Control the medium with continuity, consistency, and clarity.

**Animation Details.** Final animations must be *exactly* nine seconds in duration.
　　Size: 640 pixels × 480 pixels
　　Speed: 12 fps.
　　Final animation *must* be rendered out as a QuickTime movie.

Name the final .mov animation as: swarm_lastname.mov.

Provide storyboard PDF as well as the final .mov animation on a single CD. Label the CD as: Project 4: Swarm and include your first and last name. *Don't forget to also provide a printout of the storyboard.*

### Grading Out of 100

Storyboards: 20%. Ability to visualize an appropriate, clear, well-organized, and memorable solution to the given problem in storyboard form as outlined above. Level of finish and technical craft achieved.

Animations: 50%. Ability to visualize an appropriate, clear, well-organized, and memorable solution to the given problem in regard to multiple shape and motion tweening, motion paths, and use of layers, and an effective use of point of view, timing, speed/velocity, and a limited two-color palette.

Animation Presentation/Technical Craft: 20%. Level of technical finish achieved in final presentation of the animations as it relates to multiple shape and motion tweening, motion paths, and use of layers, and an effective use of point of view, timing, speed/velocity, and a limited two-color palette. Size of animations must be 640 pixels × 480 pixels.

Class Participation/Critique: 10%. Ability to articulate thoughts and ideas in a group setting and with the instructor about the project, in a professional and respectful manner that fosters and creates a learning environment.

## Project 5: Sound

A sound is something that is heard. Listening is an activity.

Sound design is fine-tuning the message your audience will sense. Sound may be buried in the message and only noticed if it is ever taken away. Sound may be the message. Without it we limit the use of one of our most receptive senses. Naturally, certain tones are conveyed by using certain sounds that ultimately communicate a message. It will be up to you to determine what you want to say and how you want to say it through the design of *sound*.

Below is a list of five words. Each student must compose sound from a sample or recorded means or a combination of both that communicates each word. Listen critically to how different sounds portray different messages. Each sound should be exactly ten seconds in length, exported as QuickTime .aif files. We will play each .aif one at a time through the QuickTime player.

The words to use are:

- Soft
- Global
- Digital
- Speed
- Mournful

**Details.** Five, ten-second QuickTime .aif files

Each file should be labeled with the corresponding number and sound name as well as students' initials followed with .aif (for instance, 1_soft_studentsinitials.aif). Place the files in a folder labeled "pro_5_studentslastname" and burn it to a CD labeled with your first and last name as well as "Project 5: Sound." Be prepared to load the files onto the presentation computer at the beginning of class.

### Grading Out of 100

Audio: 70%. Student demonstrated the ability to record, import, edit, compose, and export .aif files. Student also demonstrated an appropriate, clear, and memorable solution to the given problem. Level of finish and technical craft achieved.

Presentation: 20%. Student was well prepared for the final presentation.

Class Participation/Critique: 10%. Ability to articulate thoughts and ideas about the project in a group setting and with the instructor, in a professional and respectful manner that fosters and creates a learning environment.

## Project 6: Essay

Three hundred-word written essay describing a work of motion design

### Project Description

Students should first choose a work of motion design to watch, think about, and describe critically. Examples are Web sites that rely on motion to communicate their message, movie main title designs, broadcast designs such as advertising commercials that rely on motion design, station identities, or show introductions. Briefly describe what the general concept of the piece is and what compelled you to choose it. Also, using your best guess, who was the intended audience? Make succinct points about the effectiveness of the use of motion, use of sound, live action/photography/illustration, point of view, color, composition, and type choice/type design if applicable.

Please include a screen capture of a keyframe, the title of the piece, the company who produced it, if possible, and the sources you used. I will provide a diagram for layout guidelines. Because of ease and availability, I would encourage you to use a Web-based source for the keyframe example.

Using a DVD or VHS. You should make sure there is a way you can capture or obtain a keyframe from the sequence if you use these sources.

Web sites. Please feel free to use any of the examples presented in class or choose your own:

*www.motiontheory.com*

*www.brandnewschool.com*

*www.hillmancurtis.com* (Craig Frazier animations and many more)

*www.d-kitchen.com*

*www.mk12.com*

*www.imaginaryforces.com*

*www.picturemill.com*

*www.psyop.tv*

*www.epoxy.ca*

*www.planetpropaganda.com*

*www.carladiana.com*

*www.donniedarkofilm.com*

*www.modernista.com*

Other possible Web sites for material:

*www.designinmotion.com*

*www.macromedia.com* (showcase or site of the day)

*www.quicktime.com* (QuickTime trailers)

## Project 7: My Robotic World

**Required:** Initial concepts, rough storyboards, rough animation, final presentation storyboard, and final motion design.

A robot is defined as a mechanical device operating automatically in a seemingly human way. A world is defined as any sphere or domain, individual experience, outlook, secular life and interests, or people concerned with these. Create a narrative about how robots exist, move, think, sound, and act, and what they accomplish and communicate in a world you design. What will your robots look like? What are they made of? What is the tone or personality you wish to convey? Will they be good, evil, helpful, or hurtful? Is your robotic world rigid with clean vector imagery of is it organic and free form with hand-drawn or bitmap visuals?

You are challenged to design sound and motion under the theme "My Robotic World." Experiment/play, inquire, and risk what your final motion design will communicate to the audience. You may certainly reference Hollywood robots such as the Terminator, R2D2, and RoboCop, but you may also invent and challenge what a robot can be and how robotics could exist in your world from a narrative you create.

One requirement of this project is to use typography/letterforms in motion. For some students, this may mean typographic design in motion using existing fonts. For others, this may mean custom letterforms in motion such as hand-drawn letters, words, and phrases. In either case, the typography/letterforms should challenge the conventions of how we see and read type as it moves.

Animations must explore and appropriately demonstrate the following:

- An understanding and utilization of structure—the arrangement of all parts of a whole, composed of related parts and put together systematically (Note: a *structure* does not have to mean rigidity. Structure can be highly organic.)

91

- Use of motion in regard to the story's inherent conceptual structure
- Effective use of typography/letterforms in motion
- Changing the point of view throughout the duration as it relates to the narrative, velocity, speed, and timing
- Effective use of sound and motion
- Sound composition
- Synchronized sound—cutting to sound or cutting sound to motion
- Effective use of imported vector art and bitmapped imagery
- Effective use of combining vector art and bitmapped imagery in the animation
- Experimentation, inquiry, and risk in regard to self-developing the content
- Effective use of form and color, scale, and the viewing area/screen

Students may also use keyframe animation, shape/motion tween, animated graphic symbols, motion guides, transparency, the ease in/ease out feature, and anything else learned from our in-class Flash lessons.

### Initial Concepts

A minimum of three sheets (roughly 8.5 × 11 inches) of exploratory notes, image references, sketches, and writing are to be used as the basis for developing initial narrative concepts.

As you begin, start considering a conceptual framework for a thirty-second animation. This is the step where you should explore and inquire about possibilities. Describe through words and sketches how the story will eventually be told using a combination of sound, color, typography/letterforms, and motion. Write down any and all ideas. At this discovery step, don't eliminate any ideas. Notice if any of the concepts can be taken to the next level—rough working storyboard.

### Rough Working Storyboard and Rough Animations

**Required:** Rough fifteen-frame working storyboard. These can be in sketchbook form or working digital files.

Rough .swf Flash animations—Flash animations will be viewed from students computers.

This initial step of storyboarding should be done in sketch form. Sketch at least two to three, six-frame storyboards that fall out of the initial concept stage. Once you determine a direction, continue to a rough fifteen-frame working storyboard. This may be done using pencil, pen, or marker on paper or begin making frames directly in a digital environment. This stage is where you should ask questions about the work you are creating. Begin considering the sound and working out details in regard to timing, velocity, typography, color, scale, point of view, and motion that are appropriate to the inherent conceptual structure. Rough working storyboards will give much needed visual feedback before the final animation is implemented.

As you develop a rough working storyboard, begin experimenting with animation. You should start working out how you will animate many of your ideas. Bring rough animation experiments for the in-class review.

## Final Presentation Storyboard

Fifteen frames using the template provided and exported as a .pdf. Also, provide a black and white printout.

The next step is to create a complete and final storyboard. The final storyboard is a visual plan used for working out as many challenges as possible before starting the final animation. The final storyboard should show your ability to visualize an appropriate, clear, thoughtful, and memorable solution to the given problem as well as your overall craft in regard to illustration, color, and composition. Please use the template provided. Frames must be produced digitally. If you wish to draw by hand, please scan the final frames, import, and place accordingly in Illustrator.

Label .pdf as: "pro_7_strybrd_studentslastname.pdf".

## Animation

Size: 640 pixels × 360 pixels
Speed: 12 fps
Length: thirty-second QuickTime movie.

As you design and animate the final animation, ask yourself and others if all of the parts are working together as a whole. Animations should show a considered, entertaining, and engaging narrative about the chosen concept. Animations must explore and demonstrate an appropriate use of sound, timing, velocity, typography in motion, color, form, scale, use of imported vectors and/or bitmaps, an effective point of view, and use of motion in regard to the story's inherent conceptual structure as it relates to the chosen concept.

Please label final animation as: pro_7_studentslastname.mov. Place both the .pdf and a .mov in a folder labeled "pro_7_studentslastname." Burn these files to a CD and label the disc "Project 7: My Robotic World" and include your first and last name.

## Grading Out of 100

Initial Concepts: 5%. Student researched and began considering a conceptual framework for a thirty-second animation through exploratory sketches and writing.

Rough Working Storyboard and Rough Animations: 5%. Student sketched at least two to three, six-frame storyboards that lead to a rough fifteen-frame storyboard and began considering sound as well as working out details in regard to timing, velocity, typography, color, scale, point of view, and motion that are appropriate to the inherent conceptual structure. Provided rough experimental animations.

Final Storyboard: 10%. Student completes, prior to finishing the final animation, a final storyboard that demonstrates his ability to visualize an appropriate, clear, thoughtful, and memorable solution to the given problem in sequential form as well as an overall craft in regard to illustration, color, and composition.

Animation: 40%. Student demonstrates the ability to visualize an appropriate, clear, thoughtful, and memorable solution to the given problem. Animation shows all elements working together as a whole as they relate to the use of sound, timing, velocity, typography in motion, color, form, scale, use of imported vectors and bit maps, effective points of view, and use of motion.

Animation Technical Craft: 30%. Level of presentation of final execution. Software skills and exploration. Overall technical craft in regard to the use of motion and the use of sound.

Class participation and critique: 10%. Attendance, preparedness, verbal articulation, probed questions, and discussion participation effort.

## objective of class projects

All projects coincide with lessons learned in class. Each project is sequentially built upon the understanding of previous projects. The course begins with two analog projects that challenge conceptual approaches to storyboarding, which is the foundation to understanding how to design with a time-based medium. As the course progresses, students begin to create more complex motion designs while at the same time learning how to articulate thoughts and ideas verbally with the class and the instructor. Sound is always enthusiastically received. Once sound is introduced, the Flash lessons are complete, therefore students have a good understanding of what is possible with Flash and this is reflected in wide variety of solutions for the final projects.

## outcome or conclusion

Sound + Motion in Graphic Multimedia is an introductory course for motion design. Students leave this course with an understanding of storyboarding, basic Flash animation, basic sound design, and an overall conceptual growth as it relates to both time-based media as well as the other coursework within the School of Design. Students also leave with an arsenal of motion design terms and knowledge that can be a significant segue to complement the students' growth within the illustration and graphic design curriculum.

## recommended reading

Curtis, Hillman, *MTIV: Process, Inspiration and Practice for the New Media Designer*, New Riders Press, 2002.

COURSE TITLE: Motion Graphics 1: Principles

TEACHER: Matt Normand

FREQUENCY: One Semester

LEVEL: Junior/Senior

CREDITS: 3

DEGREE: Bachelor of Fine Arts, Graphic and Interactive Design

SCHOOL: Ringling College of Art and Design, Sarasota, FL

## summary and goals

This course is an exploration of the principles of motion as they apply to typography and other graphic elements. The emphasis is on the visual theory involved in designing for time and space, concept, point of view, and sequence.

Outcomes: To test certain motion graphics models while approaching the various expectations and processes of a professional motion graphics studio.

Technology:

- After Effects
- Final Cut Pro
- CINEMA 4D (This program is not taught, but some students used it for coursework.)

## week by week

**WEEK 1.** Project 1, Here is Here, is assigned. Students spend the first thirty minutes writing how they got to class, they then expand it into four frames. I tell them to start with a beginning and end, then fill in the middle, most important frames.

Students spend the week elaborating on eight frames as separate Photoshop compositions or as an Illustrator document.

**WEEK 2.** Students import each Photoshop document into an After Effects project as a separate composition. They are then asked to stagger these eight compositions into one encompassing composition. After they have this rough animatic completed, they can go in and animate the individual pieces in each separate composition.

I assign project 2, Box, and ask everyone to bring five items to class in a shoebox.

**WEEK 3.** Students exchange their shoeboxes with each other and write a two hundred-word story about the contents of the box.

The week is concluded by a series of black-and-white typographic posters that illustrate key points in the story.

**WEEK 4.** Students create storyboards from the investigations of their posters. They do this by cutting out frames from paper and cropping them over the image. With this "plan" they can either animate the layers or drive a camera over the composition. Project 3, Logo, is assigned.

**WEEK 5.** The two movies are elaborated further and a third movie is added that is the combination of all of their objects.

**WEEK 6.** The final week, movies are finished and turned in. Logo project is critiqued.

**WEEK 7.** Logo project is due. Project 4, Intelligent Stupidity, is assigned. Students are asked to pick a physics term and write a three hundred-word list.

**WEEK 8.** Students make physical experiments based on their terms and document them.

**WEEK 9.** Rough two- to three-second loops are created, and a fifteen-second documentary is started.

**WEEK 10.** Intelligent Stupidity is completed. Students are broken up into teams named after motion graphics firms in Los Angeles and New York, and project 5, Movie Titles, is assigned. Group names include Imaginary Forces, Brand New School, Prologue, Motion Theory, Blind, yU+co, etc.

**WEEK 11.** At the beginning of week, groups start pitching ideas for movies for which they want to design titles. The students are required to make preliminary storyboards in Photoshop. Teams that make the most convincing ideas are awarded the titles.

**WEEK 12.** Teams further develop storyboards and start to create motion tests of the selected scenes.

**WEEK 13.** Motion tests are critiqued and scenes are further developed during the class time. Students are encouraged to begin reworking old projects for their final montage or "reel."

**WEEK 14.** Movie Titles is due. The Final Reel, project 6, is assigned. Students utilize the last three weeks developing a sequence that highlights their best work.

**WEEK 15.** This week is devoted to studio time to further develop your final reels.

**WEEK 16.** Final reel is due. End of the semester.

# assignments and projects

### WEEK 1, CLASS 1.

### Project 1: Here Is Here

**Part One.** Everyone had an adventure today to get to this awesome classroom. What happened between closing the apartment door and walking into class? Did you go to the right classroom?

Not everyone had the same experience. *We want your story!*

For the remainder of the class I want you to write/illustrate the sequence/narrative/process/story that brought you to the classroom today. Be true to the form. Mundane is genius. Start at waking up or getting in the car; it is up to you.

After thirty minutes, you are all going to share the synopsis (summary) of your story. You are limited to two minutes.

Draw!

After forty-five minutes, you are all to share thumbnail sketches of a four-panel storyboard.

**WEEK 1, CLASS 2.** Make eight 240 pixel × 160 pixel panels that illustrate your story. The storyboard can be drawn, photographed, vector, collage, or a combination of them all. Present storyboard on 11 × 17 inch paper. *No web images.*

**Part Two.** From your writings and explorations come up with a title that relates to the nature of the first class.

Cast of classmates. I will pass out a list of your classmates. You have to determine who is what. Not everyone is going to be an actor, some people will be directors and cinematographers. It is totally arbitrary who is what, your only requirement is to use everyone's name.

**WEEK 2, CLASS 1.** Make *twelve* additional 720 pixel × 486 pixel panels. The new panels can elaborate the story with both images and/or typography. Present the twenty-panel storyboard on 11 × 17 inch pieces of paper. *No web images.*

**WEEK 3, CLASS 1.** Animatic with sound due as a QuickTime movie: Limit thirty seconds

**WEEK 4, CLASS 1.** Final Animation with sound due as QuickTime movie: Limit thirty seconds

The project will expire at this final stage, but you are encouraged to further develop it for your final reel.


## Project 2: Box

**Part One.** For the next class bring in a shoebox with five to twelve items in it. Objects must fit inside the box.

These objects can describe your past, present, or future. They can be connected to a time or place or they can be utterly useless. These objects can be distilled, intact, or destroyed. None of these objects can have any value assigned to them or any sentimental value (in the event that they are ruined or lost in our investigations).

Include two copies of an inventory list of all objects in the box as well as one paragraph for each object.

**WEEK 3, CLASS 1.** You will bring this to our next class. It will be graded, as it will be an obligatory part of what we will be doing in the class.

Please consider the fact that we will be investigating these items for a few weeks and it would help if you chose something interesting. If I think that objects were chosen in haste (and it will be obvious), I will assign you an F for the day. Have a sense of humor while choosing the objects as well; remember not to include valuables. Consider objects lost.

**Part Two.** Pass your box to the person to the left six times.

WRITE/SOUND/IMAGE. Examine the contents of the box. What items stand out? What items seem to go together or contrast each other? You are now to create sets from the contents of the box. After you determine the sets you will be asked to write short descriptions or stories of your choice.

Choose two single artifacts: You will describe each separately. This will count as two sets.

Choose two artifact pairs: You will describe the two pairs separately. This will count as two sets.

Entire contents: Investigate the box as a whole. You will describe the entire contents of the box. This will count as one set.

In the end you will have a total of five sets of information.

Some things to keep in mind:

1. Write about them. Be descriptive, but also leave something for the reader's imagination. How much needs to be said before the reader understands what you are describing? The objects may be described literally or metaphorically.

2. Describe them with sound. Use indexical sound, voice, or music. Consider the roles of language, gender, inflection, and mood. How do they change and create meaning for the objects you are describing? Translate these sounds into written form.

3. Image the artifacts. Use both still and video imaging. Try other methods of image making—illustration, rubbing, copy machine.

Consider image types, symbolic, metaphoric, and iconic. How do they change and give meaning to the objects you are describing? Translate these images into written form.

Gather information. Start combining these writings and invent stories/narratives. Formulate ideas, type out lists, illustrate with a matrix. Question typography. Be prepared to work in class on building narratives. You should have a rough draft of each set.

**Part Three.** Narrative to Poster. Create five posters—one for each set of items that you have described—that meet the specification below:

- Presented on an 11 × 17 inch landscape
- Black and white
- Use only typography

You are strongly encouraged to use a variation of type building tools including copy machine, Letraset, projections, and computer.

Consider how you would like the viewer to perceive your artifacts. Is the narrative description literal, metaphoric, or iconic?

Use hierarchy, read path, mutation, and mutilation of message to convey your communication.

The posters that you will create will evolve into storyboards and movies.

**WEEK 4, CLASS 1.** Bring in five complete posters. The next part will be assigned at this point.

**Part Four.** Poster to Storyboard. Approach! See! Read!

Use your posters to create five individual eight-panel storyboards.

Investigate different methods viewing and different reads of the posters that you have created. Ask your classmates what they are reading first. How can words take up the center of the frame? How do we read the poster at different distances; thirty feet, fifteen feet, five feet, eight inches, one inch, one millimeter, zero? What if you film your approach to the poster with a Mini DV camera and edit the footage?

**WEEK 4, CLASS 2.** Start investigating turning your poster into a storyboard.

**WEEK 5, CLASS 1.** Storyboard is due and class critique.

**WEEK 5, CLASS 2.** Work day.

**Part Five.** Storyboard to movie. Pick two storyboards you feel strongest about. Create two movies—one for each description you have developed. In these movies you may only use typographic solutions. You may only use black and white. You may not use sound.

99

The movie must be 720 pixels × 486 pixels. Each movie can only be fifteen to twenty seconds long.

**WEEK 6, CLASS 1.** Individual critiques. Work day.

**WEEK 6, CLASS 2.** Project is due.

**Part Six A.** Sound/Typography/Color/Image. Add sound, typography, color, and image to one of the movies from part five.

Sound: YOU ARE NOT ALLOWED TO USE ANY COPYRIGHTED MUSIC OR SAMPLES. You may use original music.

Color: Think about what colors connote. Think about color correction, monochromatic systems, saturation, etc.

Image: Consider the image making techniques that you were doing at the beginning of the assignment.

Make one, ten- to twenty-second movie.

**Part Six B.** Go Nuts! Consider the rules of parts one through six a and break them. Your only constraint is that you are limited to type, sound, color, and any objects in your box.

Make one, twenty- to thirty-second movie.

**WEEK 5, CLASS 1.** Work day.

**WEEK 5, CLASS 2.** Short class critique of parts six a and b. Work day.

**WEEK 6, CLASS 1.** Parts six a and b individual critiques.

**WEEK 6, CLASS 2.** Parts six a and b are due.

## Project 3: Logo

Go to *http://brandsoftheworld.com*. Find a logo of your choice. Make three different three-second animations. What do I mean by different? Simply animate different parts of the logo on or off. You may investigate up to three different concepts of the bizarro.

You are not limited to just the logo. The logo does not have to remain intact as seen on the site (for example, you may only want to use Colonel Sander's head, rather than "KFC—We Do Chicken Right!").

These pieces have the potential of being used in your motion portfolio. So treat at least two animations with a little bit of dignity and respect.

**WEEK 4, CLASS 1.** Choose a company. Individual consultation.

**WEEK 5, CLASS 2.** Rough class critique.

**WEEK 6, CLASS 1.** Individual consultation. Work day.

**WEEK 6, CLASS 2.** Individual consultation.

**WEEK 7, CLASS 1.** Logo is due.

## 100    Project 4: The Intelligent Stupidity Project

Theorize, experiment, document. In this assignment, students will learn the value of physics in motion graphics. There are many ideas that come from the physical world that can apply to four-dimensional abstraction. Students will be asked to loosely define a physics definition and draw some conclusions as to how it can be performed using video cameras, still cameras, and/or simple time-based media techniques, and finally the computer.

Goal: Interpretation of physics definition into a motion graphics test.

Demonstrate experiments for class use.

*Do not make redundant word and image pairings.*

**WEEK 7, CLASS 1.** Create a three hundred-word list and a definition, drawings, and notations for your chosen term.

**WEEK 7, CLASS 2.** Laboratory.

**WEEK 8, CLASS 1.** Present video and/or photography of experiments.

**WEEK 8, CLASS 2.** Laboratory.

**WEEK 9, CLASS 1.** After Effects translation, rough drafts of three different three-second loops and one, twenty-second documentary film essay.

**WEEK 9, CLASS 2.** Laboratory.

**WEEK 10, CLASS 1.** Due.

Choose from the following list (Note: I suggest instructors provide a list of twenty terms or more so students are not limited in their choice.):

- potential energy
- kinetic energy
- centripetal force
- inertia
- work
- mass
- lever
- pulley
- horse power
- weight
- heat
- reflection
- refraction

- gravity
- friction
- speed
- fission
- fluid
- displacement
- circuit
- attraction
- power
- vibration
- acceleration
- photon
- resistance

- fusion
- magnet
- collision
- equilibrium
- tangent
- velocity
- resonate
- repulsion
- torque
- stress
- frame of reference

## Project 5: Movie Titles

In this assignment students will be making advanced storyboards. They will be using Photoshop and Illustrator. The class will be divided into five teams. This is a partial collaboration.

Every team will pitch for one (or three) of the movies on the list below.

**Part One.** Every team will choose one film from the provided list and typeset one hundred film titles (teams are responsible to delegate typefaces and variations). Each person will create three different concepts for their team.

**Part Two.** Each team will embellish the combination of their storyboard ideas of my choosing. Each person will create an advanced twenty-panel storyboard. Each person will create one motion test.

**Part Three.** Each team will create five different motion tests. Each team will create one, forty-panel storyboard.

### Teams

Break the class into teams of four or five students depending on class size. To create added interest, name the teams after existing motion graphics studios. Studios include Blind, Brand New School, Imaginary Forces, Motion Theory, Prologue Films, and yU+co. This idea introduces students to studios that have created substantial work, and offers ideas for employment after graduation. Other studios can be found on Motionographer's Web site (*www.motionographer.com*). This Web site will be an excellent resource of examples for Project 6: Final Reel.

### Choosing Movies

Instructors must choose ten to fifteen movies that have a release date past the due date of the assignment. Only use movies that have a trailer on QuickTime's Web site (*www.apple.com/trailers*) or a full synopsis on the Internet Movie Database Web site (*www.imdb.com*).

## Project 6: Final Reel

Spend the next week editing all projects into a final reel of thirty seconds to one minute in length. This will be due on the final day of class.

COURSE TITLE: Motion Graphics 2: Projects

TEACHER: Matt Normand

FREQUENCY: One Semester

LEVEL: Junior/Senior

CREDITS: 3

DEGREE: Bachelor of Fine Arts, Graphic and Interactive Design

SCHOOL: Ringling College of Art and Design, Sarasota, FL

## summary and goals

Students will develop a personal demo reel that shows an understanding of storyboarding, animatics, art direction, and broadcast design. The course is intended for students with an interest in pursuing jobs in motion graphics at studios such as Cartoon Network, Imaginary Forces, Comedy Central, and Prologue.

Prerequisite: EL 430 New Media: Motion Graphics or instructor permission. Students will develop:

- An understanding of the storyboard planning process
- An understanding of animatic planning
- An understanding of the role of art direction
- An understanding of motion graphics and its relationship to broadcast design
- A facility with image making for motion
- An understanding of the role of motion in communication

Upon completion of this class, students will have further explored their skills in motion design tools and created multiple projects for an application demo reel. Students will have achieved a work level that meets the expectations and processes of a professional motion graphics studio for an entry-level designer position.

Technology:

- After Effects
- Final Cut Pro

Class time each week will include working on four projects for each reel as well as preparing an end of the year showcase to present at senior portfolio night.

A project will take three weeks to complete but may be further embellished or exercised. Students are required to choose four out of seven projects to complete over the course. Projects have both pragmatic and experimental intention and are open for interpretation. This class is intended to be more cerebral and will go about as far as students want to take it. Students are responsible for their own process work.

# assignments and projects

Choose four of the seven projects listed below. Project descriptions follow.

- Broadcast
- Advanced Logo
- Public Service Announcement
- Movie Title
- Journey
- Rules
- Translation

## Broadcast

With this assignment, students will be encouraged to look beyond just animating a logo to the whole series of identity marks that will carry a station's brand across many uses within its programming.

1. Choose between a television station identity and the Academy Awards or another televised event.
2. Digitally record on-screen graphics including logos, bumpers, teasers, and other branding devices.
3. Design a logo that is a play on the existing mark or invent a new identity.
4. Design as many different station identity tags as you can possibly invent.

## Advanced Logo

The goal of this assignment is to further a student's ability to create meaningful connections between company identity, branding, and signature product with the use of motion and sound design.

Go to *http://brandsoftheworld.com* and make a series of logos in motion that encapsulate the branding of a company or a product that it sells. You have the options of rebranding the company, redirecting the audience demographic, redesigning the logo, and making a social statement about the company.

In no way, shape, or form are these logos to resemble any previous class work.

## Public Service Announcement

This project is intended to give you the opportunity to contribute to a worthy cause with a powerful message.

Choose an issue of interest to you and make a public service announcement for it. It must be something that you feel strongly about and aligns with your ideas as a person.

Announcements can vary in length but cannot be more than one minute long.

## Movie Title

Students have the option to work independently or in groups on a movie of their choice. Consider making titles for a favorite book that does not exist as a movie or as a coming attraction, or that exists as a movie that has what you feel is a poor title.

## Journey

The purpose of this assignment is to investigate a hidden meaning within text. In the processing of information, too often we take ideas at their literal translation. This project gives students the opportunity to invent metaphor and a new context for an older meaning. The project's success relies heavily on the students understanding of the art direction of live-action motion graphics.

Find any piece of literature that talks about a journey. Write twenty words that are the summation, commentary, protest, or antithesis. Juxtapose any combination of these words with a journey. You are limited to using only a video camera and type. You may use After Effects and Final Cut Pro for editing. Do not use these tools to layer type into video.

## Rules

Our language is woven with unlearned rules that we understand as truths. They may apply to a word and a specific gesture or could appear in a comment from a notable figure. Nonetheless, we have these rules.

Using sound, visuals, and motion as the media, define a rule of your language.

Read/reread the excerpts from Jean-Francois Lyotard's *The Postmodern Condition: A Report on Knowledge (Theory and History of Literature Volume 10)* (University of Minnesota Press, 1984). Chapter 3: pages 9–11 and chapter 10: pages 37–41.

Choose a topic to have a conversation about.

Tape-record a conversation (with consent).

Observe the conversation.

Develop a rule based on the conversation.

Define the rule using motion.

## Translation

This project is intended to open translation based on the age/genre of audiences. It is important that we as a society understand the possibilities of our complex language. Different codes evolve from sports or games, or entertainment. They often exist as cliché or slang.

Your goal is to discover one of these words, research it, and define the word based on gender, genre, and geographic location. You are to illustrate this word and define it by three different audiences. This illustration should include inflection of voice, pronunciation, and context.

How is this presented? What happens when the audiences are mixed up? Choose a word.

106

## summary and goals

This course will explore the foundations of motion graphics. Design for screen, effective use of typography, graphical elements, sound, video, and motion are covered with simple animations, logo and shape motion, and environmental visual effects.

Although technical proficiency is expected, the primary emphasis of the course is the creation of imagery, sound, video, and animation for use in motion graphic projects. Through the application of traditional motion skills to the workspace, students will develop technical, verbal, and conceptual design skills that can be utilized effectively as part of a motion graphics project.

Upon completing this course, students will be able to:

- Apply animation techniques to create promos, stings, idents, etc., for motion graphics
- Integrate the use of design, typography, sound, space, timing, and animation within motion pieces
- Present, discuss, and articulate concepts through analysis, research, and idea development related to course topics

Technology: Adobe After Effects/Apple Motion, Final Cut Pro, and Soundtrack Pro.

Hardware: Dual processor G5 with 2 gigabytes of RAM.

Student Requirements: Students must have good working knowledge of Photoshop and Illustrator before taking this class. Prerequisites include design for Web class.

## week by week

**WEEK 1.** Introduction to motion graphics, development of sketchbook, assignment 1 announced.

Overview of After Effects 1.

Weekly reading 1: *MTIV*: Read process and introductory sections up to page 53.

Weekly reading 2: *Motion Graphic Design and Fine Art Animation*: Read chapters one and two.

**WEEK 2.** Sketchbook check, reading discussions, assignment 1 final logos due. Storyboarding lecture.

Weekly reading 1: *MTIV*: Read process pages 54–93.

Weekly reading 2: *Motion Graphic Design and Fine Art Animation*: Read chapters three and four.

**WEEK 3.** Overview of After Effects 2.

Sketchbook check, reading discussions, assignment 1 storyboard due.

Using Sound (The lab director will demonstrate the use of sound equipment.)

Weekly reading: *MTIV*: Read practice on pages 94–145.

Weekly reading 2: *Motion Graphic Design and Fine Art Animation*: Read chapters five and six.

**WEEK 4.** Overview of After Effects 3.

Reading discussions.

**WEEK 5.** Work in progress check.

Studio time.

**WEEK 6.** Assignment 1 due: Presentations and group critique.

Assignments 2 and 3 are announced. Assignment 3 is a group assignment. The assignment is a presentation by the students (in groups of two to three) and involves discussion on topics relating to motion graphics.

Weekly reading 1: *Motion Graphic Design and Fine Art Animation*: Read chapter eight.

Weekly reading 2: *MTIV*: Read pages 147–157 and 198–207.

Weekly reading 3: "Telling a visual story," *Creativity*, June 2003.

Student demonstrations of tips and techniques.

Examples of motion work.

Lab director will demonstrate Mini DV camera and using Mini DV decks.

**WEEK 7.** Overview of After Effects 4.

Reading discussions, sketchbook check, assignment 2 storyboard due.

Mid-semester critiques.

**WEEK 8.** Studio time.

Assignment 3: Group assignment presentations.

**WEEK 9.** Studio time.

**WEEK 10.** Assignment 2 due: Presentations and group critique.

Assignment 4 announced.

Weekly reading 1: *Motion Graphic Design and Fine Art Animation*: Read chapters nine and ten concerning output methods.

Weekly reading 2: Stefano Hatfield's interview with Commercial Director Frank Budgen ("The Midas Touch," *Creativity*, July/August 2002).

**WEEK 11.** Overview of Final Cut Pro HD.
Sketchbook check, research, and initial roughs due, reading discussions.

**WEEK 12.** Student demonstrations of Final Cut tutorials.
Assignment 4 storyboard due.

**WEEK 13.** Studio time.
Progress check.

**WEEK 14.** Studio time.
Progress check.

**WEEK 15.** Assignment 4 final due: Presentations and group critique. Resubmissions.
Final submission of all work on CD-R, DVD-R, and VHS Tape.

# assignments and projects

Students have four assignments.

Assignment 1: The goal of the first assignment is to produce a logo and then an ident (an animation of that logo). Students are given three subjects for their initial logo designs—an artist, a nonprofit, and a classmate—they design logos for all three subjects initially. After a critique, one is chosen, students storyboard an ident and then create it using After Effects.

Assignment 2: This assignment involves creating a set of three stings (the short animations that you see on MTV sometimes promoting a show in between programs). Usually I will give them a title to work with; for instance, I will ask them to choose from a list. One assignment included a list of stereotypes. They then have to produce a set of three ideas for creating stings in the style of MTV.

Assignment 3: This is a group assignment usually done in pairs. Students have to watch five films and analyze their structure, narrative, cinematography, lighting, etc., and then a group discussion occurs.

Assignment 4: The final assignment can be anything from an introduction for a film festival, sometimes a foreign film festival, or a promotional piece/public service announcement on a subject that they can choose from Amnesty International.

# recommended readings

*Adobe After Effects 7.0 Classroom in a Book*, Adobe Press, 2006.
Block, Bruce, *The Visual Story: Seeing the Structure of Film, TV and New Media*, Focal Press, 2001.

Bolante, Anthony, *After Effects 7 for Windows and Macintosh: Visual QuickPro Guide*, Peachpit Press, 2006.

Curtis, Hillman, *MTIV: Process, Inspiration and Practice for the New Media Designer*, New Riders, 2002.

Hatfield, Stefano, "The Midas Touch," *Creativity*, July/August 2002.

Krasner, Jon, *Motion Graphic Design and Fine Art Animation: Principles and Practice*, Focal Press, 2004.

Sheridan, Sherri, *Developing Digital Short Films*, New Riders, 2004.

Taylor, Angie, *Creative After Effects 5.0, Animation, Visual Effects and Motion Graphics Production for TV and Video*, Focal Press, 2001.

"Telling a visual story," *Creativity*, June 2003.

**COURSE TITLE:** Motion Graphics (Macintosh)

**TEACHER:** Laurie Burruss

**FREQUENCY:** One Semester, twice a week for three hours and twenty minutes

**LEVEL:** One semester of Adobe Photoshop or six months professionally using Photoshop is prerequisite

**CREDITS:** 3 (six hours)

**DEGREE:** Associate of Arts or Certificate of Interactive Multimedia Design

**SCHOOL:** Pasadena City College, Pasadena, CA

## course content

Motion Graphics (Macintosh), an intermediate- to advanced-level course, introduces theories, techniques, and practices of motion graphics and the integration of design, photo imaging, sound, video, and animation into video presentations using the Macintosh platform. Effective visual communication, creative problem solving, an understanding of the vocabulary of art, and techniques in portfolio presentation are some of the main objectives in this course.

The tutorials and projects will investigate a tool (After Effects) and its special features that include integrating images, graphics, typography, sound, animation, and video on the personal computer. The course will explore experimental and new technological approaches to creating original visual imagery for use in design, fine arts, animation, interactive media, and the Internet. In addition to receiving an introduction to compositing in a postproduction suite, students will learn some basic nonlinear editing utilizing QuickTime, Soundtrack, GarageBand, SoundStudio, Flash and Final Cut Pro.

As in traditional studio/fine art courses, the problems will deal with visual organization and communication, creative brainstorming skills, and experimentation with techniques and a variety of media. Time will be spent examining current motion graphics projects and their development from concept to storyboard to flow chart to stand-alone digital video movie. Later in the semester, projects will evolve into more complex ideas that might include nesting movies, creating digital audio and video, advanced animated special effects, and output to film, video, and CD-ROM. The class will explore the relationship and applications of art/design to our daily environment and to the contemporary art world. Members of the class will work individually and in teams depending upon the complexity of the projects. Hopefully you will take chances, experiment, share, develop self-confidence and critical thinking skills, and ultimately learn to see the world with a fresh set of perceptions.

Generally, a project is given every two to three weeks followed by a critique at the project's due date. In addition to these projects and hands-on tutorials, a one-page artist/gallery report is required by the end of the semester. (The report and a suggested format will be discussed the third or fourth week.) This course is designed to follow Photo 30 or an equivalent course. Since this course is experiential, participation is crucial. Each student in class will be a source of ideas and critical feedback to every other student. Some time will be required outside class to complete assignments. Be prepared to work—that means coming to class with the necessary materials, appropriate dress, great ideas, and enthusiasm!

## grading

Grades are based on the execution of class work and assigned homework projects. I will grade each project as the semester progresses. By being graded as we go along, you can see your strengths and weaknesses and hopefully improve. The criterion for grading is as follows:

A – Work should show outstanding creative thought and effort and execution. "A" work is not merely competent, but daring!

B – Work should show creative thought, effort, and execution.

C – Work simply fulfills the minimum requirements.

D – Work shows little or no understanding of concepts and a poor effort.

F – Failure to meet the above minimum requirements.

## materials and textbooks

The "materials list" gives a general list of materials for use throughout the semester, but with each individual project some additional materials may need to be purchased. These additional materials will be announced at the time a new project is given. Materials and textbooks are a necessary and required part of this course. The textbooks contain many of the tutorials and images that form the basis of the projects.

### Art Materials

- A personal notebook or sketch pad for notes and ideas (no larger than $8\frac{1}{2} \times 11$ inches)
- Eighteen-inch ruler with steel edge (may also use long metal bar for a cutting edge)
- X-Acto knife with blades
- Assorted BLACK felt tip pens and markers (both wide and fine lined)
- Pencils

- Erasers (pink and kneaded)
- Different colored, small pads of Post-Its (for tracking different elements on the storyboard)
- Spray mount
- Glue stick
- Matt board for presentations (black, white, or gray—NO colors, please—32 × 40 inches)

## Computer Materials

- A spool of thirty to fifty CD-R type CD-ROMs or DVD-Rs for burning yourself OR a FireWire hard drive
- A mouse pad
- Headset/microphone

## Textbook

Adobe Creative Team, *Adobe After Effects, Classroom in a Book*, Adobe Press, 2003.

# introductory assignment 1: building a movie

Organizing by Scene (sites where you can expect certain types of activity to take place):

Create a rough storyboard using markers, pencils, or colored pencils to make a labeled box for each scene you foresee building.

Make an animatronic—scan your rough drawings and place them in After Effects roughly where you think each scene will occur. Create a little QuickTime movie to give your client/audience the timing and feel of the project in the early stages. Add sound where you can even if it is not the final audio.

Pinpoint the special needs that arise from each scene.

Global considerations—What is intrinsic to the nature of the project and what is the context in which it will operate?

Brainstorming:

Sketch ideas—KEEP ALL MATERIALS for your project treatment book.

Collect source materials; collect collage materials.

Research concepts and collect collateral material.

Begin the thought process by trying to answer the following questions:

Who is the typical user? Why will they watch? How do I want to involve the audience?

Do you have to "earn" attention?

What's the frequency of play?

How deep is the content? (How many nested levels and layers will your project require?)

Building the Movie:

Step One: The Primary Flow

Step Two: Production (the work behind the scenes)

Step Three: Output to source for project (QuickTime, VHS, CD-ROM, Web, etc.)

Final Storyboard: Print selected clips from the movie to create a final storyboard for presentation. These should be printed in color with a text describing the action, sound, and direction of each scene.

# introductory assignment 2: art materials

The Good, the Bad, and the Ugly—Creating a Usage Profile

## Problem

Upon completion of the introductory lecture and the demonstrations of After Effects as a product and creative tool, each student should select two motion graphic studios that are of interest to the student. View the work of these two studios. You might want to pick what you consider are a "good" example and a "bad" example.

## Part I

Study and preview one of the selected studios. Deconstruct means to take the whole piece apart and recognize its essential elements. Identify the goals and important elements that were identified in the early stages of the project including product configuration (VHS, film, CD-ROM, etc.), project goal(s), creative considerations, technical considerations, the target audience, the frequency of play on television, attention factor, and special elements or needs of the project. Write your conclusions on one page titled "Usage Profile."

## Part II

Finally, or in a conclusion, evaluate the work (both the good points and the bad points). Evaluate whether your selected project was successful or unsuccessful in achieving its goals. Your answer may not be black and white! In some cases, different elements like interface design may have worked but the navigation was impossible and frustrating. Answer the following questions:

- Does the piece successfully communicate to the intended audience?
- Does the piece fly right over people's heads or, on the other hand, is it too simplistic?
- Does the piece go beyond its original intentions? Does it give you a powerful, meaningful, or memorable vision or visual experience with regard to its content or subject matter?
- Does the piece have "staying" power? Do the integrated elements of audio, graphic, animation, QuickTime, and storytelling leave a lasting impression on the viewer?
- Do you recognize the metaphor of the interface design, the overall design, the navigation of the piece?
- Do you find enduring or captivating qualities such as drama, humor, satire, irony, energy, mystery, sensitivity, boldness, legibility, sensationalism, understatement, etc., in the piece? How would you define the overall design sense of the work you are analyzing?

Do not write "I just liked it" or "I hated it" or "It was nice." Would you want to go out on a blind date with a description that bland? BE DESCRIPTIVE AND INSIGHTFUL!!!

If you answer these two parts concisely and specifically, you will receive a high mark! Remember that I am not an English teacher and that I am looking for your perceptions and ideas most importantly. Recognizing a good idea is the beginning of creating your good ideas! Genius and creativity do rub off, so place yourself where genius and creativity are at work.

## Motion Graphics Studios

Attik: *www.attik.com*, Belief: *www.belief.com*, BL:ND: *www.blind.com*, Built-D Media: *www.built-d.com*, D-Fuse: *www.dfuse.com*, DRAWING AND MANUAL: *www.drawingandmanual.com*, Engine: *www.engine.net.au*, General Working Group: *www.generalworkinggroup.com*, Graphic Havoc: *www.ghava.com*, Doma: *www.doma.tv*, Head Gear Animation: *www.headgearanimation.com*, The Light Surgeons: *www. thelightsurgeons.co.uk*, Motion Theory: *www.motiontheory.com*, OVT Visuals: *www. ovtvisuals.com*, Planet Propaganda: *www.planetpropaganda.com*, Motion Graphics by Bjorn Sjostrom: *www.malmo.bonet.se/bjorns*, Style War: *www.stylewar.com*, Trollbäck + Company: *www.trollback.com*, Twenty2product: *www.twenty2.com/mg_frame.html*, Unburro: *www.unburro.com*, UV Phactory: *www.phactory.com*, V2 Labs: *www.vsquaredlabs.com*, Verb: *www.verbmedia.com*, yU+co.: *www.yuco.com*

# project 1: promotional video opener

Problem: To design and animate an opening sequence.

1. Inviting Opener

Create an inviting opener for the Pasadena City College Jazz Festival in May at the campus amphitheater. This will be an opener for a promotional videotape being produced by a fictional local performing arts center. The center wants to showcase one of its performers or concerts in a video that will be distributed free to potential sponsors. You have been asked to supply a short opening animation that can be dropped in during the video editing process.

For inspiration:

- • Look at organizations like UCLA Performing Arts Series, the Music Center, etc.
- • Your performer or performance can be imaginary.
- • Look at KCET-TV openers.
- • Listen to audio track classical or jazz for ideas.

2. The Graffitti Club

Create animated titles for a Saturday morning television program aimed at children between ages eight and fourteen. The title for the program is "The Grafitti Club." It is an art and music program designed to inspire children to become creative. The whole feel of the show is one of salvage and creativity.

For inspiration:

- • Watch some kids' television on a Saturday morning. Research what's there, what works, and what doesn't.
- • Look at kids' magazines, books, and movies.
- • Listen to some chart music.

3. Pop Art—Design and Music from the 1960s

This program title involves a series of documentaries about design and music from the swinging '60s. You are asked to design something that looks like it could have been produced in that era, but, of course, you will give the sequence a modern twist that still fits the period. Be selective with the most important elements from this period and then figure out how to recombine them to build something new and exciting.

For inspiration:

- • Check out Mary Quant's stark black and white designs; beatniks dancing in seedy nightclubs;
- • Classic film titles like the brilliant Bond movie titles;
- • Think of Saul Bass's and Pablo Ferro's fantastic film titles;

- Designers for Blue Note cover art, Andy Warhol;
- Also videos like the Pink Panther animations and Austin Powers;
- And of course the Hippie culture.

## Technical Specifications

Duration: Ten to fifteen seconds

FPS: 30

Movie size: 720 × 580 square pixels, 4:3 aspect ratio

I have provided you with a choice of audio tracks. I have also included templates, a sample of the project, and a storyboard template.

You are to work entirely with still images that you generate in Photoshop, Illustrator, After Effects, Final Cut Pro, or Fractal Design Painter. You are to demonstrate skills you have learned so far, such as:

- Compositing layers
- Setting keyframes
- Animating footage layers
- Modifying properties of layers with the transformation tools (opacity, position, scale, etc.)
- Using imported alpha channels
- Applying special effects
- Adding an audio track
- Rendering the final project as a QuickTime movie

All work must be original.

Suggestion: Do not import more than five to six files to your project.

Mandatory: Include an audio track.

Please make sure everything you use is copyright free or that you have permission.

## Method and Process

**Organize Yourself.** Start by making some sketches; create a simple storyboard; listen to the soundtrack over and over. Create your still images in Photoshop and Illustrator. Consider the size you need for your movie's format.

**Create a template** either in Illustrator or Photoshop. Make it the exact size you want for your movie. Show it to the instructor in one week.

**Assemble** your project in After Effects.

**Render** your project as a QuickTime movie in order to create a stand-alone piece. Do not use compression. Use full resolution, best color, and best audio.

Be prepared to **present** the instructor both the .aep file and the QuickTime (.mov) file.

## The Brief

Most real life projects begin with a brief, given to you by the client. A brief is a set of requirements for a specific project. Information to include in the brief is, as follows:

- Target audience
- Preferred color scheme
- Information about the program itself
- Identity or mood that the program makers wish to convey

Create a brief that defines the requirements for the project you have chosen. Be sure it answers the information above.

## The Storyboard

Sketch a simple storyboard. Divide a sheet of paper into twelve, 4:3 rectangles, with space above, underneath, and between each one for comments. I have provided you with an Illustrator file so you can resize it to whatever dimensions you like without losing resolution. Print out a copy so that you develop you own storyboard for the project of your choice. (Name the file "Storyboard.ai.")

The storyboard does not need to be a work of art but a basic representation of the whole story told in four to twelve frames. Stick figures are acceptable. Use it to work out timing and camera moves.

In the space I've requested be left around the frames, fill in the following:

- Top: Timing
- Underneath: Direction notes
- Between the frames: Transitions

# project 2: animated logo

Problem: To design an animated logo for a fictional film, production, or special effects company. Establish the company's identity using your graphic design skills enhanced by the ability to animate and apply special effects over time with an audio track. The project should be created using a template created in either Illustrator or Photoshop. (This template should be approved by the instructor in one week.) The project should incorporate a fade-out at the end so the company can edit other sequences to it.

You may use still images created in Illustrator and Photoshop, as well as QuickTime files (.mov) from other sources, and audio sources. You must explore nesting compositions inside of other compositions and experiment with applying visual effects. Concepts to be explored in this project include:

- Nesting compositions
- Using a template to create animation

- Applying special effects—channel blur, fast blur, Gaussian blur, radial blur, brightness and contrast, tint, hue/saturation, color balance, bevel alpha, drop shadow, alpha levels, spherize, scatter, and glow
- Using layered Illustrator and/or layered Photoshop files as comps in the footage window
- Creating a track matte
- Using an adjustment layer
- Don't forget keyframe assistant to apply easy ease, enabling motion blur, continual rasterization, and antialiasing, and transfer modes under switches/modes

## Technical Specifications

Duration: Eight to twelve seconds

FPS: 30 for video; 15 for the Web

Movie size: 640 × 480 square pixels for video; 320 × 240 square pixels for the Web, 4:3 aspect ratio

For examples view the following Web sites:

Hillman Curtis: *www.hillmancurtis.com/hc_web/web_motion.shtml*, Enigma Pictures: *http://enigmapictures.co.za*, Imaginary Forces (type of work, identity): *http://imaginaryforces.com*. Also see the Belief, Built-D, and Twenty2product Web sites listed above.

# project 3: juxtaposition—animated collage

Problem: To juxtapose text, imagery, and sound over time to create an overall unique, meaningful experience. Through the juxtaposition of your project's element, attempt to:

- Involve the audience.
- Pose questions or create riddles that the audience must answer.
- Encourage the audience to ask questions and to draw conclusions for themselves. (For example: What meaning do I feel when certain elements are juxtaposed or collaged? Why does the type move in a certain way? Do the words do what they mean?)

You must incorporate into your project the text from the fortune cookie you randomly select. Try to develop visual imagery and typographic imagery that create a poetic experience for the viewer. This piece should feel like an animated collage with layers of imagery, interesting juxtapositions, density of meanings and readings, and ambiguity that allows the viewer to draw unique and individual conclusions. Additional text/words/letters may be incorporated in the piece.

As part of this final output for this piece, you must create a project treatment notebook. This notebook should contain the following materials:

- Usage profile
- Rough storyboard (pencil, colored pencil, marker, image with text captions)
- Animatronic (made from the rough drawings that are scanned and dropped into After Effects to show timing)
- Movie (a QuickTime movie is fine)
- Final storyboard (slick color prints with captions to be included in the notebook)
- Collateral materials such as sketches, thoughts, and ideas, research, collage materials, or source materials for images, text, and audio

To create the movie, you may use still images created in Illustrator and Photoshop, as well as QuickTime files from other sources, and audio sources. You should explore nesting, track mattes, masking, and special effects. You may also create the elements separately and then bring them all together in one final movie as we have been doing in our textbook.

## Technical Specifications

Duration: Fifteen seconds

FPS: 29.97 for video; 15 for the Web

Movie size: 720 × 560 NTSC DV1 square pixels, 640 × 480 square pixels for video, 320 × 240 square pixels for the Web, 4:3 aspect ratio

For examples view the work of directors Flavio Kampah and Kyle Cooper.

For inspiration check out *Type in Motion: Innovations in Digital Graphics* (Rizzoli, 1999) by Jeff Bellantoni and Matt Woolman.

# project 4: alphabet in motion—identifying the emotional center

Problem: To animate one letter of the alphabet using your motion graphics design skills in groups. Your team must be your sounding board and agree that you have identified the emotional center. String your short QuickTime movies together to create one long or whole movie of the alphabet. Since we do not have twenty-six students enrolled in the class, each team will take one to two extra letters. The following steps should be employed:

- Identify the emotional center. Implement the target method. Keep the four-stage processes from *Flash Web Design: The Art of Motion Graphics* by

Hillman Curtis in your thinking throughout the piece: 1) working toward a global visual language, 2) respecting the technical environment, 3) addressing the multitasking attention deficit, and 4) identifying the emotion center. For example, the letter "m" might be "motion."

- Identify the elements that have to be in the spot—text and visual elements as well as audio. The length of the project should be eight to fifteen seconds.
- Gauge whether the spot is successful or not. After viewing the work, you or the viewer should be left with any of the three key feelings you have centered on in the target.

## Technical Specifications

Duration: Eight to fifteen seconds
    FPS: 30 for video; 15 for the Web
    Movie size: 320 × 240 square pixels for the Web, 4:3 aspect ratio
    For examples view:
    Hillman Curtis: *www.hillmancurtis.com*, Roger Black at Interactive Bureau: *www.iablondon.com*, Razorfish: *www.razorfish.com*

# project 5: call to justice—identifying the emotional center

Problem: To create a public service announcement (PSA) by responding to the following design challenges, which provide content and context directions. One of the following themes may be used for this project to create a "global visual language":

- The death penalty
- Globalization
- Land mine issues
- Liberty and social justice
- Nuclear threat reduction

This project will enable you, the artist, to speak directly and creatively to national and international audiences on important issues as well as generate justice service. The hope is to amplify the voices of youth via communication arts.

## Content Development

1. Criminal Justice Reform. Create a justice service announcement that explains the injustice of the death penalty as carried out in the United States. Your primary audience is Congress.

For more information on this theme, research the death penalty online.

2. Globalization. Create a justice service announcement that advances public understanding of the process and effects of globalization. Your primary audience is consumers.

For more information on this theme, research globalization online.

3. Land Mine Issues. Create a justice service announcement that documents a story of triumph over the tragedy of landmines. Use as your subject the Preah Vihear Silkweaving Workshop, a Cambodian microenterprise project in which local artisans—many of them landmine victims—hand weave silk textiles for the United States and other overseas markets. Your primary audience is the general public.

For more information on this theme, go to Land Mine Issues and Preah Vihear Silkweaving Workshop at *http://vvaf.org/campaign/index.*

4. With Liberty and Justice for All. Create a justice service announcement that articulates and refreshes our understanding of what it means to be a nation "with liberty and justice for all." Your primary audience is youth ages eighteen to twenty-five.

For more information on this theme, research liberty and social justice online.

5. Nuclear Threat Reduction. Create a justice service announcement that highlights the urgent need to reduce the threat of nuclear weapons. Your primary audience includes policy makers in Congress and the White House.

For more information on this theme, research nuclear threat reduction online.

## The Brief

These are some points you may choose to address in your brief:

- What is your definition of justice?
- Why did you choose your particular social justice topic?
- Why did you address the topic the way you did?
- What impact do you hope to have on your audience?
- What results do you hope to achieve through your work?
- What resources did you discover in the process of creating your work (such as Web sites, books, films, speakers, etc.) that support your project's intent and emotional center?

## Technical Specifications

Duration: Fifteen to thirty seconds
FPS: 29.97 for video; 15 for the Web
Movie size: 320 × 240 square pixels for the Web, 4:3 aspect ratio

Submission summary:

1. Create your Video as a QuickTime movie.

Acceptable Software: You may use any software that is capable of generating a QuickTime movie. These include, but are not restricted to, iMovie, Final Cut Pro, and After Effects.

2. Save two versions: a compressed, low-resolution version and an uncompressed, high-resolution version.

The maximum duration should be fifteen to sixty seconds. For the maximum file size for the compressed low-resolution version, refer to the size specifications for the server on which your entry is hosted (see information about Web hosting below).

3. Optional: Your Animation can be hosted on an independent site.

If you do not already have a site on which to host your work, there are many sites that offer free hosting including *http://geocities.yahoo.com*, *http://angelfire.lycos.com*, and *www.tripod.lycos.com*.

Links to assist with content development:

Annenberg Public Policy Center: *www.appcpenn.org*, the Center for Digital Democracy: *www.democraticmedia.org*.

This project will be due on the scheduled final exam day. All prior projects must be turned in on the last day of classes.

# recommended readings

Bellatoni, Jeff, and Matt Woolman, *Type in Motion: Innovations in Digital Graphics*, Rizzoli, 1999.

Meadows, Mark S., *Pause & Effect, The Art of Interactive Narrative*, New Riders, 2002.

Ziegler, Kathleen, Nick Greco, and Tamye Riggs, *Motion Graphics: Film & TV*, Watson-Guptill, 2002.

# recommended resources

BDA (Broadcast Design Association): *www.bda.tv*

Design in Motion – The Daily Motion Design Resource: *http://designinmotion.com*

DVcreators.net: *www.dvcreators.net*

This site provides training, inspiration, networking and other resources to DV creators.

Digital Producer Magazine: *www.digitalproducer.com/pages/features_animation.htm*

This is a site of motion design tutorials.

Apple Final Cut Pro: *www.apple.com/finalcutpro*

Apple's site offers information about Final Cut Pro and examples of the program in action.

Creative Planet: *www.creativeplanet.com/*

    Creative Planet offers a network for creative professionals.

Society of Motion Picture and Television Engineers: *www.smpte.org*

Digital Video (DV) Live: *www.dv.com*

The WWUG—After Effects Worldwide Users Group: *www.dmnforums.com/html/ homeset.htm*

Adobe After Effects: *www.adobe.com/products/aftereffects*

Tech Head Stories: *http://tech-head.com*

Adobe Motion Center: *www.adobe.com/motion*

After Effects Portal: *http://msp.sfsu.edu/Instructors/rey/aepage/aeportal.html*

## motion graphics studios and organizations

Cybermotion: *www.cybmotion.com*

MGLA (Motion Graphics Los Angeles): *www.mgla.org*

124

## summary and goal of the class

- To learn how time, space, and sound can affect the meaning of a message
- To define the process of designing with motion from concept to execution
- To expand both your visual and verbal vocabularies as they relate to motion design
- To develop critical investigations into meaning and movement as opposed to relying on special effects

This class will focus on how motion affects meaning and how new meaning can be developed through time, space, and sound. We will explore the basic fundamental aspects of animation including sequence, keyframes, composition, and transition as well as look into various ways to capture and translate movement from the world around us. You are encouraged to experiment, create, and investigate within this medium.

We will begin by exploring time and motion through small exercises. After this will be a small project ending with a final larger project. Each project will be executed using After Effects. Assignments will build upon themselves as your knowledge of the processes develops throughout the semester. Although it is preferable to keep the software tool in the background of the class, it is nonetheless an important issue in creating the end product. Therefore, we will spend some time in the beginning of the semester reviewing the software to give you a chance to get comfortable. Please use this time appropriately to get up and over the learning curve. After Effects training will also be supplemented by the tutorials found at *www.lynda.com*.

## week by week

**WEEK 1.** Design: class introduction, review online links
Technology: After Effects (AE) interface, in-class tutorial
Assignments: Project 1: Motion Studies, part I

**WEEK 2.** Design: Time + Space = Motion lecture, review motion studies

Technology: AE motion tracking tutorial: playing with time, previewing movies, typography

Digital video principles: video as digital data

Assignments: Project 1: Motion Studies, part II

Take some time to reflect on today's lecture and see how those basic principles can add value to your project.

**WEEK 3.** Design: look at motion design examples, individual discussion, progress critique

Technology: AE layers, masks and alphas, audio, rendering final movies

Digital video principles: 24 fps video, digital audio

Assignments: Motion Studies project due next week. Bring final project on CD to submit. Refer to project brief for correct project parameters.

**WEEK 4.** Design: critique on Motion Studies project, music mapping lecture, review project 2

Assignments: Project 2: Choreography, part I music maps due next week

**WEEK 5.** Design: review music maps, look at examples, class discussion, project 2, part II reviewed

Assignments: Project 2: Choreography, part II critique next week

**WEEK 6.** Design: sequence, class discussion, project 2, part II reviewed, introduction to Project 3: Modern Day Nursery Rhyme

Assignments: Choreography project due next week. Bring final project on CD to submit.

Bring material for project 3 photo shoot.

**WEEK 7.** Design: critique on project 2, photo shoot for project 3, field trip to WBIR television station

Assignments: Begin to isolate footage from photo shoot you plan to use in your project. Project 3 storyboard due next week.

**WEEK 8.** Design: class discussion, in-class workday, review Project 4: Public Service Announcement (PSA)

Assignments: Continue working on project 3. Digital presentation for Project 4: PSA due next week.

**WEEK 9.** Design: review digital presentations, individual discussions, in-class work time

Assignments: Project 3: Modern Day Nursery Rhyme due next week. Bring final project on CD to submit. Project 4: PSA storyboards due.

**WEEK 10.** Design: Project 3 critique, review PSA storyboards

Assignments: Project 4: PSA animatic, and look and feel frames due

**WEEK 11.** Design: review animatics, and look and feel frames, look at examples, in-class work time

Assignments: Begin final production on project 4

**WEEK 12.** Design: review look and feel frames, in-class work time

Assignments: Continue production, individual discussion next week

**WEEK 13.** Design: individual discussion with guest critics, in-class work time

Assignments: Continue production on project 4, progress critique next week

**WEEK 14.** Design: progress critique project 4, field trip HGTV and DIY tour with DIY Design Director

Assignments: Project 4: PSA due next week. Bring final project on CD to submit.

**WEEK 15.** Final project critique with three guest critics

# class projects and project goals

## Project 1: Motion Studies

### *Part I*

For the first part of this assignment, you will need to capture ten DIFFERENT motions. Each of these motions should be a minimum of ten seconds and a maximum of fifteen seconds in length. They do not have to be one continuous movement; they can be repetitive. When filming, consider things such as:

- Cropping
- Dimension/depth
- Exploring all angles (sometimes the most interesting are the most unexpected)
- Looking at nature, the machine-made world, people, animals, or even staging something
- Aiming for a variety of scale, contrast, and hierarchy
- Lighting (be sure it is adequate so you can clearly see the movement)

These ten studies should vary in their scope. It should be clear that you are considering a wide range of possibilities. These should be transferred into the computer and brought in as QuickTime videos on a CD for class review.

### *Part II*

Now that you have your motion studies complete, one of them will serve as the basis for further study and examination. Using this one study, you will generate the following three renditions:

1. Tracking. In this version, you will track the movement with a single word. The word choice is up to you; however, it should be meaningful to the movement being

highlighted. The movement of the word should be tracked directly to the movement in the footage. The background footage should not be seen in the final rendering of this piece. This rendition is limited to two colors (one for the background and one for the word).

2. Phrase. This version will be similar to the one above; however, you should now expand the elements to use a phrase, a question, a quote, etc. The words expressed here do not have to be mapped directly to the footage; however, there should be a strong reference to it. The background footage should not be seen in the final rendering of this piece. This version will also be two-color (one for background and one for the words).

3. Interacting. This version will actually employ and include your footage. Select a single word or a phrase (it does not necessarily have to be the ones used in the previous renditions) and have it interact with the movement in the footage. Again, what is this combination communicating? The footage should be included when rendering this file.

With ALL of these you should be conscious of what you are communicating. These are not merely exercises but small explorations that study a motion and explore how it can add value to a message. Consider the following as you progress with this project:

- Be very particular about the study you choose to use for this project. Not only will you be working intensely with it, it should lend itself to the needs of all three versions. You may want to start experimenting with several before you make your final decision.
- Before you begin, you should identify the qualities that are associated with the motion you are using. Use this identification list to select the words and phrases you use in the final pieces. Be careful not to be too influenced by the visual of the footage; pay careful attention to the movement itself. The text chosen should not just say what is happening in the motion.
- Once you select the motion that will serve as the basis for the project, you should work to move past the flat, rigid exploration of the space and become more expressive—really look at how the message can be influenced by the movement through space.
- There will be no sound in any of these; how can the expression in the movement being used compensate for this?
- Can you create contrast among the three of these? Do they each convey the same thing or can you stretch yourself to discover how a single movement can convey more than one emotive quality?

Parameters:

- No more than fifteen to twenty seconds
- No sound

- No additional effects
- 320 pixels × 240 pixels
- Should be submitted on CD

## Project 2: Choreography

It is no secret that sound can make or break a motion piece. Therefore, it is crucial, when designing with sound, that you have a good understanding of how it is a part of the whole composition. This next project will cover issues related to sound and its relationship to a moving message.

### Part I: Music Deconstruction

You have been provided with seven musical selections. Listen to each closely then select the one you would want to work with. Within that song, identify a fifteen- to thirty-second snippet and isolate it using the program of your choice. Be sure to treat the beginning and end of the piece appropriately (i.e., don't just cut it off). With the piece isolated, map the music with reference to the Music Animation Machine discussed in class (*www.musanim.com/index.html*). This mapping is something that should be printed out and brought to class.

In this map of your musical selection, try and tease out individual instruments and attempt to map the following:

- Pitch
- Timing (give yourself a base scale or grid from which to work)
- Rhythm or patterns created

The point is for you to become intimately involved with the intricacies of your piece of music prior to working with it in any visual capacity.

### Part II: Application

Now that you have successfully broken down your musical selection to truly understand the layers, you will generate three choreographed sequences set to your piece. You should begin by storyboarding this in your sketchbook.

1. Punctuation. Using only punctuation, animate these symbols in accordance with your musical selection. Think carefully about the number of marks you need to have on screen. Who is the main character? Who are the supporting characters (if any)? How do scale and depth relate to what is being heard? What role does color play? What is the narrative that emerges? You are allowed to use up to five colors.

2. Image. Choreograph this piece again, this time using still or moving images, your choice. What mood/tone/emotion are you trying to convey? How do the transitions relate to the musical selection?

3. Image and Punctuation. In the final version, you should bring together both the image and the punctuation movies. Layer them so that the image is behind and the symbols are on top. Synch them up so that both are aligned with the music. Once these are aligned, you may have to go back in and do some fine-tuning for readability and hierarchy purposes. You are allowed to go in and apply visual effects AS NEEDED (i.e., ONLY if they aid in the final piece; do not just apply them to apply them). What does this layering afford you in your creative process?

Project parameters:

- No more than fifteen to twenty seconds
- Screen size is up to you
- Should be turned in on CD

## Project 3: Modern Day Nursery Rhyme

In this third assignment, you will combine what you have learned to date with a longer message. You will give a contemporary twist to a childhood classic by taking a nursery rhyme and presenting it on screen. Just because this is a nursery rhyme doesn't mean it has to be designed for children.

After your rhyme is selected, you should brainstorm to see how it could begin to shift into another context. Do you want to use humor? Do you want to make a social commentary? Do you want to target another specific audience? Do you want to question its meaning? You must work solely with the words in the rhyme and not alter it. You can choose to do only a stanza or two if the rhyme has several, so long as it is a complete thought. Once you have it chosen and have brainstormed on it, you should storyboard it out so that you have a clear plan of how you would want to begin.

All the words of the rhyme need to be represented on the screen; however, you are not to use the computer to generate them. The goal of this is for you to develop alternative ways to getting your message into the computer (rather than always allowing the computer to render it for you). This is not to say that the craft will always come across as being "hand-made." There are some beautiful things you can do to capture type and then further refine it in the computer.

We will start with a class photo shoot to begin capturing the text of your rhyme. Bring in materials to work with based on the brainstorm discussion in class. You are expected to participate in this shoot; however, you are not limited to the footage gathered that day. The point of the shoot is to help you get started so you can further refine the direction in which you would want to go. You should allow yourself the freedom to experiment during this shoot, be open to serendipitous moments. Make sure to bring enough film to do a thorough documentation and even consider bringing in multiple capture devices. You may want to shoot from multiple angles.

Keep in mind all of the issues we have discussed to date regarding composition, transition, editing, rhythm/pace, etc. Just because you are capturing all of the footage does not mean these concepts would not apply.

Parameters:

- Final time is up to you
- Screen size is up to you
- Type must be present on the screen, and captured on film and then brought into the computer
- Audio should have no lyrics
- Final should be turned in on CD

## Project 4: Public Service Announcement

### *Part I*

For this final project you will be developing a public service announcement (PSA) campaign for a randomly selected audience.

Each of you have randomly selected an audience from the list below:

- Parents of infants (birth–6 months)
- Parents of toddlers/preschoolers (2–4)
- Adolescent girls or boys (6–11)
- Teenage girls or boys (12–18)
- College-age girls or boys (18–24)
- Young adults (24–35)
- Adults (40–60)
- Senior Citizens (65– )

You will begin with identifying and presenting the subject matter you plan to cover in your PSA. This will require that you not only immerse yourself in the issues surrounding this audience but also conduct research into stats and statistics that will build or support your reasoning for development. This research will culminate in a five- to ten-minute digital presentation you will present to the class. This presentation should be broken into the following three parts and address the questions listed below:

1. Audience definition
   - Who is your audience?
   - What types of issues are of concern to them?
   - What types of communication methods resonate with them?
2. PSA topic
   - What specific issue are you going to focus on for this project?
   - Why is it relevant to your audience?

- Why does it warrant attention in a PSA campaign?
- What result would you hope to attain by highlighting this issue?
- How has this issue been addressed in the past (provide specific visuals)?
- In what venue do you foresee this PSA being played so as to reach your audience?

3. Visual approach

- What emotions does this subject evoke?
- What clichés does this topic conjure?
- How can it be defined with color? With texture? With line quality?
- What other stylistic approaches can be attributed to it?
- What photographs capture the emotive qualities?
- How does your approach to the visuals, as they relate to the content, also reach your audience? What will you need to keep in mind as you move forward?

Using the links referenced in class as a starting point, select at least two examples of other motion pieces that you feel can serve as inspiration to the visual approach of this project (they do not have to be PSAs, nor does the subject matter have to be the same).

This presentation should be a digital PowerPoint or Keynote presentation that is at least five minutes but no more than ten minutes in length. While you have been given an outline of the required information above, you can also expand on it where needed. It should not be presented in such a dry manner as to only "check off" all of the required parts. This is not an all-defining document, rather a departure point.

## Part II Storyboards

The next step is the generation of storyboards to map out the narrative. Storyboards are of great benefit to the production of a motion piece as they help you to not only organize your thoughts but also begin to indicate to you what is needed in order to produce the piece.

Format: Storyboards do not necessarily outline every single frame; rather, they include the more important keyframes. However, be sure that you get a good range of frames illustrated so as to tell the story properly.

The frame outline can be hand drawn; however, it is easier to generate the blank frames in the computer, print them out, and fill them in. Frames should be illustrated in a manner that indicates what is on screen. Any sound, narrative, or action should be written in underneath.

## Part III The Animatic

The animatic is the next stage in the production process. This is essentially your storyboard frames scanned in and set to the correct musical score. This will help you to better see the timing and pacing of your piece. It can have simple transitions and should be set to your musical selection. If you find that you have too few storyboard frames for the animatic to make sense, you will then have to go back in and generate more frames. This will look like a very crude piece due to the level of production, but it is a very important stage in the process.

Format:

- Can be done in iMovie
- Can have simple transitions
- Should have music selection to which your frames are set so as to understand any timing issues

If you have audio narration, be sure to add it in.

## Part IV Look and Feel Frames

Once you have an understanding of your narrative and what it will take to produce your piece, you should then develop a series of look and feel frames to get an idea of the visual production level you want to reach. These frames are specific frames selected from your storyboard and generated in Photoshop (or equivalent). The important thing to remember is that these are still frames. They are meant to illustrate the visual mood and tone you plan to project in your piece. You should also begin to show what type treatment you plan on employing in the piece.

Format:

- Created to the size of your final movie
- Select at least four to six keyframes (try to select a variety of moments)
- Frames do not have to be printed out and can be generated in the computer and put in a PDF for class presentation

## Part V Production and Final

Upon completion of the early production phases you will begin production as you have for the previous projects. Do not forget about what you have learned in the projects prior to this one. See how you can incorporate those ideas into this final piece.

Your final CD is due at the final critique. The final CD should be turned in with the following components:

- Digital presentation
- Storyboards (can just be scanned in and saved as a PDF)
- Animatic
- Look and feel frames as PDF or PowerPoint document
- Final PSAs saved in a single .mov or DV file with three seconds of black space separating the two

Parameters:

- Long version—minimum of thirty seconds, maximum of sixty seconds.
- Short version—minimum of ten seconds, maximum of fifteen seconds.
- Screen size determined by you
- Should be turned in as .mov file on CD or DVD

## outcome or conclusion

As with learning any new paradigm, you start with the basics. This part seems obvious. You build the foundation before you begin the building. With the democratization of the technology used to develop motion graphics, it is imperative that students be properly grounded in the foundation of what it means to work spatially.

Students begin by exploring what it means to be in motion. They run through several of the classic exercises that require they act out a particular sequence or movement to gesture what it means to be a Bold Futura "B" or an Italic Garamond "f". Literally interjecting themselves into their work loosens them up and begins to get them thinking. The initial project that follows these exercises, entitled Motion Studies, forces students to move further to collect motion examples from their environment, analyze these motions, and apply them toward specific messages. It is a three-part visualization in which they first have to literally track the movement of the video, then apply a single word to that tracking, and end with the application of a whole phrase. Limitations are lifted at points and the students can branch from the initial movement as long as it is informed by the initial capture. This project not only forces the student to really study a motion, it provides them with an understanding of how to become resourceful when looking for motion references.

The second project focuses on the understanding of sound. This is an area I learned to ease into lightly, for if I was not careful in the structure I provided students, projects would be scored to whatever was in their iPods without regard to appropriateness. While the music selections are provided for them, each one is at least four minutes long, forcing them to be critical in selecting the portion that they would like to work with. The first version is to be choreographed using only punctuation, the second using only imagery, and, perhaps the most surprisingly successful, the last version combines both of the previous two, one layered on top of the other, with little or no change to the originals. By setting up clear boundaries within which to begin and explore, ones that force students to truly examine and analyze the nuances, they have a foundation from which they can then move on to more conceptual and communicative problems.

The nursery rhyme project that follows in this sequence allows the class to explore what was learned in the previous two projects within a framework that allows for more flexibility in designing their message. Aside from a few parameters of length and screen size (to help those whose eyes are bigger than their stomachs), the only requirement is that all of the type for the rhyme has to be present; however, none of the words can be generated by the computer. So while it does build on the previous studies of movement and choreography, it also introduces the concept of generating typographic expressions beyond the stroke of a keyboard.

The final project was the most inline with the commercial application of the skills learned to date. The PSA provides students with the opportunity to spend time designing a message from storyboard to animatic, and look and feel to final production. Breaking down the core concepts of motion and sound into smaller projects earlier in the semester allows them the time to really understand the nuances of these components without being overwhelmed yet with a larger message. By the time this project is reached, students are comfortable with the basic concepts and technically proficient, allowing them to really explore what it means to design a communicative piece.

The concepts presented in each of these projects could each easily be teased out for an entire semester's worth of study. However, their sequencing within the allotted time frame has proven effective in providing a platform from which a student can further explore his interest in the medium.

## recommended reading

Woolman, Matt, *Motion Design: Moving Graphics for Television, Music Video, Cinema, and Digital Interfaces*, Rotovision, 2004.

COURSE TITLE: Type in Motion

TEACHER: R. Brian Stone

FREQUENCY: Spring Quarter, once a week for four and a half hours

LEVEL: Junior, required class

CREDITS: 4

DEGREE: Bachelor of Science in Design

SCHOOL: The Ohio State University, Department of Design, Visual
Communication major, Columbus, OH

## summary and goal of class

This course is aimed at expanding the students' typographic vocabulary through the use of time-based composition, sound, and animation. The application of kinetic media will enable the visual communication designers to incorporate motion, scale change, sequence, metamorphosis, and context (mood) to typographic communication. Students develop time- and movement-related projects using semantic typography with the objective of enhancing visual form, meaning, and communication. By experiencing the rhythmic and expressive use of type in motion, students will investigate varying type size, weight, spatial relationships, form/counter form, and movement within a word(s), while preserving sound typographic principles.

This junior-level requirement is intended to expose students to a more interpretive use of typography, which can be applied in a variety of applications; for example, film and television titles, movie previews, commercials, information kiosks, multimedia programs, Web sites, and presentations. Its focus on kinetic principles and motion aesthetics is an ideal precursor to interactive multimedia and interface design.

This course is also intended to provide exposure to current multimedia authoring applications and provide a foundation in the understanding of the stage, score, and timeline metaphors used in these applications.

Each class session incorporates a one-hour authoring application tutorial. Students are exposed to Flash and After Effects. It is the responsibility of the student to determine which application is most appropriate for his communication strategies and to continue a degree of self-directed learning.

The film titles listed below are used to illuminate specific principles regarding motion graphics and kinetic typographic messages. They are a useful supplement to course instruction in that:

1. The films are readily available.

2. They are familiar to most students and are easily related and deconstructed when the films' plots are already known.

3. The longer duration of these titles often exposes systems and structures (as opposed to commercials, etc.).

4. Their relevancies are revealed as complements or extensions of the theme or plot of the film.

5. They solicit emotional impact based on film genre (from horror to comedy).

6. The addition of motion, type, and graphics express more information about the filmmaker's vision.

# week by week

**WEEK 1.** Type in Motion—Course Overview

Lecture: Letterforms and Typography: Abstract to Concrete

Lecture: Shifting Paradigms and the Distinction Between "Flying Type" (type that indiscriminately moves) and "Type in Motion" (motion used to enhance meaning)

Introduction to Project 1: Visual Equations from Verbal Language

Concrete examples to illustrate principles:

*Scream*. A deconstructed version of the film title is used to demonstrate the layering of dimensions, for example, texture, sound, and color to amplify meaning.

*Seven*. This film title initiates a discussion of Imaginary Forces reviving the merits of "type in motion."

**WEEK 2.** Lecture: Designing with Time

Concrete examples to illustrate principles:

*Alien*. This title exhibits abstract to concrete representation of letterforms coupled with time to reveal a message of anxiety.

*King Kong*. This 1933 title establishes a historical context for type's integration with film and discusses the technological innovations used. This title considers the enormity of the stage, that is, movie screen vs. printed page.

*Psycho* and the work of Saul Bass. In this example, the agitated motion of the title coupled with the musical score sets an emotional context. The sequence concludes with a dissolve that mimics the geographic setting of the film's opening scene.

*Barbarella*. This title uses the integration of type and image while letterforms appear to interact with the leading character.

Studio: Work through project 1 concepts, review flipbooks

Lecture: How Animation Works

Lecture: Type in Motion Principles (different types of motion)

Authoring tutorial 1

**WEEK 3.** Studio: Work through project 1 concepts, review flipbooks

Introduction to Project 2: The Dialogue of Antonyms

Concrete examples to illustrate principles:

137

*Lost Souls.* This title applies the power of obscurity and amorphic forms, forcing the audience to be active viewers to interpret the message.

*Along Came a Spider.* This title uses typographical metaphors, direction, and anthropomorphism.

*Altered States.* This title applies type as integrated, layered visual effects).

Web site: *www.bemboszoo.com* shows an example of establishment of a visual vocabulary using Bembo letterforms that move from abstract to concrete representations.

Review of flipbooks or authoring

Authoring tutorial 2

**WEEK 4.** Presentation: Project 1 (critique)

Studio follow-up: Review concepts for project 2

Concrete examples to illustrate principles:

*True Lies.* This title shows a moving, visual contradiction.

*Edward Scissorhands.* This title uses object metaphor based on motion only.

*Twister.* This title demonstrates the act of independence, whereby complex behaviors are simulated with every element acting independently.

*Six Feet Under.* This title attempts to anticipate the movement of the eye and its focal points. This is a strong example of integration and interaction with physical objects—similar to *Panic Room.*

138    Authoring tutorial 3

**WEEK 5.** Studio: Work through project 2 concepts, review storyboards

Concrete examples to illustrate principles:

*Mars Attacks.* This title uses an object metaphor based on motion only with the addition of exaggerated perspective and view points.

*Me, Myself & Irene.* This title demonstrates animated antithesis; form, color, and texture are used to show the concept split personality.

*West Side Story.* This Saul Bass classic uses type and environment to reinforce the culture and context of the film.

Authoring tutorial 4

**WEEK 6.** Studio: Work through project 2 concepts, review storyboards, authoring

Introduction to Project 3: Mixing Multiple Dimensions

Concrete examples to illustrate principles:

*The Music Animation Machine.* This title by Stephen Malinowski provides a visualization of the multiple dimensions (layering) of music.

*Dr. Strangelove.* This title applies a raw, erratic, linear type treatment that does not sit as overlay to the film but is integral to it.

*Panic Room.* In this title letterforms integrate and interact with the physical elements of the film.

Authoring tutorial 5

**WEEK 7.** Presentation: Project 2

Studio follow-up: Review concepts for project 3

Concrete examples to illustrate principles:

*Island of Dr. Moreau.* This title shows an intense pacing and aggressive jump cuts that are closely in step with the musical score and visual elements.

**WEEK 8.** Studio follow-up: Development of concepts for project 3, edit music

Concrete examples to illustrate principles:

*The Art of War.* This title uses a consistent system of motion and subtlety to depict a micro to macro narrative.

*Spiderman.* This title applies perspective, angles, and depth of graphics using independently moving layers and simulated lighting effects.

*Dark City.* This title uses occlusion, masks, and lighting effects and exploits the abstraction of letterforms.

**WEEK 9.** Studio follow-up: Development of concepts for project 3, score music

Concrete examples to illustrate principles:

*Romeo Must Die.* This title integrates Chinese characters as graphics with letterforms to establish a mood and context for the film. Letterforms in the physical cityscape are juxtaposed with type overlays.

*Catch Me if You Can.* This title is a culmination of previous techniques with the addition of simulated "camera" movement. The canvas is much "bigger" than the framed area, creating a pseudo-perspective.

139

**WEEK 10.** Film: *Short Ecstasy 11* (DVD, Quickband Networks, 2000). The film is a compilation of the works of Saul Bass and includes an interview with him.

Studio follow-up: Development of concepts for project 3

Final authoring stages

**WEEK 11.** Final Presentation: Project 3

# class projects

## Visual Equations from Verbal Language

### *Enabling Words to Mimic Verbal Meaning, Visually and Kinetically*

Students are instructed to examine a word with different connotations (multiple meanings). For example, the word mercury could mean an element, a planet, or an automobile brand. Through motion, the students are charged with defining a specific meaning. Depicting the details of motion aesthetics, they are ultimately to create a narrative that is revealed over a ten-second period. The project should meet the following specifications:

- 100 pixels × 200 pixels (30 fps)
- Sans serif type, black on white background
- No audio
- Ten seconds

**The Dialogue of Antonyms**

*Creating a Visual Interaction while Kinetically Expressing the Opposite Meaning of Words*

Students are instructed to examine a pair of words with opposing meanings (antithesis), for example, slow/fast, curious/indifferent, smooth/rough. Through motion, the students are charged with defining the meanings of each word. Focus is placed on an interaction or visual dialogue between words. This narrative is created over a twenty-second period and should meet the following specifications:

- 100 pixels × 200 pixels (30 fps)
- Sans serif, black on white background
- No audio
- Twenty seconds

## Mixing Multiple Dimensions: A Kinetic Typographic Poster

This project will integrate typography and image with sound, moving in time and space. It is an exploration of the acoustical field unified with the visual field.

Using a series of three typographic posters announcing a lecture series developed from the previous quarter's typography studio, students build a kinetic extension to the series. Students are charged with building kinetic narratives that introduce the content and hierarchy of these posters (speakers, date, time, location). Type and graphic language are scored to sixty seconds of instrumental audio. The final animation should be viewed as an extension of the typographic language created in the three previous anchored solutions. Projects should be 600 pixels × 600 pixels (30 fps) and sixty seconds in length. Audio must be instrumental (and semantically appropriate).

All projects are to use the following naming convention: TIM01_lastname.ext, TIM02_lastname.ext, TIM03_lastname.ext. Upload these items to the class folder (on the department's network) entitled TIM2006.

# object of class projects

Each project builds in complexity and communication. Project 1 gives the students their first opportunity to develop storyboards, apply various principles discussed, understand the temporal dimension of communication, and familiarize themselves with the potential of specific time-based applications. Project 2 allows the students to react to constructive criticism received from project 1. Confidence and authoring proficiency will increase while the intellectual delivery of communication is enhanced. Students also begin to articulate how their projects intend to work (or not) in the kinetic space. Project 3 affords a new range of creativity and communication. The integration of several dimensions (time, movement, sound, color, texture, etc.), although challenging, allows the student to expand their typo-graphic vocabulary. They are able to take a more holistic view of their communication plans (static and kinetic) and are fully proficient in their chosen authoring application.

## outcome or conclusion

The course provides our students with their first formal exposure to time-based communication. It opens a new verbal and visual vocabulary to their armamentarium. Students discover that "type in motion" can enhance, in certain respects, visual form, meaning, and communication beyond static, anchored messages. Their project research reveals that this meaning is greatly influenced by our cultural influences, associative bonds, spoken language, and semiotic references. Additionally, it is discovered by many that kinetic typography specifically designed with the intent of enhancing meaning can evoke emotional responses. These reactions, whether they are excitement, delight, humor, agitation, or tension, make typographic communication a richer, more memorable experience, even if these reactions are momentary.

## recommended readings

Bellatoni, Jeff, and Matt Woolman, *Type in Motion: Innovations in Digital Graphics*, Rizzoli, 1999.

Carter, David, *Experimental Typography, Working with Computer Type 4*, Rotovision, 1997.

Carter, Rob, Ben Day, and Philip B. Meggs, *Typographic Design: Form and Communication*, Willey, 2006.

Carter, Rob, *Digital Color and Type (Working with Computer Type)*, Rotovision, 2002.

Curran, Steve, *Motion Graphics: Graphic Design for Broadcast and Film*, Rockport, 2000.

Kane, John, *A Type Primer*, Prentice Hall, 2002.

*A special acknowledgement goes to Daniel Alenquer and A. Chris Murnieks for assisting in the development of this curriculum.*

COURSE TITLE: Type in Motion

TEACHER: David Cabianca

FREQUENCY: One Semester

LEVEL: Junior/Senior

CREDITS: 3

DEGREE: Bachelor of Design

SCHOOL: York University, Toronto, Ontario, Canada

## summary and goals

The goal of this course is to introduce students to the creation of narrative structures outside of print-based media. The projects are not specific to any particular "use value," for example, film credits for a particular movie, or a mock television promo. To do so would be to rely on a student's preconception of what narrative structures are, which is to say, rely on what he or she has already seen on television or other media. Instead, the assignments ask students to "tell stories" or react to their own experiences. Most students find this absence of a "client" unsettling at first but soon become comfortable making work with the goal of telling a story from their own perspective, of being their own content generators. By focusing on a basic understanding of constructing a narrative—narrative at its most primary semiological and discursive levels—students are capable of adapting to any requirement in the future, whether that is a car commercial, a film title, or a public service announcement.

### Outcomes

Project 1 is intended to ease the students into the narrative possibilities of an image sequence. Equal attention is paid to the critique of the narrative content as well as the formal qualities of the images themselves. Students often forget that the camera can move from a micro relationship with its subject to a macro relationship. They also need to be encouraged to experiment with focus, depth of field, distance from the subject, and lighting conditions.

Project 2 is purposely confined to a twenty-second motion investigation. By limiting the project to a short length, students are less intimidated as they familiarize themselves with using a DV camera and using After Effects. It also allows them to concentrate on learning how to create transitions using a limited number of image sequences while they master the medium.

Project 3 is significantly longer in assignment length and semester duration. It is intended to function as a display of abilities as much as it is an investigation in content creation. Because this is considered a senior-level studio, emphasis is placed on the development of a student's individual "voice" or individual mode of expression.

## Technology

Software: After Effects, Photoshop, InDesign, Illustrator, Premiere, Final Cut Pro
Hardware: digital/analog camera, DV camera, tripod, various light sources, PC/Macintosh computers

# week by week

Student Participation (10%)

**WEEK 1.** Introduction: Review of motion graphics with sample works
Assigned reading with one-page response (2.5%): Umberto Eco, "The Poetics of the Open Work," in *The Open Work*
Assigned: Project 1: Head Shot Narratives (15%)

**WEEK 2.** Discussion of "The Poetics of the Open Work" (and collection of one-page response)
Class critique of Project 1: Head Shot Narratives
Assigned reading with one-page response (2.5%): H. Porter Abbott, "Narrative and Life," in *The Cambridge Introduction to Narrative*

**WEEK 3.** Discussion of "Narrative and Life" (and collection of one-page response)
Final review of Project 1: Head Shot Narratives
Assigned: Project 2: Video Poster (20%)

**WEEK 4.** Additional review of motion graphic work
Individual critiques of Project 2

**WEEK 5.** Additional review of motion graphic work
Individual critiques of Project 2

**WEEK 6.** Final review of Project 2: Video Poster
Assigned: Project 3: Narrative Video Sequence (50%)

**WEEK 7.** Individual critiques of Project 3: Narrative Video Sequence storyboard or drawn storyboards

**WEEK 8.** Individual critiques of Project 3

**WEEK 9.** Individual critiques of Project 3

**WEEK 10.** Class critique of a rough edit (5% out of 50%)

**WEEK 11.** Individual critiques of Project 3

**WEEK 12.** Final review of Project 3: Narrative Video Sequence (45% out of 50%)

# assignments and projects

## Project 1: Head Shot Narratives

Before creating time-based media it is necessary to consider the fixed frame of the camera, light and shadow, the transition between frames (i.e., the edit), and the manner in which these elements converge to create narrative content. To do this, the first project will use photography to explore the human head via an image series.
   Due Week 3

**Exploration:** Using a horizontal format only, create a sequence of fourteen 5 × 7 inch color images of the human head. This sequence can explore the micro diversity of numerous parts of the head or a macro focus on a single, detailed aspect. Have a rough cut presented in a horizontal, linear sequence ready for critique next class. Mount the final horizontal, linear sequence for grading.

**Goals:** to assess light, shadow, point of view, cropping, composition; to develop the ability to see through the camera; to assess the ability to create a dialogue using images and express intent

**Tools:** regular camera, digital camera, and/or digital video; tripod; various light sources

NB. Under low light conditions, a tripod is necessary to avoid shaking the camera and unintentionally producing a blurred image. Digital cameras in particular suffer from a slow shutter speed and require a fixed support. It is also recommended to make use of a quality camera that has a macro setting. York's digital cameras have macro capability. Please respect your classmates and return borrowed equipment promptly—preferably within twenty-four hours.

## Project 2: Video Poster

Posters are a consistent medium for graphic designers, and video work can be considered an extension of the poster—when each frame is composed, a frozen moment can function as a poster.

   *A picture of life brings with it multiple and varied sensations. The sight, for instance, of the cover of a book which has been read spins from the character of its title the moonbeams of a distant summer night. The taste of our morning coffee brings us that vague hope of a fine day which formerly so often smiled at us in the unsettled dawn from a fluted bowl of porcelain which seemed like hardened milk. An hour is not merely an hour, it is a vase filled with perfumes, with sounds, with projects, with climates. What we call reality is a relation between those sensations and those memories which simultaneously encircle us—a relation which a cinematographic vision destroys because its form separates it from the truth to which it pretends to limit itself—that unique relation which the writer must discover in order that he may link two different states of being together for ever in a phrase. [ . . . ] In this, as in life, he fuses a quality common to two sensations, extracts their essence and in order to withdraw them from the contingencies of time, unites them in a metaphor, thus chaining them together with the indefinable bond of a verbal alliance. Was not nature herself from this point of view, on the track of art, was she not the beginning of art, she who often only permitted me to realize the beauty of an object long afterwards in another, mid-day at Combray only through the sound of its bells, mornings at Doncières only through the groans of our heating apparatus. The relationship may be of little interest, the objects commonplace, the style bad, but unless there is that relationship, there is nothing. A literature which is content with "describing things," with offering a wretched summary of their lines and surfaces, is, in spite of its pretension to realism, the furthest from reality, the one which impoverishes us and saddens us the most, however much it may talk of glory and grandeur, for it abruptly severs communication between our present self, the past of which objects retain the essence and the future in which they encourage us to search for it again. But there is more. If reality were that sort of waste experience approximately identical in everyone because when we say: "bad weather," "war," "cab-stand," "lighted restaurant," "flower garden," everybody knows what we mean—if reality were that, no doubt a sort of cinemagraphic film of these things would suffice and "style," "literature" isolating itself from that simple datum would be an artificial hors d'oeuvre. But is it so in reality? If I tried to render conscious to myself what takes place in us at the moment a circumstance or an event makes a certain impression. [ . . . ] I perceived that to express those impressions, to write that essential book, which is the only true one, a great writer does not, in the current meaning of the word, invent it, but, since it exists already in each one of us, interprets it. The duty and the task of a writer are those of an interpreter. (Marcel Proust*, Remembrance of Things Past: Time Regained, *translated by Stephen Hudson, Vintage Books, 1927; this English translation 1931: 924–26.)*

145

Due Week 6

**Exploration:** Using a vertical format only—twenty seconds at 29.97 fps, DV/NTSC 533 × 800 square pixels—explore the statement: Synthesize your opinion about a day.

**Goals.** Consider different interpretations of your statement: what does it mean at its most basic level? What can it be at its most extreme? What can it be at its most banal? How many ways can it be expressed in different media? How many ways can it be expressed with light? Is one form of light the best manner in which to approach your reaction? Make meaningful form: make work that can sustain discussion for an hour. While the twenty-second video will be presented as a loop, there does not necessarily need to be a seamless transition between the first and last frames.

Explore the graphic qualities of type as part of your compositional concerns. Make type image studies as you work. These will help you with your ideas as you work through motion design. Note that an 11 × 17 inch image study is due for discussion in Week 5.

## Project 3: Narrative Video Sequence

The historical avant-garde revised the forms of expression artists, designers, and writers employed because they desired that culture reflect changes brought about by technological modernity. In the shift from home-based craft technique to mass-produced factory objects, the avant-garde sought forms that displayed an awareness of their construction, forms that were often stripped of ornament and reduced to reflect their machined fabrication and serialized production. These explorations by the avant-garde invigorated art's relationship with craft, resulting in new forms of painting, sculpture, architecture, graphic design, and literature, among others. The idealism of these explorations led artists to question the foundations and techniques of artistic practice. In painting, artists focused on the application of pigment to the canvas, the brush stroke, and the use of color itself. In architecture, designers created geometric shapes that took advantage of new glass, steel, and concrete methods of construction. In literature, authors reconsidered the word itself: meaning was no longer something transparent to language but something that could be shaped and crafted by the writer. In each instance, the artist was able to mold meaning to suit his or her discipline by questioning existing practices and expanding the discourse that defined tradition.

With the advent of mass media technologies—and broadcast technologies in particular—graphic designers are given yet another tool to affect the production of narrative. How a designer chooses to tell a story—the edit, frame, perspective, use of light and darkness, color, typography . . . —can equally influence a narrative as much as the text and images do.

Prior to beginning this project, read Jorge Borges, "The Garden of Forking Paths," in *Labyrinths: Selected Stories and Other Writings*, New Directions Publishing, 1964: 19–29.

Due Week 11 (5%)

Rough cut narrative sequence for group critique

Due Week 12 (45%)

Project 3 for final review

**Exploration:** Using a horizontal format only—sixty to ninety seconds at 29.97 fps, DV/NTSC 720 × 480 square pixels—produce a meaningful narrative that reflects your understanding of the path you wish to take in design. Your video may consist of a thought that you have wanted to pursue further, a use of typography that you want to explore, an examination of your interest in color, light, and pacing, and other. Consider your focus on methodology, the application of that method to studio work, and the organization of relevant work in a thoughtfully argued project. Focus on the development of a long-term thesis, a cumulative process through which each student builds a coherent, investigative, and experimental body of work.

## conclusions

The first three classes were specifically designed to introduce the vocabulary and concepts of narrative tropes to the students—both linear and nonlinear forms of narrative structures. To accomplish this, short excerpts of literature were read by the students, and then their representational qualities and the values of their narrative forms were discussed. The authors introduced included Samuel Beckett, Thomas Mann, Marcel Proust, Virginia Woolf, and Kathy Acker. Once a vocabulary was established, it was much easier to discuss the structuring of a narrative with each student relative to his or her own work.

Interestingly, while the students have all grown up in an "MTV world," they were unfamiliar with the tools necessary to conceptually recognize and analyze the culture of images. In particular they lacked the ability to draw a connection between a rapid sequence of unassociated images and the production of meaning invoked by those images. Previous to their analyses in class, for the students, the narrative structure of a Samuel Beckett novel was indistinguishable from that of Thomas Mann. The students recognized that the words were presented differently, but they had not thought about how that difference affected the experience and the meaning of the narrative.

147

It is necessary throughout the course to show the students examples of quality motion graphic work and to discuss with the students why the work is effective in typographic and image-based terms. Students are largely familiar with quality print-based work but lack the ability to discern what constitutes a well-designed motion graphic piece. The work of the firms Imaginary Forces, Brand New School, Hello Logan, Motion Theory, Wieden + Kennedy Japan/Eric Cruz, and Digital Kitchen and the work of pivotal schools such as Cranbrook and CalArts were viewed and discussed in class.

## recommended readings

Due Week 2

Eco, Umberto, "The Poetics of the Open Work," in *The Open Work*, Harvard University Press, 1989: 1–23.

Due Week 3

Abbott, H. Porter, "Narrative and Life," in *The Cambridge Introduction to Narrative*, Cambridge University Press, 2002: 1–11.

Due Week 7

Borges, Jorge, "The Garden of Forking Paths," in *Labyrinths: Selected Stories and Other Writings*, New Directions Publishing, 1964: 19–29.

**COURSE TITLE:** Type + Motion

**TEACHER:** Martin Venezky

**FREQUENCY:** One Semester, once a week

**LEVEL:** Open to all who have taken at least one previous motion class and
are familiar with the programs and equipment used

**CREDITS:** 3

**DEGREE:** Bachelor of Fine Arts and Master of Fine Arts

**SCHOOL:** California Institute of the Arts, Valencia, CA

## summary and goal of class

Welcome to Type + Motion. It may seem odd having me teach this class, since I am
not known for making type move. In fact, my portfolio has nary a moving component to be found. But what I am good at is what will set this class apart from others
you've taken. And that, my friends, is the conversation, analysis, criticism, and challenges that will happen during the creative process.

148       We will not focus on software or digital manipulation. That's not to say that
these won't be important considerations. After all, most of what you present will be
in digital form. I am simply not prepared to offer that kind of direct guidance.
Rather, we will consider motion and language in all their nuance. How they are
perceived. How they deliver meaning. How they create consequence. Learning to
ask questions and critique with eloquence will be important to you regardless of
the software, the medium, or the projects you take on.

## some thoughts on motion

It's really simple. Motion produces relationships. One thing moves, other things don't.
One thing moves, other things resist. It is this difference that attracts our attention.

      Just like in our physical world, the way things move provides us with informa-
tion about the world. What is natural? What are our expectations? What can we rely
on? As we cobble together a set of logical rules, we can negotiate the world and
understand how we function in it. When these rules are twisted or negated, we are
mystified. That's entertainment! That's theater! That's why such simple things as
optical illusions or magic tricks or flipbooks delight us.

     It is so important to keep these things in mind as you work—theater, logic,
consequence, expectation—as well as the dynamic complexity of real movement
vs. a portrayal of movement. Is there a difference? Which are you working with?
How do you want your viewer to feel?

## some thoughts on type

Type is a special case, because it is already a nest of relationships. And type, text, and language move in more ways than simply physical. Can we think of speech as the movement of language? We use metaphors like "spreading a rumor" and "delivering a message." Why do they make sense to us? Don't they suggest mobility?

And what about translation? Is that movement, too? As a text transitions from one language to another, what exactly is happening? What happens to the writer, the reader, the translator?

And then, there's type in the world. Metropolitan areas are characterized by an abundance of physical type in the environment. How do these signs and messages respond to motion? How do they respond to the traveler, the position of the sun, to each other, to the passing of time, and to the changing (and moving) environment?

## problems with motion

So much motion work is annoying and boring. Almost all of it implies a passive role for the audience. That is to say, our position remains fixed, like audience members who watch patiently as type does its tricks for them. (The television ads for Target are a good example of the opposite of this.)

And then there is the problem of the motion "look." Except for the persuasiveness of software makers and the commercial world, there is no inherent reason for motion to be massively edited with quick cuts, or for everything to be shiny and smooth, or travel on perfectly geometric paths. Watching old experimental film is sometimes a relief, since these assumptions weren't present. The hand of the filmmaker, rather than the hand of the programmer, predominates.

And there is no inherent reason why motion work has to be so segmented into "boy" and "girl" work. That is, either aggressive, metallic, fast, and futuristic or fluffy, cute, gentle, and natural.

As we work, we will take note of these issues and work our way through their temptations.

## expectations and outcome

Because I cannot teach you specific techniques, I expect all of you to have a significant knowledge of, and comfort with, the basic technologies you will be using.

I realize that each of you has a different set of skills regarding motion. I expect every one of you to be willing to move outside of what you already know and try techniques that seem daunting to you. To further that goal, I expect each of you to share your knowledge with patience and consideration. I am not opposed to collaboration as long as it isn't an excuse to have a comrade do your work for you.

Because of the time-based nature of the medium, critiques can take longer than expected. Please be prepared before class by having your work ready to be displayed. Please edit down long takes, or at least be ready to pinpoint highlights for us to see. Please be prepared to talk about your process, present artifacts, or show stills of setups. Please participate in discussions, offer considered criticism, and challenge my opinion.

# class projects

The class will not be unlike the Form classes I've taught in the past. The projects will hinge on experiment → result → analysis, which is a highly disciplined format. I am more interested in a battery of short focused studies than long, epic, wandering complexity. By limiting ourselves this way, we can travel much further and much deeper in our explorations.

I will do my best to emphasize hand skills, especially drawing, building, set creation, and materials study. Understanding the quality of the hand is valuable, even when your work remains completely within the digital realm.

## Project One: Assimilated Properties

1. Choose a single letterform and a single object or material.
   a. The letterform should be from a conventional typeface. Don't be clever. Be ordinary. You can embellish your choice as the project progresses.
   b. The object or material should be mundane and unexceptional. Choose something that, if destroyed, can be easily replaced or procured in quantity without hardship.
   c. Don't choose a combination that seems to conveniently "go together" or "match." That isn't the point at all.
   d. Don't try to imagine the finished project.
2. Explore the properties of the material or object.
   a. Concentrate on visual representation, but don't just consider how it looks on film. Also consider properties such as its movement, size, weight, utility, mark-making. Avoid properties that are overtly language based. We are not trying to make beautiful films. We are trying to use film to discover properties and their documentation.
   b. Do not use color. Do not use sound. Do not get fancy.
3. Explore the properties of the letterform.
   a. Start by examining the letter by itself.
   b. Continue exploring the letter through film and motion. How does it move? Why? How do you create a "logical world" for the letter?

4. Now begin a conversation between the letter and the material.
   a. How do they talk to each other? How can the properties of one be assimilated into the other? How does one translate its thoughts to the other?
   b. What kind of process works best for you in this project? Do you draw out thumbnails? Do you begin directly with the camera or computer?
5. Although this is meant to be a quick project, I do want to use it as a base for further exploration. For example, how do you define the space in which this conversation is taking place? If you now remove the material, has the letterform learned new properties? How are these manifested physically?

## Project Two: Type in the Environment

No matter how firmly type is affixed to its environment, it will move as we move around it, past it, through it, or beneath it. It changes as we approach. It is obscured by larger or closer objects. It changes as the day changes, as the weather changes, as it ages or is revised (the price of gasoline for example).

Type can be illuminated at night or hidden by darkness and shadow. It might swivel on its structure or turn on its axis. It can explode, degrade, or disappear. It can be made of permanent or temporary materials, machined or handwritten.

1. Choose a typographically rich location somewhere in the world that you can visit often, observe, and film.
   a. Don't try to be clever. The place can be completely ordinary. Pick somewhere that genuinely interests you.
   b. Typographically rich doesn't have to be type-filled. It only needs to sustain your interest and provide a rich and surprising resource.
2. Use motion to explore the type in numerous situations.
   a. Focus on how the type is experienced.
   b. Do not use color (again). Do not use sound (again). Do not get fancy (again).
3. Try to remove the type from its location. There are many possible strategies to accomplish this.
   a. You can build a model or set to re-create the type in a pure setting.
   b. You can tweak the footage.
   c. You can invent some other method.
4. Remember the importance of:
   a. Light
   b. Relationship to viewer
   c. Craft

**COURSE TITLE:** Integrative Typography

**TEACHER:** Louise Sandhaus

**FREQUENCY:** Spring Semester

**LEVEL:** Junior/Senior/Graduate

**CREDITS:** 5

**DEGREE:** Bachelor of Fine Arts or Masters of Fine Arts

**SCHOOL:** University of California, Los Angeles, Design | Media Arts, Los
   Angeles, CA

## overview

This studio class investigates the relationships among content, formal expression, and media as typography migrates among print, computer-based, motion, and environmental contexts.

The class begins with the basics of working with type including: visual composition and contrasts; understanding how words and visuals work in tandem to make and convey meaning; and the structuring and organizing of information. Following these exercises will be a series of short projects applying these understandings to typographic projects in different media. The final project will be a documentation of the class.

Prerequisite: Typography 1

## week by week

**WEEK 1.** Survey of Typography

In class: Review syllabus and guidelines. Look at examples of type in different environments. Discuss relationship of form, function, and context. Develop criteria for evaluating "good typography."

Assignment: Bring to class one photograph that "speaks to you" and one typography example that you're fond of. Also bring black paint (tempera, gouache, India ink), brushes, and 8.5 × 11 inch white paper. Wear your work clothes.

**WEEK 2.** Composition and Space

In class: Do compositional analysis of images and texts. Discuss use of contrasts: scale, weight, negative/positive space, values, etc. Do compositional exercises.

Assignment: Read about how the visual conveys meaning in *Stop Stealing Sheep & Find Out How Type Works*. Find typefaces that exemplify an assigned adjective (such as sloppy, uptight, whimsical, dignified).

**WEEK 3.** Words, Voice, and Meaning

In class: Discuss denotation, connotation, legibility, and style. Look at examples of letterforms and talk about "screaming signifiers." Review the design process, which includes research and brainstorming, thumbnails, roughs, comps, variations, and refinement.

Assignment: Read Raymond Queneau's *Exercises in Style*. Write a denotative and a connotative help-wanted ad for some "help" that will make your life better.

**WEEK 4.** Organization, Structure, Vocabulary, and Grammar

In class: Discuss reading from *Exercises in Style* and help-wanted ads. Discuss organization and structure; do structuring exercises for the ads and establish a visual vocabulary. Look at examples of interesting ad design.

Assignment: Read "Chapter V, Structure" from *Type & Typography*. Design two ads; one denotative and one connotative. Use design process.

**WEEK 5.** Words in Print

In class: Group critique of ads. Look at examples of poster design.

Assignment: Design a 18 × 24 inch, black-and-white help-wanted poster. Present three different roughs of three different approaches.

**WEEK 6.** Print Ad

In class: Group critique of poster comps.

Assignment: Refine your help-wanted poster. Present three comps for one approach.

**WEEK 7.** Print Ad to Web Ad

In class: Review posters. Discuss how a help-wanted ad would change in other media: How does the intended audience help shape decisions of form and content (what it says, what it looks like, where it appears)? Do organization and classification game. Reconsider how to rewrite your help-wanted text for the ad as it next becomes a three- to six-page Web site.

Assignment: Create a structure for the ad on the Web and create roughs of the Web pages.

**WEEK 8.** Web Ad

In class: Review Web site roughs. Desk critiques while site design development continues. Discuss music structure and storyboarding.

Assignment: Complete design for the ad Web site. Find a small bit of music to go with your ad. Consider the connotations of the ad and how they affect the intended message.

**WEEK 9.** Motion: Tutorial on Sound-Editing Software

In class: Learn sound-editing software and edit your sound to ten seconds.

Assignment: Create a drawing showing the music structure of your sample.

**WEEK 10.** Motion: Tutorial on After Effects

In class: Tutorial on After Effects.

Assignment: Read the article by Michael Worthington, "Entranced by Motion, Seduced by Stillness." Storyboard your concept for an ad in a motion environment. Use your music to structure the ideas of your ad. Adjust/rewrite copy as needed.

**WEEK 11.** Web Ad to Motion Ad

In class: Review Web sites and storyboards (with music).

Assignment: Build a rough of your motion ad in After Effects. Include sound.

**WEEK 12.** Motion Ad

In class: Desk critiques of motion roughs.

Assignment: Refine your motion ad.

**WEEK 13.** Motion Ad to Environmental Design: T-shirt

In class: Critique of motions ad. Discuss metaphor and analogy. Look at examples of fashion and environmental design.

Assignment: Design a T-shirt with your ad. Demonstrate three different concepts by applying them to the drawing of the T-Shirt. Use Illustrator. (Consider how the T-shirt will be produced: Silkscreen? Iron-on? Sewn? Consider how the method will affect the meaning.)

**WEEK 14.** Environmental Design: T-shirt

In class: Discuss three concepts for T-shirts.

Assignment: Refine your T-shirt design. Storyboard your presentation concept for the class fashion show.

**WEEK 15.** Environmental Design: T-shirt

In class: Discuss refined designs and presentation concepts.

Assignment: Produce the T-shirt.

**WEEK 16.** Environmental Design: T-shirt

In class: Fashion show dress rehearsal.

Assignment: Refinement.

**WEEK 17.** Environmental Design: T-shirt Fashion Show

In class: Fashion Show! (Make sure to have someone document your work.)

Assignment: Gather all the processes and projects from class assignments.

**WEEK 18.** Final Documentation

In class: Discuss narrative structure and pacing. Rough out documentation of class projects. Discuss documentation in different media: print, Web, video.

Assignment: Storyboard/thumbnail the narrative/documentation of class projects to show what your have learned during this class.

**WEEK 19.** Final Documentation

In class: Present storyboards/thumbnails of your documentation.

Assignment: Develop a comp of the documentation in final media.

**WEEK 20.** Final Documentation

　　In class: Present and critique your documentation.

　　Assignment: Refine your documentation.

**WEEK 21.** Final documentation due.

## required readings

Baines, Phil, and Andrew Haslam, *Type and Typography*, Watson-Guptill, 2002. (Required Week 2.)

Queneau, Raymond, *Exercises in Style*, New Directions, 1981. (Required Week 2.)

Spiekermann, Erik, and E. M. Ginger, *Stop Stealing Sheep & Find Out How Type Works*, Adobe Press, 1992.

**COURSE TITLE:** New Media

**TEACHER:** John Bowers

**FREQUENCY:** Fall and Winter Quarters

**LEVEL:** Junior, required class for graphic design majors (sophomore graphic design block of courses is prerequisite)

**CREDITS:** 4

**DEGREE:** Bachelor of Fine Arts in Graphic Design

**SCHOOL:** Oregon State University, Corvallis, OR

## class summary and objective

This course is an introductory studio experience to the methodologies, theories, visual and audio principles, social and cultural issues, and technical considerations employed in the design of digital motion and interaction.

The objective of the course is to analyze, articulate, and design engaging, strategic, and appropriate interactive motion experiences. The course stresses project development, collaboration, and an understanding of how digital experiences shape visual culture.

## session description

Students in the ten-week course meet for two, three-hour sessions per week. Each week's first class is reserved for lectures, critiques, and/or discussions; each week's second class is given to studio work sessions, small group meetings, and/or software instruction. The majority of work is done outside of class; students work, critique, and present extensively in teams.

## week by week

A key component of the course is to create community among students as an aid to learning. Students are active participants in the creation and presentation of course content.

**WEEK 1.** Students become acquainted with one another, an introductory lecture that outlines course learning outcomes and objectives is given, and readings on transitioning from the familiar to the unknown are assigned. Flash and HTML/Dreamweaver instruction begins with an overview of their basic conventions (new material for most students). Software instruction is participatory. After concepts are introduced, individual students or student teams will demonstrate aspects of the software to the class.

Session 1. Lecture (introduction to course)

Session 2. Software instruction (Flash and HTML/Dreamweaver conventions)

**WEEK 2.** A lecture on the basics of motion is given, followed by an exercise that requires students to visualize their commuting route and accompanying influences on speed and direction. The first project (Audible Motion) is introduced, and a large group discussion of the first reading is conducted. Flash and Dreamweaver instruction continues with a focus on integration.

Session 1. Lecture (introduction to Project 1: Audible Motion)

Discussion (reading 1 written responses due)

Session 2. Software instruction (Flash and HTML/Dreamweaver integration)

**WEEK 3.** A large group critique is held on the conceptualization phase of the first project. A lecture on collaboration methodologies is given, and the first collaborative exercise (Feedback Study) is assigned.

The first large group studio work session and "walkabout" critique is held in which students write reviews of their classmates' work.

Session 1. Critique (project 1 conceptualization due)

Lecture (collaboration methodologies)

Session 2. Work session and walkabout critique                                    157

**WEEK 4.** The first project is due and discussed in a large group critique in which students present the work of a fellow classmate to the group. The first collaborative presentations and a lecture on the basics of interaction are given. The second project (Conceptual Buttons) is introduced. Students are assigned related readings on the shaping of identity through digital interaction (writing assignment 2). Large group software instruction is given on the conventions of Flash action scripting.

Session 1. Critique (project 1 file and process book due)

Collaborative Presentations (exercise 1 due)

Lecture (introduction to Project 2: Conceptual Buttons)

Session 2. Software Instruction (Flash action-scripting conventions)

**WEEK 5.** A large group critique on the conceptualization phase of the second project is held. A large group discussion of the second reading is conducted, and the second collaborative exercise (Web Site Analysis) is assigned. A large group studio work session is held with impromptu small group discussions and software instruction.

Session 1. Critique (project 2 conceptualization due)

Discussion (reading 2 written responses due)

Session 2. Work session and small group discussions

**WEEK 6.** The second project is due and discussed in a large group critique, and the second collaborative presentations are given. A lecture on audience strategy and integrating interaction and motion is given, and the final project (Coded Phenomenon Web Site) is introduced. Large group instruction covering the basics of HTML/CSS conventions (new material for some students) is given.

> Session 1. Critique (project 2 file and process book due)
> Collaborative presentations (exercise 2 due)
> Lecture (introduction to Project 3: Coded Phenomenon Web Site)
> Session 2. Software instruction (HTML/CSS conventions)

**WEEK 7.** A large group critique is held on the conceptualization phase of the final project. Students are assigned related readings on how digital experiences have changed our sense of place (writing assignment 3). A large group studio work session and walkabout critique is held.

> Session 1. Critique (project 3 conceptualization due)
> Session 2. Work session and walkabout critique

**WEEK 8.** A large group critique is held on the ideation phase of the final project, a large group discussion of the final reading is conducted, and the final collaborative exercise (Usability Study) is assigned.

Large group instruction on the integration of HTML and CSS is given.

> Session 1. Critique (project 3 ideation due)
> Discussion (reading 3 written responses due)
> Session 2. Software instruction (HTML/CSS integration)

**WEEK 9.** A large group critique on the final project architecture is held, and the final collaborative presentations are made. A large group studio work session is held during which digital files are further developed.

> Session 1. Critique (project 3 architecture due)
> Collaborative presentations (exercise 3 due)
> Session 2. Work session and small group discussions

**WEEK 10.** A large group critique is held to review student progress on the digital files through written and oral commentary. A large group studio work session is held to resolve final details and assess usability.

> Session 1. Critique (project 3 initial digital file due)
> Session 2. Work session

**FINALS.** The final critique is held and the final project, along with any revised work, is due. Students complete instructor evaluations and individual self-assessments.

> Session 1. Critique (project 3 file and process book due)
> Instructor evaluations and self-assessments

# class projects

The course is divided into three sections, each with a project, a collaborative exercise, and a writing assignment. Each section's activities begin with an exploration of a related activity whose function and conventions are familiar. For example, tracking and visualizing the actions and feedback when interacting with an ATM or vending machine can segue into the study of flowcharts, visual movement, and digital buttons.

Each project draws from students' personal experiences. Project statements are open ended enough to allow for individuality and experimentation. Students are encouraged to explore and develop their own visual language while designing for the targeted audience.

## Projects

There are three projects in which students design a series of related and increasingly complex motion and interaction studies:
- Project 1: Design of an Audible Animation

Ten-second, nonrepresentational motion study based on a recorded sound from the students' immediate environment (e.g., alarm clock or street noise) with accompanying flipbook
- Project 2: Design of Conceptual Buttons

Two buttons, each expressing related or opposing attributes (e.g., playful and aggressive, or "us" vs. "them") through formal elements and motion, triggered by interactions of mouse over, mouse down, and mouse up, with accompanying flipbook
- Project 3: Design of a Web Site Analyzing a Coded Phenomenon

Web site contains student-authored photographs and text documenting and analyzing local public and private messaging (e.g., vernacular, political, temporary, tribal, migratory, or official) using previous motion and interaction explorations

## Collaborative Exercises

There are three collaborative exercises in which student teams work on a series of basic and familiar social patterns and interactions in their immediate environment:
- Collaborative Exercise 1: Feedback Study

Analysis of interaction with an ATM, vending machine, or other automated-service machine
- Collaborative Exercise 2: Web Site Analysis

Analysis of given Web sites (e.g., audience and strategy)
- Collaborative Exercise 3: Usability Study

Analysis of given organizational or navigational methods (e.g., tabs or numbers)

## Writing Assignments

There are three writing assignments in which students respond to posed questions about select readings:

Steven Heller, "Give Me and E" and Loretta Staples, "The New Design Basics" in *The Education of an E-Designer*

Marshall McLuhan and Quentin Fiore, "Printing, a Ditto Device" in *The Medium is the Massage*

Jessica Helfand, "Dematerialization of Screen Space" in *Screen*

Anne Burdick, "Ways of Telling or The Plot Gets Thicker, Fragments, Reconfigures, Branches, Multiplies . . . ," in *New Media, New Narratives?*, Louise Sandhaus, editor

Nicholas Negroponte, "Bitmapping: An Introduction" in *Being Digital*

William J. Mitchell, "Spatial/Antispatial," in *City of Bits: Space, Place, and the Infobahn*

- Writing Assignment 1: Experience

Responses to questions about select readings from *The Education of an E-Designer* and *The Medium is the Massage*

- Writing Assignment 2: Identity

Responses to questions about select readings from *Screen and New Media, New Narratives?*

- Writing Assignment 3: Place

Responses to questions about select readings from *Being Digital* and *City of Bits: Space, Place, and the Infobahn*

160

# overview of course learning

Students will be able to demonstrate the ability to do the following:

Concerning issues and history

- Analyze and articulate contemporary digital design issues of experience, identity, and place
- Analyze and articulate their values, beliefs, and responsibility to others
- Analyze and articulate ideas in writing and verbally in critiques

Concerning theory and methodologies

- Analyze and apply digital interaction theories, usability principles, information organization theory, and semiotic theory
- Analyze and apply processes and methodologies of attribute listing, morphology tables, mind maps, site maps, and strategic positioning
- Research, manage, develop, document, and assess a project, both individually and collaboratively

Concerning design and communication

- Determine and apply visual and audio principles of organization, structure, hierarchy, continuity, sequencing, transitions, and rhythm

- Analyze, create, and apply screen-based typography and imagery
- Analyze and apply narrative structures, visual signals, cues, and metaphors

Concerning technology and software

- Apply Photoshop, Flash, and Dreamweaver skills to create digital motion graphics and interactions
- Apply appropriate HTML/CSS coding and Flash action-scripting skills across Mac and PC platforms
- Analyze and articulate basic format conventions of programming languages and platforms

## conclusion

### Projects

Each project begins with a conceptualization phase that includes making mind maps, creating morphology tables, listing attributes, and writing concept statements. This phase is followed by off-computer sketches and free studies (with found images), and then the creation of storyboards, sitemaps, wireframes, and visual architecture studies. After students build, code, and script files, the first two projects culminate in SWF files. The final project is either SWF or HTML/CSS files posted online. Projects are evaluated on concept, development, design, technical execution, documentation (process book), and classroom participation.

### Collaborative Exercises

Students form groups of four for each collaborative exercise. Group members choose their respective team roles, execute and present exercises, and assess their team interaction and learning. The end results are presentations given to the entire class accompanied by PDFs designed by the group. Exercises are evaluated on thoroughness, design, presentation, and team assessment.

### Writing Assignments

Students are assigned readings and posed a series of related questions in advance of class discussions. Question responses are used as the basis for a class discussion on the respective reading and evaluated on thoroughness and insight.

## required reading

Heller, Steven, ed., *The Education of an E-Designer*, Allworth Press, 2001.

# recommended readings

Bellantoni, Jeff, and Matt Woolman, *Type in Motion: Innovations in Digital Graphics*, Rizzoli, 1999.

Bowers, John, *Introduction to Two-Dimensional Design: Understanding Form and Function*, John Wiley & Sons, 1999.

Helfand, Jessica, *Screen: Essays on Graphic Design, New Media, and Visual Culture*, Princeton Architectural Press, 2001.

McLuhan, Marshall, *The Medium is the Message*, Ginko Press, 2005.

Negroponte, Nicholas, *Being Digital*, Random House, 1996.

Nielsen, Jakob, *Designing Web Usability*, Peachpit Press, 1999.

Sandhaus, Louise, ed., *New Media, New Narratives?*, American Center for Design, 2000.

COURSE TITLE: Digital Video

TEACHER: Hajoe Moderegger

FREQUENCY: One Semester

LEVEL: Junior/Senior, required course for BFA students (Digital Photo 1
or Computer Imaging are prerequisite)

CREDITS: 3

DEGREE: Bachelor of Arts in Art and Bachelor of Fine Arts in Electronic
Design and Multimedia

SCHOOL: The City College of New York, Art Department, New York, NY

## course description

This course is an introductory class and covers a range of topics related to digital video. Students should gain a basic understanding of the history and development of motion graphics.

Through projects, lectures, discussions, and demonstrations, the students will get a comprehensive understanding of the conceptual, technical, and aesthetic issues of digital video planning, production, and postproduction.

Assignments in narrative structures, animation, and abstraction encourage the exploration of the digital video medium.

Analysis and discussion of contemporary and early video works, ranging from experimental artist videos to commercial music videos and classical short films will provide the foundation to position and contextualize students' work for in-class critiques.

Additionally, the course will address the following:

- The history of video
- Digital video project planning
- Output and deployment planning
- Storyboarding and previsualization
- Basic videography
- Capturing digital media using FireWire
- Use of Final Cut Pro editing software
- Use of After Effects for compositing and animation
- Common output options: CD, DVD, video for the Web

## week by week

Readings/assignments noted in this outline are subject to change and may be supplemented by additional handouts.

**WEEK 1.** Introduction to the class

Concepts: Syllabus, class objectives, and grading policy

Introduction to the history of video and its specifications (framerate, interlaced format, resolution, video systems)

Editing techniques, terms and conceptual approaches:

From Muybridge to *Memento*: 130 years of innovative moving images

View *Man with a Movie Camera* by Dzigha Vertov

"Montage—leads us to rhythm, representation, memory, desire—visioning instruments, the camera being one of them—to perception, cognition, language, presence—and projection—to the consideration of architecture and space" (Marc Lafia, "In Search of a Poetics of the Spatialization of the Moving Image," from the Eyebeam Annual Online Forum, "The (Re) Structured Screen: Conversations on the New Moving Image," November 11–December 13, 2002).

Tools and techniques: Lecture and samples

Sample images for resolution and interlaced frames shown

Discussion about the change of perception and the use of time-based images since the 1920s

Assignments: For next session get login information and books

Read: "Dzigha Vertov" by Jonathan Dawson and "Sergei Eisenstein" by Dan Shaw (Senses of Cinema, *http://www.sensesofcinema.com/contents/directors/index.html*), and Eduardo Kac's interview with Nam June Paik ("Satellite Art: An Interview with Nam June Paik," *http://www.ekac.org/paik.interview.html*)

**WEEK 2.** Introduction to Final Cut Pro and concepts of editing

Concepts: The user interface of Final Cut Pro, What is nonlinear editing?, montage

Tools and techniques: Final Cut Pro (lecture and demonstration)

Introduction to nonlinear editing (NLE) systems, setting up a project, setting up a sequence, resolution settings, importing files, and simple editing techniques

Assignments: Edit the footage located on the shared video drive to create a narration/story (montage)

Read: Chapter 6, "Editing," in *Looking at Movies*; see how to set up a new project, organizing the clips, and working with clips accessible via Final Cut Pro help topics

**WEEK 3.** Introducing After Effects and animation

Concepts: Critique of the projects

Discussion of the work of Michel Gondry

Tools and techniques: Discussion and critiques

Looking at the projects; preparing images for motion graphics; compositing techniques; introduction to After Effects (AE) including setup, composition preferences, layer, keyframes, and layer properties

Assignments: Create a layout for a title sequence/movie credits to be animated in AE (layout size 720 pixels × 540 pixels). Think of text or symbols you could use and which elements of your design will move. The Photoshop composition will become the final frame of your animation.

Read: Chapter 1, "What Is A Movie?" in *Looking at Movies*

**WEEK 4.** Effects, still images, and text

Concepts: Critiques of the animation composition

Discussion of project feasibility

Explaining animation through the work of Michel Gondry, Oskar Fischinger, and Jan Svankmajer

Recap After Effects layer properties

Tools and techniques: Discussion, lecture, and hands-on exercises

Analyzing symbols for their potential to be animated

Effects and text in After Effects; export options

Assignments: Using After Effects, animate the movie credits using your layout.

**WEEK 5.** Storyboard, script, and group project

Concepts: What is a storyboard? What is a script?

Discussion of the work of Peggy Ahwesh and Machinima

Explanation of the group project

Tools and techniques: Discussion and samples

Feedback on the assignments, explaining the camera device, explaining the camera, What is a storyboard? and What is a script for a story?

Dividing into groups, explaining group project:

- Create a short video using a "got . . ." as a theme
- No longer than sixty seconds
- Who is doing what (camera, acting, editing, sound, story)

Assignments: Pick one of the "got. . . ." themes (such as "got lost," "got it," "got more," "got up," or "got milk") and create a storyboard. EACH member of the group creates one storyboard for the next class! (A jury will decide which idea will get realized.)

In-camera edit (one to three minutes). Description: Create a storyboard, then go shoot the video. All editing is done by shooting the scenes in the right order. This assignment is done entirely without using Final Cut Pro.

Read about cutting and editing in Final Cut Pro and how to get your material in Final Cut Pro (capture, import, and presets), accessible via the Final Cut Pro help topics.

**WEEK 6.** Camera and capture

Concepts: Presentation of the storyboard and ideas, critique of the in-camera-edit, How does a camera work? What exactly is capturing? film without edits (e.g., *The Russian Arc* by Aleksandr Sokúrov, 2002)

Tools and techniques: Discussion and hands-on practical exercise

Looking at the storyboard and ideas (jury selects the final storyboard to be realized by the group)

Recap of Final Cut Pro

New topics covered: explaining the capture process, editing techniques, making a movie from still images, additional export options

Assignments: Shoot your group video for next week

Read: "Types Of Movies" in chapter 1, "Framing Of The Shot" in chapter 4, and chapter 3, "Mise en Scene," in *Looking at Movies*

**WEEK 7.** Log, capture, and project setup

Concepts: Introducing contemporary video art part 1

Capturing demonstration

Tools and techniques: Lecture, practical exercise, and demonstration

Studio setup, analog vs. digital, editing techniques (trim mode), alpha channel, fades, video transitions

Assignments: Log and capture all necessary footage of your group video (capture only what you need!)

Title files (Photoshop or Illustrator files to import) should be 720 pixels × 540 pixels, 72 dpi, RGB

Watch the movie *Run Lola Run*

Read: Tutorials for Final Cut Pro or After Effects can be found at: *www.2-pop.com, www.desktopvideo.about.com, www.lafcpug.org, www.designinmotion.com, www.creativecow.net,* and *www.mgla.org.*

**WEEK 8.** Title creation and effects

Concepts: Introducing contemporary video art part 2

Analyze parts of the movie *Run Lola Run*

Tools and techniques: Discussion and hands-on practical exercise

Group discussion covering title creating, using Final Cut Pro titler (effects), using After Effects effects, and using Photoshop files

Assignments: Edit your group video and add title/credits

Read: Melanie Crean's interview with Tom Tykwer (Eyebeam Annual Online Forum, "The (Re) Structured Screen: Conversations on the New Moving Image," November 11–December 13, 2002)

**WEEK 9.** Midterm Review

Individual meetings with each student

Assignments: A list of current gallery or museum shows with video works will be provided. Visit at least three of them, pick one, and write a brief essay about one of them.

**WEEK 10.** Class critique day

Concepts: In-class critique of the group projects

View music videos by Michel Gondry, Oskar Fischinger, Chris Cunningham, Busby Berkeley, and Spike Jonze

Tools and techniques: Discussion and feedback

Looking at the Projects

Exercises and demonstrations of stop motion and photo animation, markers, and waveforms

Assignments: Create a music video (pick only a part of song between sixty and ninety seconds)

Read: Esther Leslie's "Where Abstraction and Comics Collide" about Oscar Fischinger (*www.tate.org.uk/tateetc/issue7/fischinger.htm*); and "Animated Films and Experimental Films" in chapter 1 of *Looking at Movies*, page 46–52

Further reading: See the article "The Machine-Art of Dziga Vertov and Busby Berkeley" by Nicole Armour about two great film directors, creating rhythm in various forms (accessible via *http://imagesjournal.com*)

**WEEK 11.** Advanced editing techniques

Concepts: Critiquing of the music video

Introducing contemporary video art part 3

François Truffaut's *Les Mistons*

Exercises: rotoscoping, frame animation, editing

Briefing for next project

Tools and techniques: Critique, lecture, and practical training

Dissecting of a segment of *Les Mistons*

Briefing for last project

Assignments: A short video about "YOU" (final QuickTime due in three weeks!)

Make a production schedule!

Read: Chapter 9 "How to Do Things with Pictures," in *The Reconfigured Eye: Visual Truth in the Post-Photographic Era* by William J. Mitchell (MIT Press, 1994): 190–223

Further reading: about shots, editing and sound in Final Cut Pro's help topics.

**WEEK 12.** Film theory and DVD production

Concepts: Introducing contemporary video art part 4

The editing process

Film techniques

Introduction to DVD: discuss DVD authoring and compression

Tools and techniques: Other ways to create a moving image

Discussing Mitchell's essay

In-class experiment with still photography

Advanced masking techniques

DVD authoring: discuss layout sizes, menus, and compression

Assignments: Continue to work on the short video about "YOU"

Start mpeg compression for previous projects

Create a layout for a DVD menu. Image size: layered Photoshop file, 720 pixels × 540 pixels, 72dpi, RGB. If you create buttons within the Photoshop comp, make sure you create four states for each button: on, over, active, and inactive.

Read: Torben Olander's interview with Jeremy Blake (*http://www.artificial.dk/articles/jeremyblake.htm*)

**WEEK 13.** The final DVD

    Concepts: Critique of the last assignment

    DVD authoring

    Tools and techniques: Critique and demonstrations

    Class critique of last project

    DVD: discuss layout sizes, menus, and compression

    Assignments: Finish the short video about "YOU"

    Create a DVD containing all projects

    Read: "Elements of Narrative" in chapter 2 of *Looking at Movies*, pages 57–77

Comparing linearity in video games; examples of nonlinear and linear storylines (see "The Linearity Question" by Reverend Anthony at *http://www.destructoid.com/the-linearity-question-29983.phtml*)

**WEEK 14.** Working class

    Concepts: Recap

    Finalizing the DVD

    Review

    Tools and techniques: Working class

    Solving hardware and software issues

    Assignment: Prepare presentation for final

**WEEK 15.** Finals

    Individual presentation of selected works (maximum length is seven minutes) followed by a question and answer session

## required readings

Barsam, Richard, *Looking at Movies: An Introduction to Film*, W. W. Norton, 2006.
Monaco, James, *How to Read a Film: The World of Movies, Media, and Multimedia*, Oxford University Press, 2000.

## recommended readings

After Effects:

    Weinman, Lynda, *Adobe After Effects, Hands On Training*, Peachpit Press, 2006.

Final Cut Pro:

    Any textbook covering Final Cut Pro; consider Peachpit Press, CMP Books, Hungry Minds, etc., or the Final Cut Express manual (a PDF file accessible via Apple's Web site, *http://manuals.info.apple.com/en/Final_Cut_Express_HD_User_Manual.pdf*)

Video Editing:

    Wohl, Michael, *Editing Techniques with Final Cut Pro*, Peachpit Press, 2003.

COURSE TITLE: Design Film

TEACHER: James Kenney

FREQUENCY: Fall Semester, twice a week for three hours

LEVEL: Junior/Senior

CREDITS: 3

DEGREE: Bachelor of Fine Arts in Graphic Design

SCHOOL: California College of the Arts, San Francisco, CA

## summary and goal

In this class students will learn to produce short graphic documentaries that inform, surprise, and communicate universal meaning. The students are encouraged to express a point of view and to write a statement of purpose that describes what their audience will understand and feel from the film.

## week by week

**WEEK 1.** Students choose their film's topic in the first class, without time for debate or switching. What students can do with their topics is more important than what they chose. Ideally, the final film should become about more than the topic.

**WEEK 2.** Research the topic from a contemporary, historic, and graphic perspective.

**WEEK 3.** Edit and/or animate the research. Add voiceover and/or typographic content. Present the edit for critique.

**WEEK 4.** Find an authority(ies) on the topic. Schedule interviews. Discuss interviewing techniques. A colleague will interview students about their topics.

**WEEK 5.** Film the authority(ies) speaking about the film's subject matter.

**WEEK 6.** Edit the interviews together with the previous research edit for critique.

**WEEK 7.** Brainstorm a public (typo)graphic performance. Scout a location(s). Consider your audience. Prepare the physical graphic elements and materials.

**WEEK 8.** Perform and document the first performance.

**WEEK 9.** Perform and document additional performances. Edit the performance together with your previous exercises for critique.

**WEEK 10.** Evaluate graphic and titling needs. Prepare the text and storyboard.

**WEEK 11.** Animate your graphics, considering using After Effects 3-D.

**WEEK 12.** Finish animations and edit them together with your previous exercises for critique.

**WEEK 13.** Consider which sections of the previous exercises to include in the final edit.

**WEEK 14.** Tighten editing and transitions.

**WEEK 15.** Postproduction: color correction, sound, music, lower-thirds, end-credits, etc.

**WEEK 16.** Render. Output. Present. Critique. Archive.

## class projects

Exercise 1: Research Short Film. Students produce a short film via animated or filmed graphics that encompasses the preliminary research of their chosen topic. Additional information is presented through voiceover and typography. For example, in a recent student film, the chosen topic was "mice." In the first exercise, the student gave a history of man's relationship to the small animal.

Exercise 2: Interviews Short Film. Students produce a short film with interviews of an authority(ies) on the topic of their film and an additional interview of themselves with questions asked by a colleague. In the "mice" film example, the student interviewed a biologist regarding our use of mice in science and the diseases that mice can spread. In the self-interview, the student discussed how she lives in a small room with fourteen mice in various cages. She also discussed how the mice represent a world of beings that she can control, unlike her family, who have a history of mental illness.

Exercise 3: Performance Short Film. Students produce a short film that performs a visual graphic communication of their topic in a public space. For the "mice" film example, the student performed a ritual burial for a recently deceased mouse. She exhumed the box, which contained the bodies of tens of deceased mice and created a graphic tombstone that lists all of their names. She also filmed taking her emotionally distanced mother to a children's amusement park.

Exercise 4: Animated Graphics Short Film. Students produce a short film of digitally animated graphics for their film, including important research sections and main title sequences. For the "mice" film, the student finessed the animation of her research by utilizing digital cameras and lighting. She also animated a main title sequence, wherein scurrying mouse eyeballs became the counters of her title's typography.

Final Project. Students edit together selections from the previous exercises and produce new components as needed. In this postproduction phase, music is produced or secured, sound is mixed, picture is color corrected and output is completed. For the "mice" film example, the final film was a rich intersection of biological information with the history of a schizophrenic family and the meaning found in a young girl's search for control and caring.

## recommended readings

Lamott, Anne, *Bird by Bird*, Anchor Books, 1995.
Murch, Walter, *In the Blink of an Eye*, Silman-James Press, 1995.
Rabiger, Michael, *Directing the Documentary*, Focal Press, 1998.

## goals and objectives

Imaging IV builds on the introduction to motion graphics from the previous module in Imaging III (courses introducing still photography, montage, interaction design, and motion ideas are presented in a two credit support class structure that are divided into modules in the sophomore and first semester junior years for undergrads).

Imaging IV covers sound design, time-based identity, and narrative-based visualizations of information:

- Introduction to sound as representation: montage, layering, editing, etc., ambient environment, physical positioning of the viewer, etc.
- Introduction to a simple semiotics of sound, gesture, and video (film), including digital "effects"
- Introduction to simple editing of sound/video
- Introduction to simple ways of thinking about visual information

The course includes technical support on simple editing, sound and sound manipulation, video camera operation, and file preparation for different formats, including advanced After Effects, Peak, and Final Cut Pro. Studio use and lighting are also covered, including green screen techniques.

## week by week

### Project One, Part One—Motion Typography and Sound

Follow this link for examples of past students' projects: *www.ncsu.edu/graphicdesign/ html/undergrad/explore/index.html* (click on Imaging IV)

**WEEKS 1–2.** Introduction and explorations of the following in a film title (students choose from a list of potential titles supplied by the instructor):

172

- Rhythm—often dictated by sound
- Animation—as a transition (going from one formal state to another)
- Gesture—the motion creates an indexical level of representation, for example, a "ratchet-like" movement suggests the motion of a wrench, etc.
- Intonation—size, scale, weight, and placement (tied in part to traditional ideas of typography)

Due: Ten explorations, three to five seconds in length (After Effects as animation program)

**WEEKS 3–4.** Introduction to sound

Describe an activity in a space through recording and editing. Sound is self-generated and recorded by the student based on the environment, ambience, or "intervention" (i.e., creating sound by intervening in the environment).

Terms for describing some of the phenomena: physicality and depth; point of view (movement and placement of the listener); rhythm; representation outside of the visual frame; and indexical (for example, the mental image created of a radio newscaster).

Due: Two final thirty-second edited clips (based on a minimum of twenty separate samples)

## Project One, Part Two—Videography and Editing: Synthesis into a Final Film Title

**WEEKS 5–7.** Introduction to previsualization: sequence, storyboarding, and ideation, the directorial aspect of camera, point of view (POV), light and camera movement, plus the postvisualization ideas of editing.

Students adapt their previous experience with still photography (framing, lighting, and formal composition) from Imaging I and II to include motion as 1) motion in front of the camera and 2) motion with the camera. Students are encouraged to develop simple, multiple-frame (syntactical) relationships between the representation in motion typography "gestures" and look for connections to the apparent content in the film title. They develop simple keyframe sequences and edit sound clips, video, and motion type into two final twenty- to thirty-second film titles.

Introduction to a narrative-based visualization: "Deep Time"

Charles and Ray Eames developed late in their careers a highly successful short film and book called *The Powers of Ten*. In it, they attempted to take an abstracted mathematical notation and relate it to a general audience through scale changes.

In this assignment students explore visualizations of "Deep Time." "Deep Time" is the idea of geological time: theories of cosmology, evolution, and the history of the earth are based on a time scale that is not easily graspable in terms of a human lifetime or even of the span of human history. The students will develop a short (one and a half minute max.) informational video that relies on a script to explain some aspect of "Deep Time," while developing a motion-based visual timeline and analogy. The students will develop a simple script creating a voice-over narrative. The script must contain an introduction, the excerpted quote from a source of research, writing that supports the timeline and visual analogy, and a conclusion.

**WEEKS 8–9.** Introduction to narrative and visualization. Begin research, script development.

**WEEKS 9–10.** Keyframe ideas: analogy and timeline—three-frame sequences tied to script in outline format. Begin development of shooting list and variations on framing and lighting.

**WEEK 11.** In-progress critique of visual representations of analogy and timeline— keyframe as composition and simple thumbnail sequences: progression, transition, etc.

**WEEKS 12–13.** In progress: quick screenings and discussion of shots and simple editing, brainstorming related to storyboard ideas.

**WEEK 14.** Comprehensive editing including animated graphics, video, sound, and voice-over narration.

**WEEK 15.** Open

**WEEK 16.** Final critique

174

# recommended readings (plus lecture sources)

Allen, Robert C., *Channels of Discourse, Reassembled*, Routledge, 1992.
Eisenstein, Sergei, *Film Form*, Harvest Books, 1969.
Kunz, Willi, *Typography: Macro- and Micro-aesthetics*, Niggli, 2004.
Smith, Keith, *The Structure of the Visual Book*, K. Smith Books, 2003.
Tufte, Edward, *Envisioning Information*, Graphics Press, 1990.

# filmography

Saul Bass: various film titles
Saul Bass/Alfred Hitchcock: *Psycho* film sequences
The Office of Charles and Ray Eames: *The Powers of Ten*
R/Greenberg: excerpts from film title *Alien*
Imaginary Forces: excerpts from film titles for *Bicentennial Man, Arlington Road*
Leni Reifenstahl: excerpts from *Olympia*
Alain Resnais: excerpts from *Hiroshima Mon Amour*
Dziga Vertov: *Man with a Movie Camera*

COURSE TITLE: Time-Based Design: Typography and Narratives

TEACHER: Isabel Meirelles

FREQUENCY: One Semester, fourteen weeks, once a week for three
and a half hours

LEVEL: Junior, required class

CREDITS: 4

DEGREE: Bachelor of Science in Graphic Design

SCHOOL: Northeastern University, Department of Art + Design,
Boston, MA

## summary and goals

The course introduces undergraduate graphic design students to time-based design in a studio setting. The focus is on kinetic typography and visual/aural narratives. The course enhances previous knowledge of typography and visual language while examining how temporal structural elements such as rhythm and simultaneity affect visual communication in a dynamic medium. Studio practice is supplemented by examination of historical, theoretical, and perceptual aspects of motion graphics. Historical and contemporary time-based works from different fields are presented and analyzed during the course. Examples of work cover a wide range, among them choreography (e.g., M. Cunningham), music video (e.g., M. Gondry), Web video (e.g., H. Curtis), historical animations (e.g., O. Fischinger, N. McLaren), contemporary animations (e.g., Z. Rybczynski), historical title design (e.g., S. Bass, P. Ferro), and contemporary title design (e.g., K. Cooper, Imaginary Forces, Trollback), to mention a few.

The coursework consists of three assignments that examine principles of communication design in a time-based medium. The purpose is to explore how to effectively communicate messages along time. All projects require a significant amount of experimentation and work, from content definition, research of the topic, and storyboard to production of the movie/message.

The course meets once a week for three and half hours. Class activities include presentations, discussions, software tutorials, one-on-one meetings, class critiques, and readings.

The goals of the course are:

- To investigate the nature of time-based media
- To learn the fundamentals of time-based design
- To explore relationships between visual, aural, and kinetic vocabularies
- To develop strategies and methods for solving time-based design problems

- To develop and use objective critical language for analyzing and communicating messages along time
- To explore effective solutions for communicating in a time-based medium

## outcomes

Students are evaluated on quality of concept development, quality of design solution (how well it solves the problem and communicates information), quality of design process, and participation in class activities. Students are expected to systematically experiment and explore design solutions, to demonstrate week-to-week progress, and to actively participate in class activities.

## evaluation

Grades are based on:
Concept development and design solution: 50%
Process and class participation: 30%
Production and craft: 20%

## technology

A series of tutorials is offered throughout the course to familiarize students with After Effects, which is the recommend authoring tool. The objective is to enable students to acquire the necessary skills to solve the given problems. For the great majority of students this course is their first design experience in a time-based environment. The course doesn't require specific software. Students can use any technical means to develop their projects.

## week by week

**WEEK 1.** Introduction to assignment 1: Kinetic Typographic Message.
Lecture: Introduction to time-based design with presentation of works.

**WEEK 2.** Assignment 1: Class critique of the first version of the flipbook.
Tutorial: Introduction to After Effects (AE) and how to work with type in AE.
Lecture: Presentation of title design examples.

**WEEK 3.** Assignment 1: Class critique of the first version of the movie.
Tutorial: Working with type in After Effects.
Lecture: Presentation of choreography examples.

**WEEK 4.** Assignment 1: One-on-one meeting to discuss revisions of the project.

Tutorial: Using masks and images in After Effects.

Introduction to assignment 2: Preview of a Graphic Design Exhibition.

Lecture: Presentation of short movies presenting designers and exhibits.

**WEEK 5.** Assignment 1: Final class critique and delivery of flipbook and movie.

Assignment 2: One-on-one meetings to discuss research development and storyboard.

Tutorial: Using sound in After Effects.

**WEEK 6.** Assignment 2: One-on-one meetings to discuss revised storyboard and the first version of the movie (at least the initial twenty seconds).

Tutorial: Advanced features in After Effects.

Lecture: Presentation of music videos.

**WEEK 7.** Assignment 2: Class critique of the first version of the movie (at least the initial forty seconds).

Lecture: Presentation of Norman McLaren's animations.

**WEEK 8.** Assignment 2: One-on-one meetings to discuss the first complete version of the movie.

Introduction to assignment 3: Social Message.

Tutorial: Advanced features in After Effects.

**WEEK 9.** Assignment 2: Final class critique and delivery.

Assignment 3: One-on-one meetings to discuss research development and storyboard.

**WEEK 10.** Assignment 3: One-on-one meetings to discuss revised storyboard and the first version of the movie (at least the initial twenty seconds).

Lecture: Presentation of short documentaries.

**WEEK 11.** Assignment 3: Class critique of the first version of the movie (at least the initial thirty seconds).

**WEEK 12.** Assignment 3: One-on-one meetings to discuss revisions of the movie.

Lecture: Presentation of short animations.

**WEEK 13.** Assignment 3: One-on-one meetings to discuss the first complete version of the movie.

**WEEK 14.** Assignment 3: Final class critique and delivery.

177

# assignments and projects

## Assignment 1: Kinetic Typographic Message

The first assignment begins the exploration of fundamentals of time-based design by focusing on kinetic typography. Students have to design and present a kinetic typographic message—a short quotation. The goal is to effectively communicate the message along time. The audience is someone in her early twenties.

Students start by selecting a quotation from a list. Examples of quotations: "It is human nature to think wisely and act foolishly" (Anatole France); "The meaning of life is that it stops" (Franz Kafka); "The pure and simple truth is rarely pure and never simple" (Oscar Wilde); "Television: chewing gum for the eyes" (Frank Lloyd Wright).

The project has two phases and two outputs. In the first phase students create a flipbook communicating the message. Then, they use the flipbook as the storyboard for the development of the movie/message (second phase). Students are encouraged to examine the semantic and rhythmic qualities of the sentence by exploring the kinetic and typographic vocabularies.

Solutions are exclusively typographic and Berthold Akzidenz Grotesk is the only typeface allowed. Colors are restricted to gray scale, and if necessary, students can use one other color. Pictorial elements such as photos and drawings are not allowed. The dimensions of the flipbook are four by two inches. It should be a minimum of fifty pages and a maximum of one hundred pages. The dimensions of the movie should be 320 × 240 pixels, 30 frames/second, with a duration between twenty and thirty seconds.

## Assignment 2: Preview of a Graphic Design Exhibition

The second assignment explores the use of image, type, and sound in communicating messages along time while examining narrative structures and strategies. The task is to create a preview for an imaginary graphic design exhibition. The goal is to communicate information about the exhibit and ultimately to seduce the audience to go and visit the show when it opens. Students define the audience according to their subject matter.

In this assignment students have a double role: they are both the "curator" of a graphic design exhibition and the designer of the exhibition's preview. Students start by first selecting a graphic designer, studio, or a graphic design theme. Students research their topic (e.g., the designer's creative process, conceptual and formal qualities of the works) and select visual and verbal information that will be displayed in the project. There must be a minimum of seven representative works. The second step involves the structure and visualization of the concept in the form of storyboards. Finally, students design the preview using typographical, visual, and aural elements. The visual components can be any combination of still images, video clips, and abstract forms. Images can be used in any desired way, such as collage, superimposition, etc. The movie should have an aural component that can be any combination of narration, sound track, and audio effects. Students are encouraged to explore the relationships among visual, aural, and kinetic vocabularies: rhythm, sequencing, interval, synchrony/asynchrony, predictability/unpredictability, etc.

The following text must be part of the trailer as typographical elements (in any order): title of the exhibition, name of graphic designer or studio (if not in the title), name of museum, the location and period of exhibition, credits for the use of images and sound, and themselves as the designers.

The movie/preview can be any size within 320 × 320 pixels (either the height or width should be 320 pixels). The duration has to be between sixty and ninety seconds at most. Students can use up to two typefaces of their choice.

## Assignment 3: Social Message

The third assignment extends the exploration of relationships among visual, aural, and kinetic vocabularies in the construction of narrative, linear structures. The task is to create a message that communicates and elicits social, cultural, or environmental awareness in the general public. The goal is to inform the audience about a social issue and ultimately to have the viewer adopting the value of the message.

First, students select and research a topic. Research involves finding information about both the nature of the selected problem and how it has been communicated in different media (e.g., posters, television ads, articles, documentaries, etc.). Students are responsible for creating both the visual and the verbal components of the message. The structure of the narrative is first discussed in the form of storyboards. The movie/message should be communicated using typographical, visual, and aural elements. Visual components can be any combination of stills images, video clips, and abstract or figurative forms. In a few particular cases students are allowed to use and manipulate found images. The movie should have an aural component in any combination of narration, sound track, and/or audio effects.

The following text must be part of the message as typographical elements (in any order): the social cause, a memorable message related to the cause, credits for the use of images and sound, and themselves as the designers.

The movie/message can be any size within 320 × 320 pixels (either the height or width should be 320 pixels). The duration has to be between sixty and ninety seconds at most. Students can use up to two typefaces of their choice.

# required readings

Arnheim, Rudolf, "Movement," in *Art and Visual Perception: A Psychology of the Creative Eye*, University of California Press, 1974.

Dorfles, Gillo, "The Role of Motion in Our Visual Habits and Artistic Creation," in *The Nature and Art of Motion*, ed. Gyorgy Kepes, George Braziller, 1965.

Helfand, Jessica, "Electronic Typography: The New Visual Language," in *Screen: Essays on Graphic Design, New Media, and Visual Culture*, Princeton Architectural Press, 2001.

McCloud, Scott. "Time Frames," in *Understanding Comics*, Harper, 1994.

## recommended readings

## (related to issues discussed in class)

Arnheim, Rudolf, *Art and Visual Perception: A Psychology of the Creative Eye*, University
of California Press, 1974.

Codrington, Andrea, *Kyle Cooper*, Yale University Press, 2003.

Curtis, Hillman, *Hillman Curtis on Creating Short Films for the Web*, New Riders Press,
2006.

Curtis, Hillman, *MTIV: Process, Inspiration and Practice for the New Media Designer*,
New Riders Press, 2002.

Dondis, Donis A., *A Primer of Visual Literacy*, MIT Press, 2000.

Eisenstein, Sergei, *Film Form*, Harvest/HBJ Book, 1977.

Eisenstein, Sergei, *Film Sense*, Harvest/HBJ Book, 1974.

Helfand, Jessica, *Screen: Essays on Graphic Design, New Media, and Visual Culture*,
Princeton Architectural Press, 2001.

Kepes, Gyorgy, ed., *The Nature and Art of Motion*, George Braziller, 1965.

McCloud, Scott, *Understanding Comics*, Harper, 1994.

Meyer, Trish, and Chris Meyer, *Creating Motion Graphics with After Effects*, 2 vols.,
CMP Books, 2004–5.

Murch, Walter, *In the Blink of an Eye: A Perspective on Film Editing*, 2nd ed., Silman-
James Press, 2001.

COURSE TITLE: Advanced Time-Based Media

TEACHER: Danielle Aubert

FREQUENCY: One Semester, fifteen weeks, twice a week

LEVEL: Junior/Senior

CREDITS: 3

DEGREE: Bachelor of Fine Arts

SCHOOL: College for Creative Studies, Detroit, MI

## summary and goal of class

This course will provide students with the opportunity to explore the affect of time on image and type. We know that time-based media lend themselves well to narrative structures (e.g., films and television shows), yet much of the work done by graphic designers in this field is nonnarrative in structure (e.g., "bumps" and "interstitials" designed for television channels; many film titles). In this class we will talk about the role of structures, and sequencing, in leading an audience through both narrative and nonnarrative time-based pieces. We'll talk about the roles of timing, audience, perceived logic, boredom, and interest. Students will be encouraged to think critically about the boundaries and possibilities of the medium.

By the end of this course students will be adept at developing ideas from storyboards into finished motion graphic pieces. Students will gain fluency with software (i.e., After Effects) and become comfortable working with type in motion.

## week by week

**WEEK 1.** Introduction. Administrative stuff. Assign Project 1: Family Histories, Part 1. Work in class, one-on-one meetings.

**WEEK 2.** Project 1 due. Class critique. Assign Project 2: Family Histories, Part 2. After Effects refresher demonstration.

**WEEK 3.** Project 2 due. Class critique, students submit project on disk. Assign Project 3: About Time. Presentation of artists and designers who use time as a system of production. Work in class, one-on-one meetings to discuss approach to project 3.

**WEEK 4.** Students introduce their ideas for project 3 to the class. Preliminary storyboards are due. One-on-one meetings to continue discussing ideas.

**WEEK 5.** Class critique on first draft of motion work and desk critiques. After Effects demonstration: "Working with Masks."

**WEEK 6.** Go over near-final drafts of motion pieces. Project 3 due. Students submit project 3 on disk. A visiting critic is invited to show work to the class and to participate in class critique.

**WEEK 7.** Assign Project 4: Re-creation. Students select footage to work with for project 4 and bring it to show and discuss in class. One-on-one desk critiques to discuss approaches to the assignment.

**WEEK 8.** Watch Lars von Trier's *The Five Obstructions*. Meet for desk critiques of work thus far. Students should show clear progress and direction in the form of storyboards or early drafts of motion work.

**WEEK 9.** Process critique with the class on work thus far. Continue working in class and meeting for one-on-one discussions.

**WEEK 10.** Work in class, develop projects, desk critiques.

**WEEK 11.** Project 4 due. Students submit project 4 on disk. A visiting critic is invited to show work to the class and to participate in class critique. Assign Project 5: Money and Weather. Presentation on the prevalence of screens in the environment and the flexibility of the term "time-based media." Class discussion about the assignment.

**WEEK 12.** Desk critiques, students should come prepared with three to five ideas for project. Class field trip to the Cranbrook Academy of Art for studio visits of the 2-D department.

**WEEK 13.** Students develop one idea and present research to the class. Continue working and developing sketches, storyboards, screen tests.

**WEEK 14.** Work in class, meet one-on-one for desk critiques. After Effects demonstration: "Working With 3-D Animations."

**WEEK 15.** One class meeting to review near-final drafts. Project 5 due on last day of class. Cranbrook students invited as guest critics for final project.

# class projects

### Project 1: Family Histories, Part 1*

In Class: Take twenty minutes to write your "family history." Trade your writing with a classmate.

Assignment: Create a one-minute slide show using the text written by your classmates. You can use all or part of each text. Use images that correspond with the text. Do not use type; use only images. Feel free to fictionalize.

---

* *Family Histories assignments are adapted from an assignment given in Chris Pullman's graduate-level, time-based media class at Yale University.*

You will read each text (excerpt) aloud and trigger image changes with a keystroke as you speak. Think about how the meaning of the text is affected by your choice of images and their sequence.

- Work in a single format (e.g., 720 × 540 pixel images).
- Use still images only.
- Use cuts only between images.
- Be simple.
- Think about spoken word/image interaction.
- Think about timing and phrasing, which words go with images.
- Practice to get the timing right.
- Do your best to stay within the one-minute time limit.

## Project 2: Family Histories, Part 2

Assignment: Use an excerpt from the texts from project 1 to tell an abbreviated (fifteen to thirty second) version of a family history. For this project, use only sounds (no words or language) for the audio. Use only type (no images or video) as visuals.

Once again, think about simultaneity and the interaction of the words on the screen with the audio. Consider ways to tell a different story than the one you told in project 1.

- Work simply, using only a few sounds, serially or overlapping, and a few words as images.
- Think about timing (when things happen) and simultaneity (which things happen at the same time).
- Think about how the combination of what you see on the screen and what you hear in the audio can add up to a third thing.
- How can the form of the words or their behavior in time and space affect their meaning?
- Think about dominance and how to express hierarchy both aurally and visually.
- Change one variable at a time and see what happens.
- Work from simple to more complicated.
- Record and edit your sound outside of After Effects. Use After Effects to control the behavior of the words.
- Edit the sound and type together in After Effects.

## Project 3: About Time

Assignment: Design a thirty-second screen-based piece that records the daily passage of time over two weeks.

Look at time-keeping devices: clocks, calendars, watches, stopwatches, public clocks, cell phone displays, scoreboards, and also, newspapers, magazines, bills, time stamping devices.

Look for other "screens" that record the passing of time and the environments those screens inhabit.

Listen to the way sounds change over time, or the way we hear time elapsing—in films, on the radio, outside, inside, on television, in elevators.

Look at your own time. How do you measure your time? What signs do you look at to tell the time? What does "the passage of time" look like?

1. Make a plan. Decide what you will record and how you will track it. Think about how you will represent what you track. Don't use filters, unless you have a very good reason. Use common sense rather than styling to determine what your piece should look like.

2. Begin collecting your daily "data." Pay attention to your data's properties. In the meantime, think about how you will remediate it for video. Sketch and develop storyboards for your sequence. Include image, type/content, sound description, and durations. Use screen captures if that makes sense for the way you're working.

3. Assemble, edit, and refine your motion piece.

Objective: This exercise is designed to explore the way time-based media exist in our lived environment as well as the passage of time during the very process of designing and making. The goal is to create a video that explores representations of time using image and typography.

Required readings/references: The following texts deal with the representation of time and also with graphic design more generally. The first two are required readings. The rest are for reference.

- Jessica Helfand's "The Myth of Real Time" in *Screen: Essays on Graphic Design, New Media, and Visual Culture* deals specifically with time and screens and with changing systems for mapping time.
- Robin Kinross's "More Light! For a Typography That Knows What It's Doing," in *In Alphabetical Order (Werkplaats Typograpfie)* is a call for rational thinking in design rather than "stylishness."
- Andrew Blauvelt's "Strangely Familiar: Design and Everyday Life," from a book of the same name, was published in conjunction with an exhibition at the Walker Art Center. It is about the incorporation of design objects into our daily lives—the ways we use them, where their forms come from.
- Look at various projects by Sophie Calle.
- Mary Ellen Carroll's *Federal* (24-hour film) and *Without Intent*.
- Claire Colebrook's "Cinema: Perception, time and becoming," in *Gilles Deleuze* is kind of difficult to understand *but*, if you struggle through it, could really have an enormous impact on your work.

- Look at Daily Type (*www.dailytype.ru*).
- John Watkin's *On Kawara* is published by Phaidon. On Kawara has been making his Date Paintings since 1966. Every day he paints the date on a canvas. All his work deals in some way with the passage of time as it is recorded through the works he leaves behind. It's worth looking at this book.
- See Ahree Lee's "Me." This is a motion piece that can be found at *www.ahreelee.com*.
- Chapters 3 and 4 from *Understanding Comics* by Scott McCloud could be useful if you haven't already read them.
- See various books and videos by Dieter Roth.
- Wolfgang Schivelbusch's "Railroad Space and Railroad Time" in *The Railway Journey* is about the beginnings of the railroad industry and the way that connecting towns to one another affected the way people thought about time and space.

## Project 4: Re-Creation

Assignment: Re-create fifteen to forty-five seconds of found footage. The footage you choose must include dialogue. Observe the following restrictions:

- You must shoot any video/photographs you use yourself.
- Your final piece must have exactly the same duration as the original.
- You must reproduce the dialogue outside of the audio (i.e., you cannot have spoken dialogue in the audio, you must find some other way to reproduce it).

Make the new clip as similar as possible to the original while observing the restrictions. We will view the original clip and the re-creation side by side for the final review.

Objective: To dissect an existing scene and to work within restrictions to create a "copy" of existing footage.

Required visual text: Lars von Trier's *The Five Obstructions*.

## Project 5: Money and Weather

Assignment: This is potentially a two-part assignment.

Part 1: Design a display for current and/or forecasted weather or stock market conditions—either for a single city (e.g., Detroit) or for multiple places. Your display should appear somewhere other than a personal computer screen. What weather or financial information will you choose to display? Will it appear indoors or outdoors, on a cell phone or on a Jumbotron, projected in a vacant lot or on a set of screens in a hotel lobby? Will it appear on a television channel? Who will be your audience?

Insomniacs? A homeless population? Business executives? Migratory birds? In After Effects, design a segment of the weather/stock market content that will appear on your display. Work to scale if possible.

Part 2 (optional assignment for extra credit): Create a short "promotional" piece that demonstrates the way your display works. You can think of this second piece as a proposal (e.g., to this college, to the city of Detroit, to a cell phone company) that explains why someone should want to install your display. Or think of it simply as a documentation of the functionality of your display. This can be print and/or screen based.

Objective: To think about your agency as a designer in determining the way information "looks"—what is filtered out and what is emphasized. Also, to imagine a context for screen-based work outside the classroom.

Required readings for this project:

- Dunne, Anthony, and Fionna Raby, "Designer as Author," in *Design Noir: The Secret Life of Electronic Objects*, Basel, 2001.
- Hall, Peter, "People as Pixels," *Trace*, the AIGA Journal of Design, 1, no. 2, 2001. (Article available at *www.typotheque.com/articles/people_as_pixels*.)
- Elliman, Paul, "Designed Screens," *Dot Dot Dot*, no. 2, 2001. (Article available at *www.typotheque.com/articles/designed_screens*.)
- Manovich, Lev, "About 'Little Movies,'" *www.manovich.net/little-movies/statement-new3.html*.

COURSE TITLE: Advanced Time-Based Media: Special Projects

TEACHER: Liisa Salonen

FREQUENCY: Fall Semester

LEVEL: Junior/Senior

CREDITS: 3

DEGREE: Bachelor of Fine Arts

SCHOOL: College For Creative Studies, Detroit, MI

## summary and goals of course

This special projects course provides students the opportunity to explore and work with narrative and nonnarrative time-based structures at an advanced level. The course is designed to develop concepts and methodologies that are applicable to the design of motion graphics. Projects will further expose students to certain elements of cinematography, editing, typography, composition, special effects, sound, etc., and to the strategic use of design elements and rhetorical devices that contribute to the communication of meaning in kinetic environments. At least one project will focus on developing screen-based typography. Assigned readings in time-base and design theory, methodology, culture, and technology will be applied in the creation and critical assessment of work.

187

Critical analysis of student's work will focus on the appropriateness of communication choices: image, typography, color, scale, repetition, and space, as well as sequence, tempo, sound, rhythm, transition, speed, duration, etc., and their associated meanings.

## week by week

**WEEKS 1–3. PROJECT ONE: LOGIC, EDIT, AND EFFECT.** This short introductory exercise is designed for students to work with narrative construction and to develop a logic for the editing process. It uses an unedited film clip that has been digitized.

Independent filmmaker Otto Buj discusses the intent of the scene in the film from which the clip is taken, and critiques the editing of the extracted clip and how the edits affect meaning.

**WEEKS 2–6. PROJECT TWO, EXERCISE ONE: IN-CAMERA, ANALOG TYPOGRAPHY.** This exercise is designed to explore typography in a motion environment and to create typography that is both process driven and conceptual.

Using portions of randomly assigned literary texts as conceptual starting points, students explore process as it relates to appropriate conceptual choices. The exercise concludes with the creation of ten to twenty analog typographic explorations.

**WEEKS 6–8. PROJECT TWO, EXERCISE TWO: COMPUTER-GENERATED TYPOGRAPHY.** This exercise is an extension of the concepts and experimentation developed in project two, exercise one. Students add computer-generated typography to the previous analog exploration in order to add content, build more complex typographic hierarchies, and consider more carefully the structure of the typographic message. The exercise concludes with the creation of ten to twenty more structured, edited, and compiled typographic explorations.

**WEEKS 7–11. PROJECT THREE: THE EVERYDAY.** Students research and create a video regarding a poignant aspect of the "everyday." They are encouraged to consider processes, activities, user participation, adaptation, reconfiguration, reuse, recontextualization, consumption, multifunctionality, the portable, and mass customization. Students read the assigned articles and consider preconceived ideas about how design functions in everyday life, as well as the role of the designer. Projects are intended to challenge commonly held ideas and assertions about the experience of the everyday.

# project one: logic, edit, and effect

**Objective.** This exercise is designed with two objectives: first, to start working with narrative construction and, second, to develop a logic for the editing process. You will be working within the constraints of traditional film editing techniques. Design, as well, is often about editing. How you decide what to leave in and what to take out are decisions that serve a certain need—in this case, the development of a logic between what proceeds and what follows an edit in order to communicate an idea efficiently and effectively. Carefully consider narrative construction and the affects of time and motion on the communication intent.

Conceptually, the edit needs to make sense. For example: Does it serve a purpose? Do you understand visually what you're looking at? Does it trip up the momentum? If so, is it intentional?

It is also designed for you to start working in Final Cut Pro with simple editing and three kinds of cuts: a straight cut from one scene to another, a dissolve, and a fade up or fade out. You will want to think about timing and how the duration of a dissolve, for example, will affect the momentum of the piece.

**Assignment.** This exercise uses the assigned QuickTime file that has been digitized from the raw footage of a black and white film clip. Independent filmmaker Otto Buj will discuss the intent of this scene in the film, *The Eternal Present*, from which the clip is taken. Please take notes on the filmmaker's intent, the context of the scene within the entire film, etc. Using Final Cut Pro and, if necessary, a tutorial of your own choosing, edit the raw footage to a clip thirty to fifty seconds in length.

**Outcome.** Your final film clip should be thirty to fifty seconds in length, and edited to the intent of the filmmaker and to how the scene functions within the entire film.

## Recommended Readings

Klotz, Heinrich, "Video Art," *Mediascape* (exhibition catalog, Guggenheim Museum Soho, June 14–September 15, 1996), Guggenheim Museum Publications, 1996: 8–11.

Boggs, Joseph M., and Dennis W. Petrie, "Cinematography" and "Editing and Special Effects," chapters 5 and 6 from *The Art of Watching Films*, 7th ed., McGraw-Hill, 2006.

Bordwell, David, and Kristin Thompson, "Narrative as a Formal System," chapter 3 from *Film Art: An Introduction*, 5th ed., McGraw-Hill, 1996.

# project two, exercise one:
# in-camera, analog typography

**Objective.** This exercise is designed to explore typography in a motion environment and to work with typography that is both conceptual and process oriented. Conceptually, typographic choices need to communicate appropriately. The objective is to explore process as it relates to appropriate conceptual choices. Portions of randomly assigned literary texts are used as conceptual starting points.

You will also begin to develop a methodology for working with kinetic media through the cultivation of personal concepts and processes that are open to changing conditions and parameters, including collaboration.

**Assignment.** Begin by looking at the typography in the short film *I . . . Dreaming* by Stan Brakhage and the title sequence to the film *A Woman is a Woman* by Jean-Luc Godard.

**Conceptualize.** Using the randomly assigned literary text as a starting point, decide quickly on a concept to work with.

**Consider.** Think about what you already know about typography in print or other media, including font choice, hierarchy, sequence, scale, space, legibility, etc.

**Record/Make.** Working off the computer and using a video camera, make and/or shoot typography that reflects or relates to your concept. Experiment with multiple processes.

Find type in the environment. Make it by hand. Use xerography, photography, collage, diazo prints, photograms, scans, computer prints, light, and so on. Develop your own process, system, method. Work back and forth between analog and digital processes. In this part of the exercise, the goal is to do as much process as possible off the computer before you bring it into Final Cut Pro for editing. You are NOT creating computer type.

**Read.** See chapter 5, "Cinematography," and chapter 6, "Editing and Special Effects," in *The Art of Watching Films* by Joseph M. Boggs and Dennis W. Petrie. Explore cinematic methods of working with motion and image in your experiments on type. You could, for example, use an alternation of objective and subjective viewpoints, as outlined on page 115 of the text. Or you could work with reflections, etc. There are many techniques that could be explored from the point of view of process, and also in terms of how they affect or connote meaning.

**Remember.** Keep in mind compositional issues in two and three dimensions as well as in time: rhythm, scale, contrast, line, shape, color, white space, negative space, repetition of formal elements, texture, pattern, etc. Consider depth.

And remember issues that relate to compositions that unfold over time: rhythm, transition, speed, duration, pause, sequencing, etc.

190    **Special Effects and Rhetorical Devices.** Framing, cropping, positioning, sequencing, dissolving, montaging, morphing, slow-motion, fast-forward, instant replay, juxtaposition, superimposition, split-frame, freeze-frame, voice-over, jump cut, and so on, can be considered critically in their relation to concept. (This list of rhetorical devices is originally published in: Andrew Blauvelt, "Unfolding Information," *Emigre, The Info Perplex* 40, Fall 1996).

**Outcome.** Your final product should be ten to twenty time-based, analog typographic explorations assembled in Final Cut Pro. Successful clips will use process to develop a conceptually appropriate message.

## Recommended Readings

The following essays include selections on theories, processes, technologies, etc., that relate to typography and/or motion graphics.

Elliman, Paul, "City of Words," *Eye* 10, no. 40, Summer 2001: 62–69.

Kindel, Eric, "Marked by Time," *Eye* 10, no. 40, Summer 2001: 48–49.

Worthington, Michael, "Entranced by Motion, Seduced by Stillness," *Eye* 9, no. 33, Autumn 1999: 28–39.

Owen, William, "Bodies, Text and Motion," *Eye* 6, no. 21, Summer 1996: 24–31.

Ihde, Don, "Image Technologies and Traditional Culture," from *Postphenomenology: Essays in the Postmodern Context*, Northwestern University Press, 1995: 43–55.

One page excerpts from the following anthologies will be randomly assigned to develop concept, as inspiration, and in some cases, formal experimentation:

Borges, Jorge Luis, *Labyrinths: Selected Stories and Other Writings*, New Directions, 1981: 32–33 and 246–247.

Jabes, Edmond, *The Book of Margins*, University of Chicago Press, 1993: 166–167 and 40–41.

Marquez, Gabriel Garcia, *Collected Stories*, Harper Trade, 1999: 46, 48, and 109.

# project two, exercise two:
# computer-generated typography

**Objective.** This exercise is designed to add computer-generated typography to your previous analog explorations. The goal in project two, exercise one was to explore process as it relates to appropriate conceptual choices. This time, the goal is to add content, build more complex typographic hierarchies, and consider more carefully the structure of the typographic message. Formally, the computer-generated type must relate to the clip to which you are adding content. You may work with your edited pieces or the raw footage from project two, exercise one. You may also shoot additional footage.

**Assignment.** Using the concepts from project two, exercise one, you will add content created on the computer.

**Consider.** Think about the feedback you received in the critique of your typography explorations from project two, exercise one. Consider also what you know about typography in print or other media, including font choice, hierarchy, sequence, scale, space, legibility, etc.

**Add Typographic Content.** Working on the computer this time, add typographic content to your previous clips, or start with the raw footage and add content. Use Photoshop, Illustrator, Dreamweaver, Flash, Final Cut Pro, After Effects, and so forth.

**Reread.** Go back to chapters 5 and 6 from *The Art of Watching Films* assigned in the previous exercise. Consider how elements discussed in these chapters affect and connote meaning.

**Work with Time Structures.** Explore the use of momentum, rhythm, transition, speed, duration, pause, sequencing, etc. In motion design, time is a structuring element and functions in building hierarchies. Work with time as well as two-dimensional space, color, scale, form, etc. Consider structures like AB, AB, AB; or ABC, ABC, ABC; or ABCDEF; or 2, 4, 8, 16; and so forth.

**Special Effects.** Work specifically with rhetorical devices and effects. See "Special Effects And Rhetorical Devices" in Project Two, Exercise One.

**Sound.** Add verbal content in the form of voice.

**Remember.** Keep in mind compositional issues in two dimensions as well as in time: rhythm, scale, contrast, line, shape, color, white space, negative space, repetition of formal elements, texture, pattern, etc.

**Outcome.** Your final product should be ten to twenty time-based typographic explorations in which computer-generated typography adds content and relates formally to the clips developed in project two, exercise one.

# project three: the everyday

**Objective.** The objective is to create a video, one to five minutes in length, exploring an aspect of the everyday. In some way, your project should challenge commonly held ideas and assertions about the experience of the everyday. The video could be a complete piece or could serve as a model if it were expanded into a longer piece. In your approach, the form and content should be indistinguishable and concept driven. You must use typography in this project. Remember, this is a design project and a communication vehicle.

**Assignment.** Read the assigned articles carefully and consider your preconceived ideas about how design functions in everyday life and the role of the designer.

**Brainstorm.** Begin brainstorming on tactics and/or strategies for how you might "transform the ordinary into the extraordinary, acknowledging that the everyday is a participatory realm where design is essentially incomplete, knowing that people will eventually inhabit and adapt what is given" (Andrew Blauvelt from *Strangely Familiar: Design and Everyday Life*). Consider processes, activities, user participation, adaptation, reconfiguration, reuse, recontextualization, consumption, multifunctionality, the portable, mass customization, etc. Note that these are processes and unfinished activities and *may* function more as questions than as solutions.

**Research.** Choose a SPECIFIC area of the everyday that you are interested in researching.

Conduct your research in multiple modalities: visual/photographic/motion/video, sound, writing/language/voice, etc. Consider sound recordings of spoken voice as well as written and more conventional research sources such as books, the library, the internet. Your research should relate to the tactics/strategies you uncover in your brainstorming.

Write a one page brief, and include:

- A statement of your goal (This statement is brief and could be one sentence about what you want to explore and elicit in the audience. For example: "My goal is to make a one-minute commercial that examines the banality of routine by describing a day in the life of Character X. The intended effects in the audience are . . .")
- A description of audience (For example: "The demographic I want to reach is . . ." Who is your audience? What effect do you wish to create IN your audience? Consider audience as participant.)
- Written and visual research
- A short summary of your research and/or processes (Cite your sources.)

**Conceptualize.** Develop a concept from the goal statement of what you want to produce/elicit.

**Visualize.** Create a mental image and describe three ways you could achieve your goal. For example: "I will do this by looking at 1) how character X is caught up in instant messaging; 2) how character X uses a computer interface to write/delete/rewrite/delete/rewrite/etc., a completely banal statement; 3) etc.

**Create Content.** Develop content. Your content could be all fiction. Or you could work with nonfiction material (recordings) as in a documentary. Or you could use nonfiction research sources and write a short narrative, scenario of use, etc. Consider using dialog as well as other forms of language. Remember, information can be provided in many channels: image, sound, on-screen type, dialog, etc.

**Be Specific.** Choose something small and specific: a component that represents a greater idea.

Limit what you work with. You are not working with huge amounts of content, though you could be working with the theme of an entire documentary. It could be a small clip of a longer piece.

**Write.** Create the written/spoken/image content. Write the typographic content that will be seen on screen.

**Storyboard.** Develop storyboards for your sequence. Include image, typographic content, sound description, durations, lighting, camera angles, etc.

**Capture.** Using the storyboards as a beginning point, shoot video footage, capture sound, work with typography in camera and on the desktop.

**Include Sound.** Sound can have different relationships to image and text: it can be the same thing, as in dialog that you see someone speak; it can be parallel; it can be incongruous; and so forth.

Possible genres to develop: documentary style video, public service announcement, title/credit sequence, trailer, commercial, product demonstration/how-to video/training video/corporate video/trade show video, video incursions/installation (presenting the familiar in unconventional locations), in-store video promotion

## Considerations:

- Consider performance and participation as message-building acts.
- Consider your audience and how the performer relates to, and identifies with, the audience.
- Consider the signification of rhetorical devices, or special effects, and how a critical use helps develop meaning. See "Special Effects and Rhetorical Devices" in project two, exercise one.
- Consider how motion develops content and cognitive issues, for example, the difference in meaning between slow-motion and fast-motion.

**Outcome.** Your final product will be a one- to five-minute video that critically explores a commonly held idea about the experience of the everyday. Form and content should be indistinguishable and concept driven.

## Recommended Readings

Blauvelt, Andrew, *Strangely Familiar: Design and Everyday Life*, Walker Art Center, 2003. The following sections:

- Blauvelt, Andrew, "Strangely Familiar: Design and Everyday Life."
- Betsky, Aaron, "The Strangeness of the Familiar in Design."
- Hunt, Jamer, "Just Re-do It: Tactical Formlessness and Everyday Consumption."
- Bell, Jonathan, "Ruins, Recycling, Smart Buildings, and the Endlessly Transformable Environment."

## Additional Readings

Codrington, Andrea, "Custom Made Miracles," *Metropolis*, March 2002: 59.
Hall, Peter, "Magic Touch," *Metropolis*, February 2003: 76.
Hall, Peter, "Title Wave," and "Reel Classics," *I.D.*, March/April 1999: 60–64 and 65–66.
Kelly, Dennis Joseph II, "Human Intervention," *I.D.*, June 2002: 50.
Ramakers, Renny, and Gijs Bakker, *Droog Design: Spirit of the Nineties*, Uitgeverij, 1998.
Szabo, Julia, "Wear House," *I.D.*, May 1999: 58.
Van Zijl, Ida, *Droog Design—1991–1996*, Centraal Museum Utrecht, 1997.

COURSE TITLE: The Music Video: A Real World Workshop

TEACHER: Graham Elliott

FREQUENCY: Fall and Spring Semesters

LEVEL: Junior/Senior

CREDITS: 3 per semester

DEGREE: Bachelor of Fine Arts

SCHOOL: School of Visual Arts, New York, NY

## goal and purpose

The class teaches the art and craft of making music videos.

The genre is vast; so the course covers a lot of bases, namely, live action, animation, motion graphics, and basic special effects.

The course is structured around actual production, that is, students coming up with a concept for a particular brief, going out and shooting, bringing the footage back, and then editing.

Students work on individual projects, which are dissected, discussed, and critiqued by everyone. This gives students a great breadth of experience by following through, in depth, the process of making a varied number of films.

We start by plunging into a project that puts the student in front of the camera.

The assignment is Video-Karaoke.

Brief: Make a music video in which you are the star. Choose a song with strong vocals, you'll have to break down the lyrics and learn how to lip sync. Be as much of a rock star, rapper, etc., as you want; you can also use friends as band members, dancers, etc. Even if you don't play instruments you can fake it. Borrow a guitar, dress up, go crazy with make-up—whatever you want—most of all, have fun and be creative.

## semester one: week by week

The following is a basic guide but is somewhat flexible depending on the complexity of the concept and weather issues.

During class the weekly assignment and workflow are discussed.

Every week an introduction to a new topic is covered, for example, storyboarding, scheduling, shooting, etc. Guest lecturers come in from time to time to discuss production, lighting, etc.

**WEEK 1.** Course introduction, professor introduction.

All students introduce themselves, by way of a three and a half minute "talking head" video timed by an egg timer. Not only is this a great icebreaker it also starts getting students used to being on camera and working within the format's average length. Students will take turns operating the camera.

Students will also fill out a questionnaire indicating their knowledge of computer programs and musical and other interests.

Introduction to music videos. We look at the early Panoram Soundies of the 1940s and the European Scopines of the 1960s. Beatles promotional clips and the French Video Jukebox format of the 1970s are covered. We show landmark video examples such as Peter Gabriel's "Sledgehammer" and Michael Jackson's "Thriller" as well as old DEVO videos.

Discuss brief: Video-Karaoke

Discuss anyone's initial ideas.

Homework: Choose a song, print the lyrics, and write a concept for your video.

Each student is given a production book: a blank, sectioned school exercise book for keeping together all music video workshop notes, course work, and homework.

These books are submitted at the end of the semester as part of the grading structure.

**WEEK 2.** Music video influences are screened including clips of films such as Luis Bunuel's surrealist film *Un Chien Andalou* (1928), Bruce Conner's "found footage" collage *Cosmic Ray* (1961), and Nam June Paik's mass-media meditation *Global Groove* (1973).

Review homework: Play your song, discuss lyrics, and present concept.

Class discusses each idea and, as a group, we try to "tighten" or "loosen" the concept (as per your idea).

Class is shown real, written video treatment examples, followed by the finished video.

Homework: Write a treatment and collect style frames from magazines and the Internet that fit your concept.

**WEEK 3.** Introduction to storyboards, examples shown alongside finished projects.

Homework: Produce a full up storyboard for your treatment.

**WEEK 4.** Ten golden rules. Camera operation basics. How to prevent your shots from looking like home movies:

- Go manual whenever possible: manual aperture, manual focus
- Keep motion of the camera steady (brick method: students practice "shooting" with a real brick)

- Vary the shots: close up, medium, wide/establishing, aerial, low
- Try to incorporate motion: dolly/track, pan/tilt, crane
- Shoot cut-aways
- White balance the camera in every set-up
- Light: try to supplement dark lighting conditions
- Use a tripod or monopod
- Keep lens clean
- Check audio levels with headphones

An introduction into scheduling a shoot and other preproduction issues such as securing permits follows. Lip sync, track breakdown (i.e., verse/chorus/hook/break), and organizational skills are covered.

Low budget production techniques and tricks are demonstrated by guest filmmakers and producers.

Students present storyboards.

**WEEK 5.** Green screen workshop, shot exterior or interior (weather dependent).

Footage shot is then digitized into Final Cut Pro. Next, selects are output to After Effects for a demonstration of pulling keys and making mattes.

Homework: Make a production book for presentation at the preproduction meeting next week. The production book is the collated treatment, style frames, storyboard, lyrics and track breakdown, location scout, talent/props/wardrobe photos, schedule, crew, and shot list.

**WEEK 6.** Preproduction meeting. Students present their project formally to an industry professional with their production book. The presentation is also filmed on video for later critique.

Shoot; review dailies.

**WEEK 7.** Shoot; review dailies.

**WEEK 8.** Introduction to Final Cut Pro. Editing techniques, workflow, and outputting.

**WEEK 9.** Introduction to After Effects. Adding filters, basic special effects, basic motion graphics.

**WEEK 10.** Stop-frame animation workshop. This class we will animate an armatured model, interacting with a person in a stop-motion environment. The footage will be imported into After Effects and manipulated.

**FINAL WEEKS.** Editing and editorial issues. Class review of rough cuts.

Students who complete their films before the end of the semester will then make ten- or thirty-second promos for KickA$$tv, the in-class "TV station," which is the medium for showing student work (*www.kickasstelevision.com*).

# end of semester deliverables

One QuickTime (uncompressed) movie of Video-Karaoke
One DVD of Video-Karaoke with cover and menu page
Video-Karaoke production book
Breakdown of costs
KickA$$tv promos as applicable
Class production book

# semester two

The second semester is devoted to "Adopt-a-Band."

Brief: You've all made a video in which you are the talent. Now go out and find a band and make their music video. You will be coming up against a number of potential problems.

The first is finding a band that wants a free music video. This is usually easy, but if you need help, we have many resources. These include college radio, record label contacts, Craig's list postings, MySpace postings/research, and putting flyers up in the East Village, etc.

Next is coming up with a concept that both you and the band are excited about and can be fulfilled within the resources at hand.

Then, and quite possibly the hardest part, you must maintain a band's interest and coordinate the whole preproduction and shoot.

"My band didn't show up" is not an excuse. So you have to be aware of the new dynamics involved. The resources of the knowledge base and support of other students and the professor are valuable commodities here.

Collaboration with another student is accepted here, as the workload is greater.

# breakdown

The weekly breakdown is structured to meet the varied demands of working on a large project and roughly follows the schedule outlined in semester one. A great deal of the time is spent prepping the students so they feel confident with their ideas and skills to go and talk to the band. We invite the band/artist to the class for presentations and, when possible, the class will take field trips to recording studios, practice venues, and live gigs.

As this enters a whole new dimension, the course is flexible enough to accommodate the preshoot and postproduction aspects of the assignment. Weather is also a factor here and an emphasis is put on back-up plans if shooting exteriors.

Again, when students finish up, they will make more KickA$$tv promos and KickA$$tv Awards packaging.

# end of semester deliverables

One QuickTime (uncompressed) movie of Adopt-A-Band Video

One DVD of Video-Karaoke, Adopt-A-Band Video, and KickA$$tv promos with
  cover and menu page KickA$$tv Awards promos

Adopt-A-Band Video production book with breakdown of costs

Class production book

# supplementary notes

A basic editorial introduction to using Final Cut Pro and an introduction to After Effects
are also on the syllabus. However, this class does not teach these programs; it shows
their part in the process. Many of the students who participate are also taking in-depth
Final Cut Pro and After Effects classes or have previously. But this is not a prerequisite.

Depending on interest, an intensive weekend class can be set up covering
Final Cut Pro and/or After Effects.

The three main aspects of the class are creativity, presentation, and production.

**Creativity.** Students are encouraged to develop their ideas and push them to the
boundaries of their creative expression. Our mantra is: "If you can't do it in art
school, where can you do it?" The class is not about making formulaic music videos
but is geared to expressing ideas and learning the skills of the presentation of ideas.

**Presentation.** Presentation of initial concepts, storyboards, treatments, and production
reviews are a key element of the week-to-week structure of the course. Students are
given insight into the dynamics of presenting to the artist or band, on the creative
side, and the "suits," on the record label end.

For preproduction presentations, we often bring in an industry professional and
videotape the presentation for critique later.

Good presentation of an idea dovetails directly into good production.

**Production.** And finally, these ideas and presentations go nowhere without the final
production. Students are encouraged to get as much production value out of the limited resources at hand. This is New York City, the home of a million wanna-be camera-
men, actors, and musicians: people who crave the experience to be involved in the
creative process and have a portfolio piece. So we spend a lot of time nurturing the
skills to communicate a great idea and get other people as excited as we are and actually make short films.

**Show and Tell.** Students are encouraged to bring in their favorite music videos,
show their favorite Web sites, short films, virals, etc., on a weekly basis.

Finally . . . if you don't have the time or inclination to "put in a lot of sweat,"
this is not the course for you. But if you are ready to dive into the exciting world of
filmmaking, then take the plunge!

COURSE TITLE: Information Architecture 1

TEACHER: Brian Lucid

FREQUENCY: Fall Semester, once a week

LEVEL: Junior, required course

CREDITS: 3

DEGREE: Bachelor of Fine Arts

SCHOOL: Massachusetts College of Art, Boston, MA

## summary

How does one prepare for the role of editing, organizing, and contextualizing the information that surrounds us? Information Architecture 1 is an introductory course into the basic concepts and methods of information architecture (the ordering, structuring, and relating of data) and information design (the visualization or representation of information).

200

Information Architecture 1 addresses issues of visualizing information and transferring knowledge within the frameworks of static, temporal, and dynamic media. Students break complex information down into manageable pieces, then search to discover the most effective way to present that information so that it is clear, concise, and effective.

Course assignments expand outward from static media, allowing students to investigate how animation and interaction aid in the clarification of complex concepts and processes. The first assignment explores the representation of motion within a static medium. The second employs animation to illustrate facts and figures. The third results in an animated prototypical interface. All three assignments are designed to put time-based design in the context of visual explanation.

## goals of the course

- To explore the visualization of information across a variety of media
- To investigate various methods of organizing and presenting data
- To become adept at the transfer of complex information in a clear, concise, and visual way
- To consider design from a user-centered point of view
- To become sensitive to the strengths and limitations of differing communication media

- To effectively use motion and sound in the presentation of information over time
- To promote clarity and usability in the creation of on-screen interfaces.

# Deadlines

Important course deadlines are below. See projects for week-by-week schedule.

**WEEK 1.** Introduction to assignment one.

**WEEK 4.** Final critique for assignment one. Introduction to assignment two.

**WEEK 9.** Introduction to assignment three.

**WEEK 10.** Final critique for assignment two.

**WEEK 12.** Final critique for assignment three.

# assignment process and schedule

## Assignment One

**Overview.** Students will create a printed diagram that visually explains the correct operation of a simple object to a person who has never encountered that object before and does not know its need, its function, or its use.

201

The core of this assignment is learning to communicate a complicated sequence of ideas and events through purely visual means. It will require you to test and observe how a familiar object is used, then explore a variety of visual treatments to convey that process to an audience in the clearest and most communicative way.

**Objectives.** Students will learn to communicate fluently without words; to become familiar with ordering, presenting, and sequencing information; to explore methods of conveying time, action, and sequence across a static medium; to challenge assumptions about what your audience does, and does not, know; to render objects in the most appropriate and approachable way; to examine the use of abstract—and not so abstract—symbols in instructional applications.

**Specifications.** The format and orientation of this diagram is dependent upon the chosen object. All diagrams are to be output at 11 × 17 inches or larger. Use of words or numbers is strictly forbidden. Limit yourself to a maximum of two colors (in an unlimited amount of tints).

**Reading List:**
Mijksenaar, Paul, and Piet Westendorp, *Open Here*, Joost Elffers Books, 1999.
McCloud, Scott, *Understanding Comics*, Perennial Press, 1994.

**WEEK 1.** Discussion: Introduction to assignment one. Discussion about visual narrative and the "language" of comic art.

Project Notes: Select an object that has a singular function. Observe and consider its use. Ask the following questions: How do I explain the value of the function of this item? Why would one use it? How do I illustrate how this object interacts with the human body? How do I show its scale? How do I explain the process of using the item? Can its use be broken down into a set of logical steps? If so, what is the most important element or action that needs to be explained in each step?

Start your investigation with photography. Document the object with a digital camera to identify how many steps are necessary to portray your object's use. Add or delete photographs as needed to establish a series of essential points in time that clearly illustrate the process from beginning to end. Once complete, photograph the same points in time from varied points of view (close-up, extreme close-up, long shot, viewed from above or below, etc.). Explore as many vantage points as possible.

Review your photographic materials and consider the following questions: What vantage point and scale is most useful to illustrate each particular action in the sequence? Are certain steps more important than others? How can emphasis and hierarchy be shown within each step and within the composition as a whole? How does one illustrate motion, action, and intent? How does the user understand the result or resolution of the process? How can the eye be guided through the process correctly? What is the most appropriate graphic form in which to represent this object?

Answer the questions above by drawing. Using the photographic footage as a template, begin sketching. Work large. Consider the differing strengths of realistic, hyperrealistic, and abstract forms of representation in explaining your process. Can certain objects or actions be simplified, exploded, made transparent, made larger or smaller, etc., in service to the overall clarity of the explanation? Work through several iterations of the diagram. When the sketch is working effectively, create—using pencils, markers, and other hand tools—one single, clean, large (18 × 24 inches or larger) diagram to bring for critique. Do not use the computer in the creation of the preliminary diagram.

Next Steps: Large hand-rendered sketch due for next critique.

**WEEK 2.** Critique: Hand-rendered usage diagrams.

Next Steps: Based upon feedback during critique, make necessary corrections to the hand-drawn diagram. Once complete, use the sketch as a template to produce a vector drawing in Illustrator. Use only two PMS colors in the construction of the piece. Consider the composition of your diagram in relation to the page as a whole. Think carefully about how color, texture, and shading can guide the user, show hierarchy, and create focus. Bring a carefully tiled, full size, color diagram for next critique.

**WEEK 3.** Critique: Large-scale, digitally-produced diagrams.

Next Steps: Based upon feedback received in critique, complete diagram to final form.

**WEEK 4, Part A.** Critique: Final digitally-produced diagrams.

## Assignment Two

**Overview.** This assignment investigates the transformation of raw data into comprehensible information. The first phase of the assignment entails gathering a simple data set and defining methods to structure that data. The second phase involves extracting findings from the data and conveying that information clearly (through numeric representation) and engagingly (through design and metaphor) via time-based media.

**Objectives.** Students will gather a collection of abstract data; develop unique and appropriate methods of structuring and filtering data; become familiar with ordering, presenting, and sequencing information within static and dynamic media; consider the appropriateness of each medium in relation to given content; transfer complex information visually in a clear and concise way; use motion and sound as tools to clarify and contextualize visual information.

### Reading List:

Tufte, Edward R., *Envisioning Information*, Graphics Press, 1990.
Tufte, Edward R., *The Visual Display of Quantitative Information*, Graphics Press, 2001.
Wurman, Richard Saul, *Understanding USA*, TED Conferences, 1999.

**WEEK 4, Part B.** Discussion: Introduction to assignment two.

Project Notes: The assignment begins with a thorough documentation of your music collection, DVD collection, or video game collection.

Create a detailed record of your collection, noting specific details for each item. What should be recorded for each object? Contemplate the context of how the items in the collection are created, marketed, and used. Do not limit yourself to general facts such as dates and genres, consider personal interactions with these items as well.

Once you have completed a thorough accounting of the items, use the principles of Richard Saul Wurman's L.A.T.C.H. (location, alphabet, time, category, hierarchy) to identify seven unique methods with which you can organize or sort your collection. A certain amount of creative interpretation should be applied when choosing organizational methods. For example, in a collection organized chronologically, items could be put in order by their release date or by the date of purchase. Both methods of organization clarify the collection. One is personal. One is not. For this assignment, both methods are constructive. Be creative in your selection of organizational methods. Pushing beyond the expected will reveal deeper insight into your collection.

Identify seven useful ways with which you re-sort your collection, then design a poster that clearly presents your collection while illustrating how each "entry" in your database (i.e., album, DVD, or video game) relates to each of your seven organizational schemes.

Unlike a computer database, data on paper cannot be re-sorted at will. The challenge of designing this poster lies in creating an understandable structure of information that clearly presents all seven data relationships simultaneously. This requires placing the chosen sorting methods into a hierarchy. What organizational methods are most important based upon your opinion as to how others should view this collection?

For example, if a record collection is organized by the following seven parameters (i.e., each album is tagged with the following "metadata"):

1. Name of artist
2. Name of album
3. Date album released
4. Number of tracks
5. Genre
6. Number of times played (personal)
7. Date album purchased (personal)

the designer may decide that item one is the most useful method of organizing the collection, six is the second most important, and five is the third most important. This hierarchy might lead to a tabular chart with the albums listed in alphabetical order with subgroupings like five visualized within the overall structure via formal relationships— color, scale, typography, etc.

This poster should clearly present the collection and allow an audience to compare and contrast the various methods of organization that have been established. It should be a model of typographic design, easy to use, easy to understand, and easy to look at. The chart may be necessarily tabular, but consider how to handle such forms in an engaging and visual way (but not at the expense of usability!).

Next Steps: Preliminary poster sketches due for next critique.

**WEEK 5.** Critique: Draft poster sketches.

Next Steps: Based upon feedback received during critique, complete your diagram to final form.

**WEEK 6.** Critique: Final posters.

Project Notes: The second phase of the assignment comprises extracting meaning from the organized data and presenting it via a time-based medium.

Identify three facts, stories, or threads made apparent through the organization of your data that convey the nuances of your collection. These facts should be quantitative in nature (relating to, measuring, or measured by the quantity of something, rather than its quality) and supported by some type of empirical or measurable data. For example, your analysis may reveal that "while less than one percent of my collection is of The Beatles, over 30 percent of the collection are artists who have stated they were heavily influenced by The Beatles." Consider many different ways that quantitative relationships can be pulled out of your collection. Do not limit yourself only to simple percentages.

Each of the three facts must stand on its own as an understandable unit of information while relating to others in the series. The facts should be written so that they work together outlining a specific point of view or observation about your entire collection.

Once the three factual statements are identified, consider how each can be transformed into a simple narrative or motion sequence. Sequences must convey the quantitative information of the fact—via a chart, graph, or other clear visual representation of mathematical data—while conveying an emotional or expressive (qualitative) perspective or point of view. Carefully consider your overall concept in the way that these sequences build to a climax. How can these facts be placed in context for an average audience? How can viewers be influenced to feel a certain way about this information?

Begin with a storyboard. Draw a linear sequence of rectangles in the proportion of the computer screen on a large sheet of paper. Working left to right, fill these rectangles with keyframes—important points in time in your movie. Work chronologically. Make notes alongside the sequence regarding issues of motion and sound. Be attentive to how sound is applied. Why show something that is more easily understood through listening?

Traditional narratives have a clear beginning, middle, and end. Consider this in your sequence. You are not required to have a traditional "plot," however. Your information might be better served (and your animation more forceful) with a sequence that simply sets a scene (visualizes some data) and then breaks the scene (transforms that data) to make your point. A clear, elegant sequence will have a great deal more impact than a long, complex narrative. Keep things simple.

Be mindful about how motion, transformation, scaling, depth, color, typography, and sound are utilized throughout your sequences in support of your concept. Examine some of the quantitative properties of your medium as well—the size of the screen or the running length of the sequence—as these values can be put into service to help illustrate numeric relationships.

Next Steps: Preliminary storyboards due for next critique.

**WEEK 7.** Critique: Discussion of factual concepts and preliminary storyboards.

Next Steps: Produce three draft animatics in After Effects for next meeting. Draft QuickTime files are to be produced at NTSC/DV aspect ratio and resolution. Total running length of the combined three sequences must be thirty seconds or less.

**WEEK 8.** Critique: Animatic sequences.

Next Steps: Based upon feedback received during critique, move your animated sequences toward final form. Polished sequences, with sound, are due for next class meeting.

**WEEK 9, Part A.** Critique: Animated sequences.

Next Steps: Based upon feedback received during critique, produce animations to final form. Final animations should be rendered at full NTSC/DV aspect ratio and resolution and compressed with the DV codec.

**WEEK 10, Part A.** Critique: Final animated sequences.

## Assignment Three

**Overview.** When learning to create experiences that effectively transform information into knowledge, it is beneficial to analyze objects and processes that fall short or are otherwise unsuccessful. This assignment requires the examination of a powerful interactive tool hampered by a confusing interface and challenges you to improve its effectiveness.

The Godine Library of the Massachusetts College of Art is a member of the Fenway Libraries Online Consortium (FLO), a collaboration between nine libraries within the city of Boston that allow students of the member organizations to treat them as one large virtual institution. The online catalog for this consortium is an essential tool for this collaboration, allowing students to search for library materials throughout the city.

Unfortunately, few students take advantage of these shared resources. Many are not willing to move off their own campuses to retrieve their research materials, even if those materials are located in a neighbor institution right down the street. Exacerbating this problem is the online catalog itself, which does not facilitate easy searches, returns confusing results, and does not promote the ease in which many of these materials can be retrieved.

Your assignment is to undertake a careful audit of the current search experience and, based upon your observations, propose a new interface that meets the following goals:

- Clarify the entire search process.
- Reconsider the current methods for specifying how search results are generated (keyword, author, subject, etc.) based upon your research into the specific libraries in the consortium and their unique user bases.
- Refine how search results are grouped and presented, with a focus on clarity and ease of use.
- Facilitate the filtering of search results by the physical location of the materials within the city of Boston.
- Visualize search items in the context of where they are located in physical space.

Possibilities include organizing materials by library, showing the location of the selected material in relation to the user's location, or identifying where the book is located within a specific library's physical space.

**Objectives.** Students will analyze a current interface to information and identify its strengths and weaknesses; examine the experience of an interface and evaluate the processes that comprise it; present data and information in a clear and usable way; develop a consistent system of visual hierarchy and grouping for search results; explore how information can be contextualized via its representation within physical space; design and produce a prototypical interface that can be tested and critiqued.

**Specifications.** Preliminary interface designs are to be sketched in Photoshop or Illustrator. Once the visual design of the user scenario is complete, an interactive prototype will be authored in Flash. Interfaces are to be sized at 800 pixels wide by 600 pixels tall.

## Reading List:

Krug, Steve, *Don't Make Me Think: A Common Sense Approach to Web Usability*, New Riders, 2000.

Garett, Jesse James, *The Elements of User Experience*, New Riders, 2002.

**WEEK 9, Part B.** Discussion: Introduction to assignment three.

Next Steps: First, identify the key processes that this catalog requires and reconsider how users are led through those steps. Second, analyze how returned information is presented and experiment with different methods of clarifying the results. When complete, transform your thinking into a draft user scenario that illustrates, screen by screen, a newly redesigned and clarified visual search process. Your scenario should illustrate the process of a single user identifying and locating the library resource she needs by working her way step-by-step through the interface.

**WEEK 10, Part B.** Critique: Preliminary user scenario.

Next Steps: Based upon feedback during critique, make necessary corrections and additions to your user scenario. Once the core usability issues are solved, import the screens into Flash and create a basic click-through prototype of your interface.

207

**WEEK 11.** Critique: Interface prototypes.

In Class: User testing.

Next Steps: Based upon feedback during critique—and insight received via testing—make necessary modifications to your prototype to bring it to final form.

**WEEK 12.** Critique: Final interface prototypes.

# section 4

seniors

COURSE TITLE: Animation Action Analysis 2

TEACHER: John Canemaker

FREQUENCY: One Semester, once a week

LEVEL: Junior/Senior

CREDITS: 3

DEGREE: Bachelor of Fine Arts in Film

SCHOOL: New York University, Tisch School of the Arts, Kanbar Institute of Film and Television, Animation Studies, New York, NY

## objective

A workshop exploring personality animation; applicable to both 2-D and 3-D techniques.

- INJECT the spark of life into your animated characters.
- GIVE your cartoons, puppets, and computer creatures individuality.
- ANIMATE characters that appear to think and express emotions.

## format

The course consists of lectures, analyzing of live-action/animated films, and demonstrations of technique by the teacher. Students will present assigned exercises endowing a thought-process and emotions to characters.

## evaluation

Each student will be graded upon the following criteria:

- Attendance and class participation: 50%
- Homework assignments and completion of film/video project: 50%

## week by week

Below is the weekly class schedule. Lectures are subject to change, but student tests are due during the classes indicated.

**WEEK 1.** Orientation. Reiteration of principles of character animation. Screen excerpts from *The Rescuers Down Under* (boy and eagle); *Felix the Cat*.

**WEEK 2.** Student video test #1 due: a character drinks a cocktail and then discovers it is milk.

**WEEK 3.** Lecture on Vladimir Tytla. Screen excerpts: *Snow White* (Grumpy's kiss); *Pinocchio* (Stromboli sequence); "Night on Bald Mountain" (Devil) from *Fantasia; Dumbo* (bath sequence).

**WEEK 4.** Student test #2 due: a villain gloats over stolen treasure, then becomes suspicious and hides it.

**WEEK 5.** Student test #3 due: character enters with vase, trips, and vase breaks.

**WEEK 6.** Lecture on Chuck Jones: *What's Opera Doc?*; *One Froggy Evening*; *Duck Amuck*; Wile E. Coyote.

**WEEK 7.** Student test #4 due: shy character offers a flower and is rejected.

**WEEK 8.** Lecture on Frank Thomas. *The Sword in the Stone* (squirrels); *Snow White* (dwarfs weep); *Bambi* (ice skating).

**WEEK 9.** Student test #5 due: a character mails a love letter.

**WEEK 10.** Lecture on Milt Kahl. *Pinocchio* (Jiminy gets dressed); *The Rescuers* (Medusa); analyze the narrative structure and its movement in *The Jungle Book*.

**WEEK 11.** Student test #6 due: witch/fairy tries magic wand that, at first, doesn't work.

**WEEK 12.** Lecture on Ward Kimball: *The Three Caballeros* (title song); *Alice in Wonderland* (Cheshire Cat); *Cinderella* (cat and cups).

**WEEK 13.** Student test #7: lip sync of witch from *The Wizard of Oz*.

# recommended readings

Canemaker, John, *Walt Disney's Nine Old Men and the Art of Animation*, Disney Editions, 2001.

Hooks, Ed, *Acting for Animators*, Heinemann Publishing, 2001.

Jones, Chuck, *Chuck Amuck*, Farrar, Straus and Giroux, 1999.

Thomas, Frank, and Ollie Johnston, *The Illusion of Life: Disney Animation*, Hyperion, 1981.

**COURSE TITLE:** Pictorial Background Illustration

**TEACHER:** Cliff Cramp

**FREQUENCY:** One Semester

**LEVEL:** Senior

**CREDITS:** 3 (six studio hours)

**DEGREE:** Bachelor of Fine Arts

**SCHOOL:** California State University, Fullerton, CA

## course description

This course will be both an individual and a collaborative effort through the exploration of rendering and painting background environments. The following concepts will be discussed as they relate to story: design, use of color, value, perspective, theatrical composition and lighting, and stylization. We will also further your abilities in drawing and painting processes, and discuss portfolio presentation.

**Objectives.** This course will expose you to the conception and development of background environments for figurative images through a variety of pictorial strategies in landscape, architecture, and objects. It will demonstrate how the background can enhance your subject and teach skills applicable to animation, picture books, illustration, comic art, and any art that requires a setting for a subject.

**Prerequisites.** Traditional Illustration (ART 363A) plus three upper-division units in area emphasis (Illustration or Entertainment Art/Animation) or equivalent.

## coursework

1. A completed sketchbook journal (please draw fast and furious during the first half of the semester so that when crunch time comes, you won't be filled with regrets). Your sketchbook is a record of your notes, research, and conceptual studies. Bring it to each class meeting.

2. The sharing of your visual research with the class by posting photocopies on the classroom wall of your work and of found visual resources so others can draw inspiration from your efforts.

3. Five or more painted sky studies

Five or more painted texture studies

One painted copy of a provided color work

One painting from a provided layout

Six environments in graphite or Prismacolor, then four painted

4. The work listed above and several of your preliminary studies will make up your final portfolio, which you will turn in on the day of the final.

5. Regular class attendance.

6. A compilation of images by ten or more artists who produce environments for film (live action or animation), stage, television, and book illustration. Give each artist a minimum of three pages, which will include a title page, information on each artist, and several relevant reproductions of their work. Turn this in on the day of the final. This project will be worth 10% of your grade.

## grading

All grading is based on the quality of the finished art and the support sketches produced. The following elements are considered.

- Quality of concepts relative to the stage that is set
- Quality and understanding of techniques
- Quality of compositional arrangement/design
- Quality of presentation

## course breakdown

The semester activities will be broken down into three phases:

1. Research and painting practices. Research is the gathering of material information you use as visual references. We will jump into painting practices right away, developing technical and conceptual painting skills.
2. Layout and layout transfer. Development of your own layouts, architectural and landscape.
3. The painted background. We will continue the process by combining phases one and two to produce a finished piece based on your layout.

## week by week

**WEEK 1.** Introduction

**WEEKS 2–7.** Research and Development
The vast majority of your research should be gathered at this time.

1. Sky studies. Five or more finished paintings of skies with consideration for time of day and atmospheric conditions.

2. Texture painting. Five or more finished texture paintings of rocks, stones, bricks, wooden planks, and so on, with consideration for weathering, age, and lighting.
3. Copy painting. We will combine the techniques learned in our first two exercises to produce a copy of a finished painting. You will need to match the painting precisely.
4. Painting from provided layout. Produce three different color keys. We will discuss which color key provides the strongest story elements. Complete the final painting.

**WEEKS 6–11.** Development of the Layout

1. Emphasis on perspective drawing
2. Development of props
3. Value studies with a concentration on dramatic lighting and staging
4. Continued development of atmospheric conditions

The layouts produced during this section of the course will deal with both architectural elements and landscape treatments.

**WEEKS 9–16.** Paint Application

Continued development of atmospheric conditions, color theme, paint application, value, texture, etc.

# health and safety

Many art materials are potentially dangerous. For your good health and for those around you, please read all labels and exercise good judgment. If you are working with an airbrush, make sure that you wear a respirator. Spray adhesives and fixatives must be used at home.

# studio care

This room is used by a variety of classes, so please pick up after yourself. Anything brought in with you should leave with you. Cutting with X-acto blades directly on desk surfaces is not permitted.

# penalties for academic dishonesty

Students who submit work that is not theirs, that is for another class but is claimed to be for this course, or that is plagiarized from another artist will receive an F on that project and their final grade for the course will automatically be lowered one full letter. If it happens on more the one project, the student will receive an F for the semester grade.

COURSE TITLE: Film Language

TEACHER: Carl F. (Skip) Battaglia

FREQUENCY: Winter Quarter

LEVEL: Senior

CREDITS: 2

DEGREE: Bachelor of Fine Arts

SCHOOL: Rochester Institute of Technology, College of Imaging Arts and Sciences, School of Film and Animation, Rochester, NY

## course description

A screenings, readings, and writing course designed to give the student the opportunity to trace the development of the techniques and forms of communication in what now constitutes the classic cinema.

Topics covered:

- The basics of style: formalism vs. realism
- The growth of narrative detail and intimacy on films: the psychological close-up
- Editing for ideas: Soviet montage
- *Mise-en-scene* and meaning: surrealism and German expressionism
- Narrative "story" and narrative "voice": the development of first-person narrative, the "cover" or "frame" story
- Motifs and their purposes
- *Citizen Kane* as a textbook of film usage
- The influence of *Citizen Kane*: film noir, American expressionism, the mixture of film styles, the reliance on technique
- Film genre and audience purpose
- The moving camera and its uses
- Every film makes its own style

At the conclusion of the course, the student will be able to:

- Apply the correct term for a specific media effect
- Comprehend a variety of narrative possibilities and a number of audio-visual solutions to a problem
- Develop the ability to make reference to and discuss a body of "classic" films

- Analyze, in writing, specific thematic problems as they relate to film
- Understand that film is a cultural product created by the interrelations of artists, audience, and technology

Except for handouts, all readings are from Giannetti's *Understanding Movies* (9th edition). "G" indicates the assignment pages from the 8th edition. If you have purchased a more current edition, you will have to identify the appropriate sections for study.

# week by week

There are two types of class meetings: the class lecture (in which often a short film will be screened) with class discussion Monday mornings and a separate class screening of a feature-length film to be attended on Monday evenings. Classes begin on time.

## Photography, Frame, Movement

**WEEK 1 LECTURE.** Lumière shorts, directed by Louis and Auguste Lumière (France) 1895–1903

"Excerpts from *Lumière & Co.*, various directors (France) 1995

Reading: Chapter 1: "Photography," chapter 2: "Mise-en-Scene"

**WEEK 1 SCREENING.** *The General*, directed by Buster Keaton (USA) 1927

**WEEK 2 LECTURE.** Editing 1: Continuity and The Psychological Close-Up
Méliès' shorts, directed by Georges Méliès (France) 1901–4
*Dream of a Rarebit Fiend*, directed by Edwin S. Porter (USA) 1908; or *The Great Train Robbery*, directed by Edwin S. Porter (USA) 1903
Reading: Chapter 3: "Movement" and pages 359–64 for "The Classical Paradigm" in chapter 8: "Story"

**WEEK 2 SCREENING.** *The Battleship Potemkin*, directed by Sergei Eisenstein (USSR) 1925

**WEEK 3 LECTURE.** Editing 2: Vectors, Graphics, Associations, and Rhythms
"The Odessa Steps Sequence" from *The Battleship Potemkin*
Film Graphics: Abstract Aspects of Editing
Also: A short animated film by Paul Glabicki
Reading: Chapter 4: "Editing," especially the *North by Northwest* storyboard
Compare the written script sequences in G.: Chapter 9: "Writing," pages 404–9 and see caption under production still from "Caligari" on page 327

**WEEK 3 SCREENING.** *The Cabinet of Dr. Caligari*, directed by Robert Wiene, (Germany) 1919

**WEEK 4 LECTURE.** American Expressionism I

"Lullaby of Broadway," excerpt from *The Golddiggers of 1933*, directed by Merwyn LeRoy, choreography by Busby Berkeley (USA) 1933

*Metropolis*, directed by Fritz Lang (Germany) 1927?

PAPER 1 DUE in class

Reading: Chapter 12: "Synthesis: *Citizen Kane*"

**WEEK 4 SCREENING.** *Citizen Kane*, directed by Orson Welles (USA) 1940

**WEEK 5 LECTURE.** American Expressionism 2: Germany and the USA

Excerpt from *Citizen Kane*, directed by Orson Welles (USA) 1940

*Parataxis*, directed by Skip Battaglia (USA) 1980

Reading: Chapter 5: "Sound," chapter 6: "Acting," and handout: "Some Visual Motifs of Film Noir" by Janey Place and Lowell Peterson from *Film Comment* (vol. 10, no. 1, January–February 1974)

**WEEK 5 SCREENING.** *Double Indemnity*, directed by Billy Wilder (USA) 1944

**WEEK 6 LECTURE.** The American Film after *Citizen Kane*: film noir, gothic, and first-person narrative

*A Touch of Evil* (opening), directed by Orson Welles (USA) 1956

A short animated film from "Cartoon Noir" (DVD) compilation (USA) 1999

Readings: Chapter 11: "Critique," pages 474–88

**WEEK 6 SCREENING.** *Psycho*, directed by Alfred Hitchcock (USA) 1960

**WEEK 7 LECTURE.** Realism and The Western

Excerpt from *Paisan*, directed by Roberto Rossellini (Italy) 1946

PAPER 2 DUE in class

Reading: Chapter 7: "Drama," chapter 8: "Story"

**WEEK 7 SCREENING.** *Unforgiven*, directed by Clint Eastwood (USA) 1992

**WEEK 8 LECTURE.** Fantasy and Naturalism

*Moulin Rouge*, directed by Baz Luhrman (USA) 2001

*Invasion of the Body Snatchers*, directed by Don Siegel (USA) 1956

Reading: Chapter 11: "Critique" (remainder), chapter 10: "Ideology"

**WEEK 8 SCREENING.** *What's Eating Gilbert Grape?*, Lasse Halström (USA) 1993

**WEEK 9 LECTURE.** American Realism

Excerpts from *What's Eating Gilbert Grape?*

Excerpts from *Pleasantville*, directed by Gary Ross (USA) 1998

Reading: Chapter 9: "Writing"

**WEEK 9 SCREENING.** *Wings of Desire*, directed by Wim Wenders (West Germany) 1988

**WEEK 10 LECTURE.** Alone

*Life Wastes Andy Hardy*, directed by Martin Arnold (Austria) 1997

PAPER 3 DUE in class

FINAL EXAM on readings and terminology to be taken in morning class

"That's all, Folks."

## grading

Paper 1: 15%
Paper 2: 25%
Paper 3: 35%
Class final exam: 25%

The papers are assigned throughout the quarter; each paper assigned has increasing numerical importance. These papers are to be short and to the point: three pages each, maximum. Each paper will be designed to answer a specific question raised by the viewings, the readings, or the lectures.

## a final note

Although the class material is entertaining, the films are not offered for enjoyment alone. The films and videos must be regarded as data to be examined. If you attend all screenings and view the materials in the passive-responsive state of a "naive" movie audience, and you have not prepared yourself with study and a critical eye, much of the educational purpose of these screenings will be lost.

You must not only view the films *but also* view yourself, examining your responses and anticipations, as you view the films.

I look forward to working with you all.

## required readings

Giannetti, Louis D., *Understanding Movies*, 9th ed., Prentice Hall, 2001.

*All* of Giannetti will be read out of sequence. One week of course work covers topics roughly related in theory and production to one decade of the development of syntax in the hundred-year history of motion pictures. It is *essential* that you read the assigned selections and handouts for the next week's class discussion and view the provided films with a questioning, critical frame of mind. Attendance is required.

## recommended readings

Read the national and local movie reviews available on current films, especially and always those that you view in the theaters. Such journals would be the *Democrat and*

*Chronicle, City Newspaper*, the *New York Times*, the *Village Voice, Premiere, Film Comment, Time, Newsweek*, various Web blogs and postings, etc.

Read everything to do with filmmaking, film theory, and critique. Filmmakers and video makers read and discuss what other producers have written and said. To read the primary insights of a filmmaker will assist your own production as it forms your opinion and sharpens your critical ideas. Read so that you will not expensively repeat the mistakes of others.

COURSE TITLE: Advanced Time-Based Design: Typography and Imagery

TEACHER: Peter Byrne

FREQUENCY: Spring Semester

LEVEL: Senior, ten weeks, twice a week for three hours (Introduction to Time-Based Design or permission of the instructor prerequisite)

CREDITS: 3

DEGREE: Bachelor of Fine Arts

SCHOOL: Rochester Institute of Technology, Rochester, NY

## description

This course will provide students with an opportunity to refine and develop time-based design skills. Students will develop their skills using time, motion, and sequencing as they apply to typography and imagery. Projects will include typography and imagery components, storyboard planning, and computer-based applications as they apply to graphic design problem solving.

219

## goals and objectives

Specific competencies:

- To develop and refine planning and organizing skills for time-based projects
- To develop and refine visualization skills through storyboard planning
- To develop and refine motion and sequencing skills for graphic design problem solving
- To explore and develop time-based image manipulation and compositing techniques
- To effectively combine type with imagery
- To demonstrate technical familiarity with relevant time-based software

General competencies:

- To demonstrate creative problem solving, concept development, and critical thinking skills
- To intelligently select and use appropriate tools, materials, and production methods
- To show a refinement of skills in research, verbal and written articulation, and presentation

- To demonstrate an ability to effectively analyze and critique solutions based on established criteria and goals
- To demonstrate an ability to work effectively as a team player—in project teams or as an individual class participant

# project 1: typographic sequence—conversation*

Intonation is the sound pattern of phrases and sentences produced by pitch variation in the voice, the modulation of the voice.

Intonation can be used to express meaning. Think of the many ways you could say the word "yes" to convey meaning. You could shout it out as an expression of joy, you could utter it as a question to express doubt, or you could use it as a reply to communicate affirmation. Words can be animated to communicate intonation.

Using typography, sequencing, and animation, design and produce a visual conversation between two or more people. Visually differentiate each voice or character. Utilize type characteristics, sequencing, composition, movement, timing, rhythm, and pace. The emphasis in this project is typographic.

You may use simple imagery or graphic support elements. The final project will be in QuickTime movie format.

Objectives:

220

- Develop planning and organizing skills through storyboarding.
- Develop and refine typography motion and sequencing skills.
- Effectively use timing, rhythm, and pace to visually communicate intonation.
- Become familiar with using After Effects software.

Process: Working from a video, DVD, script, or play, find a short conversation between two or more people and transcribe it. Write a short paragraph describing the conversation and outline your design concept. Make a list of keywords that apply to your project.

Design a storyboard, outlining and describing the sequence. The storyboard should be in black marker. Use notation symbols such as arrows and other vectors to indicate movement (motion vectors). Do the notations in red. The storyboard will be refined and developed as you move through the project. Produce and refine your piece in Photoshop and After Effects. Present the finished work in class.

## Week by Week

**WEEK 1.** Project overview, lecture

Lecture, demonstration

In-class exercise: One Word, Many Intonations

*This project was inspired by a project example in the book* Moving Type: Designing for Time and Space *by Jeff Bellantoni and Matt Woolman.*

**WEEK 2.** Outline, keywords and storyboard due for review, work on project

Work on project

**WEEK 3.** Review, work on project

Project due, critique

# project 2: imagery sequence—sense of place

Sense of place is a quality that makes a place special or distinctive. It is a characteristic that fosters a sense of genuine attachment and belonging.

Using digital photographs, design and produce a motion sequence that communicates and depicts a sense of place. It could be your dorm room, apartment, the campus, your neighborhood, where you work, etc. Choose a place that you are very familiar with.

Use still digital photographs as your source files. Take high-resolution digital photographs. Images that are of a larger pixel dimension than the movie format can be panned and zoomed (change of scale) to simulate camera movement.

Incorporate simple transitions. Use image manipulation to emphasize visual, formal continuity and contrast. The emphasis in this project is on the imagery. Incorporate typography using words from your keywords list. The final project will be in QuickTime movie format.

221

Objectives:

- Develop planning and organizational skills through storyboarding.
- Develop and refine motion and sequencing skills.
- Effectively use panning and zooming techniques for motion sequences using still imagery.
- Effectively use timing, rhythm, and pace.
- Explore and develop image manipulation and compositing techniques.
- Effectively combine type with imagery.
- Become familiar with using After Effects software.

Process: Find a place that you want to depict. Write a short paragraph describing the place and outline your design concept. Make a list of keywords that apply to your project. Take a series of digital photographs. Design a storyboard outlining and describing the sequence. Produce and refine your work in Photoshop and After Effects. Final projects will be presented in class.

## Week by Week

**WEEK 4.** Project overview, lecture

Lecture, demonstration

In-class exercise: One Image, Panning and Zooming

**WEEK 5.** Outline, keywords and storyboard due for review, work on project
Work on project

**WEEK 6.** Review, work on project
Project due, critique

# project 3: typography and imagery sequence

Select either a poem, lyrics from a song, or a short passage of prose. Design and produce a typography and imagery sequence based on your chosen text. Focus on communicating and evoking the tone, ambience, and atmosphere of the text.

Create your own imagery (photographs, graphics, drawings, illustrations, etc.) Working with sound is an option. If you do, select your sound early, as it will guide your transitions and editing. The final project will be in QuickTime movie format.

Objectives:

- Develop planning and organizational skills through storyboarding.
- Develop and refine motion and sequencing skills.
- Effectively use panning and zooming techniques for motion sequences using still imagery.
- Effectively use timing, rhythm, and pace.
- Explore and develop image manipulation and compositing techniques.
- Effectively combine type with imagery.
- Effectively integrate sound, type, and imagery
- Become familiar with using After Effects software.

Process: Choose your text. Write a short paragraph describing the tone of the text and outline your design concept. Make a list of keywords that apply to your project. Design a storyboard outlining and describing the sequence. Produce and refine your piece in Photoshop and After Effects. Final projects will be presented in class.

## Week by Week

**WEEK 7.** Project overview, lecture
Lecture, demonstration

**WEEK 8.** Outline, keywords and storyboard due for review, work on project
Work on project

**WEEK 9.** Work on project
Review, work on project

**WEEK 10.** Work on project
Project due, critique

## summary and goals

This course is an introduction to time-based screen typography and motion design. We explore design issues related to animating type: character, context, emotion, montage, motion, narrative, rhythm, time, transformation, and voice. The emphasis of the course is creating meaning with motion, based on content.

Outcomes: Understanding After Effects, principles of animation, and screen/motion design

Technology: Macintosh OSX, After Effects, Illustrator, Photoshop, and Apple iMovie

Student requirements: Basic knowledge of Illustrator, Photoshop, and typography

## week by week

**WEEK 1.** Introduce project assignment 1, Explaining Resolution: Context and Understanding

Discuss After Effects interface, preparing and importing footage

Video: Eames, *Powers of Ten*

**WEEK 2.** Discuss managing footage and compositions; creating and modifying layers

Sketches due to class Weblog

**WEEK 3.** Discuss properties and keyframes; playback and previews

**WEEK 4.** Discuss rendering

Submit and discuss completed assignments

**WEEK 5.** Introduce project assignment 2, Seeing Voices: Typography and Music

Discuss type, legibility and color; drawing from external sources (Hiebert, "Drawing from Music" from *Graphic Design Sources*)

**WEEK 6.** Discuss visualizing sound and music (Armstrong, "Hearing Type" from *Baseline*); space: structure and frame
> Sketches due to class Weblog
> Video: Malinowski, *Music Animation Machine*

**WEEK 7.** Discuss typographic form and meaning; character, emotion, rhythm, and voice (Ishizaki, "On Kinetic Typography" from *Statements*)
> Submit and discuss completed assignments

**WEEK 8.** Introduce project assignment 3, Playing Sports: Force and Motion
> Discuss kinetics: force and motion; keyframe interpolation

**WEEK 9.** Discuss transformation and sequence: time and motion
> Sketches due to class Weblog

**WEEK 10.** Discuss masks and effects

**WEEK 11.** Discuss managing complex projects
> Submit and discuss completed assignments

**WEEK 12.** Introduce project assignment 4, Telling Stories: Metaphor and Montage
> Discuss metaphors (Shedroff, "Metaphors" from *Experience Design*); narrative: film and theater (Helfand, "New Media, New Narrative: The Lost Legacy of Film" from *Screen*)

**WEEK 13.** Discuss montage (Eisenstein, "Methods of Montage" from *Film Form and Film Sense*); screen space (Helfand, "Dematerialization of Screen Space" from *Screen*)
> Sketches due to class Weblog

**WEEK 14.** Discuss dynamic language (Helfand, "Electronic Typography: The New Visual Language" from *Screen*); context and content (Worthington, "Entranced by Motion, Seduced by Stillness" from *Eye*)

**WEEK 15.** Discuss form and content
> Submit and discuss completed assignments

# projects

### Project 1: Explaining Resolution: Context and Understanding

This project assignment will introduce fundamental concepts of animation and working with After Effects. Explaining complex information through dynamic diagrams is an important application of time-based media. The *Powers of Ten* video-animation provides a context that enhances the meaning and understanding of changes in the frame of reference. In the area of digital prepublishing, resolution is one of the most difficult concepts to understand because there are three distinct frames of reference (nested levels): dots-per-inch, lines-per-inch, and pixels-per-inch. Create a twelve-second animation using static images and typography to explain the relationship between the three nested levels of resolution.

## Project 2: Seeing Voices: Typography and Music

This project assignment will introduce fundamental concepts of typographic form, space, structure, gesture, and voice within the context of an animated typographic composition. Acoustic (spoken) languages and music are rich with variation in emphasis, gesture, rhythm, and tempo. Since typography is a visual representation of our spoken language, we'll explore analogies between acoustic and visual space.

Select a twenty-second segment of nonvocal music and a brief written text (prose or poetry) or quotation. Translate the text into a time-based, synchronized typographic composition that expresses the meaning of the message. Demonstrate how elements of time and motion can change and enhance meaning. Consider each of the following spatial and temporal design issues (Ishizaki, "On Kinetic Typography" from *Statements*) in the development of your composition:

- Character: a similarity of typographic characteristics (font, size, color, etc.), creating unity and a unique identity for a single voice among a series of messages
- Emotion: a typographic gesture (qualitative), created by modifying spatial or temporal properties
- Kinetic form and content: creating a correspondence between spatial and temporal properties, context and the intended meaning of a message
- Rhythm: temporal organization of typography, created by variations in the duration of presence and absence within the frame of a composition
- Tone of voice: variations in degree of emphasis (quantitative) within a message, created by modifying spatial or temporal properties

225

## Project 3: Playing Sports: Force and Motion

This project assignment will introduce fundamental concepts of physics (kinetics) and sequence within the context of a time-based composition. Since the motion of objects in physical (three-dimensional) space is based on the application of various forces (gravity, etc.), understanding this process will help you to animate typography in a two-dimensional space (through a sequence of frames) in a way that more closely resembles the movement of actual objects and is more consistent with a viewer's expectations. Sports, particularly ball games, contain myriad examples of force and motion with variations in emphasis, rhythm, and tempo.

Create text (what, when, and where) and design a promotional animation for a fictitious traditional (basketball, baseball, soccer, tennis, volleyball, etc.) or extreme (mountain biking, skateboarding, snowboarding, etc.) sporting event. Your time-based typographic composition should demonstrate a balance of kinetic form and content: motion that expresses the meaning of the message.

## Project 4: Telling Stories: Metaphor and Montage

This project assignment will introduce fundamental concepts of visual storytelling (narrative): metaphors and montage in the context of a time-based composition. Telling visual stories implies the passage of time and requires viewers to suspend their tendency toward disbelief. A storyteller creates or modifies meaning by associating or comparing one visual image with another—a spatial or temporal juxtaposition—using context, metaphors, and montages.

Design a film title sequence for an existing film of your choice, integrating text (film title and the name of the director and/or lead actor/actress), sound, and video-graphic images. Actively search for ways to communicate the emotional tone and essential aspects of the film through characteristics of typographic form and motion. Make your composition a unified, multisensory experience, choosing images and music or sounds that reinforce your typographic message and make it more memorable. Create dynamic metaphors or other symbolic images (fragmented or abstracted connotations) for your composition with a digital-video camera. Imagine the frame as a window rather than a room; close-cropped images are usually more effective for title sequences than environmental scenes.

# recommended readings

226

Armstrong, Frank, "Hearing Type," *Baseline*, Autumn 2003, 42.

Eames, Ray, and Charles Eames, *Powers of Ten*, Pyramid Film & Video, 1978.

Eisenstein, Sergei, "Methods of Montage," in *Film Form and Film Sense*, Meridian Books, 1968.

Helfand, Jessica, "New Media, New Narrative: The Lost Legacy of Film," *Screen*, Princeton Architectural Press, 2001.

Ibid., "Dematerialization of Screen Space."

Ibid., "Electronic Typography: The New Visual Language."

Hiebert, Kenneth, "Drawing from Music," in *Graphic Design Sources*, Yale University Press, 1998.

Ishizaki, Suguru, "On Kinetic Typography," *Statements*, newsletter for The American Center for Design 12, no. 1, 1998.

Malinowski, Stephen, *Music Animation Machine*, DVD, Malinowski, 1990.

Meyer, Trish, and Chris Meyer, *Creating Motion Graphics with After Effects*, vol. 1, 3rd ed., CMP Books, 2004.

Shedroff, Nathan, "Metaphors," in *Experience Design 1*, Waite Group Press, 2001.

Woolman, Matt, *Motion Design: Moving Graphics for Television, Music Video, Cinema, and Digital Interfaces*, Rotovision, 2004.

Worthington, Michael, "Entranced by Motion, Seduced by Stillness," *Eye*, Autumn 1999, 33.

COURSE TITLE: Motion Graphics Portfolio

TEACHER: Jeffrey Metzner

FREQUENCY: Fall and Winter Semesters

LEVEL: Seniors (working knowledge of Final Cut Pro and After Effects
   prerequisite)

CREDITS: 3

DEGREE: Bachelor of Fine Arts

SCHOOL: School of Visual Arts, New York, NY

## summary and goals

Art directors/designers composed a page or a poster over a period of time, usually days. They tried the type big, tried the type small, tried different fonts, moved it to the left and to the right, photo-stated photos of art (big, small, medium, color, black and white), and then, with the help of rubber cement and thinner, they moved graphic design elements around until they finally (refined) felt they were communicating what they wanted to communicate and called a project finished.

It was then stopped—frozen in flat time and space on the page.

NOW motion graphics allows you to explore the placement of graphic design elements in time and space with a sound track (sound: which was never a part of graphic design before).

The video may end but it is never stopped—never frozen; always moving.

Motion graphics is the next dimension of graphic design. A student can shoot a video or import a film or video, add typography, photography, animation, art, and a multitude of graphic design elements.

All this, along with a sound track that the student can create or import, results in endless possibilities.

Motion graphics is a new palette and a new form of communication. Because the medium is so new, I insist that the student embraces the idea and ideal of experimentation. My goal for the class is to help the student to be relaxed enough to have the courage to make a personal statement—something emerges.

## assignments

My assignments are geared to force the student to use typography and graphic design elements, as opposed to making short films. This is not a film class or a computer arts class; this is graphic design. First and foremost it is conceptual.

227

Because of the time-consuming nature of motion graphics, I don't have a weekly schedule of events. But there is a proper work order and I allow students to move at their own pace (except for slackers).

**1. The projects.** An example of an assignment could be The ABCs of a pop culture subject that you are interested in (e.g., The ABCs of Graffiti, The ABCs of Poker, The ABCs of Clandestine CIA Activities). See *http://sva-dv.com*.

**2. The treatment.** At least three different ideas need to be submitted to me in written form (a simple paragraph). Because this class meets once a week, the students communicate with me via Internet. We send jpegs and mpegs and QuickTime movies. We have a server where we can post our work.

**3. The storyboard.** The accepted idea is now storyboarded by hand so the student can begin to visualize the sequencing of his idea, and it can be discussed.

**4. Style frames.** Using Photoshop, the student chooses a few frames of the video and creates a close approximation of the way he wants the video to look. This *vision* needs to be created and begun in Photoshop and then extended into the unlimited possibilities of animating in After Effects.

**5. Sound track.** The student needs to create or find the sound track that he wishes to work with. My approval is needed in all these categories. If I am going to work on a project with the student I want to like everything about it, because I'm going to listen to it and see it so many hundreds of times.

Once the idea and storyboard have been approved (2 and 3) the student may begin to shoot video—import film or video—gather all information and convert it to digital. This information is carefully and orderly labeled and batched in Final Cut, allowing easy access to the many files (shots).

**6. Begin the long process of animation using After Effects.** The first five steps occur more or less over the first month of the semester depending on my approvals. The animation process depends on the difficulty of what the student is trying to accomplish.

It is a long, arduous creative process, and even rendering each sequence is extremely time consuming. The project is finished when I say so; it can take anywhere from weeks to months, depending on the scope of the idea.

# the projects

All solutions to projects start with an idea. The following projects are abstract and do not apply to the world of business. They give the students an opportunity to express themselves.

Here are a few examples:

- The Opposites Project. Good/Evil; Empty/Full; Ugly/Beautiful; Big/Small; Outside/Inside

- The ABC Project. Choose a pop culture event that interests you and create a video using the format of the ABC books of your childhood (i.e., The ABCs of Pie. A is for Apple Pie, B is for Blueberry, C is for Cherry, etc.). This project is no longer than two minutes and doesn't go further than A–F.
- The e. e. cummings Project. Choose a poem written by the poet e. e. cummings and create a video that is true to his poem in spirit.
- Nonsense Poetry of Lewis Carroll and Other Nursery Rhymes. Reinvent what nursery rhymes mean.

The following projects are related to possible uses of motion graphics in the business community.

- Cable Television Station Promo. I supply a list of cable stations (Comedy Central, Food Network, Sci-Fi Channel, etc.) and students produce a ten- to twenty-second promo.
- Title sequence for a new James Bond Movie based on *The Man with the Red Tattoo*.
- Choose a vintage movie and create a promo for it for Turner Classics or AMC Channel (e.g., *Maltese Falcon*).
- The two-minute mini-documentary. Choose an animal that you are interested in and tell something about it; or choose a person that you are interested in and tell something about him; or choose an aspect about New York City that you are interested in . . . etc.

The class projects are designed to give the students three to four diverse samples of work so that they will graduate with a reel of work that is considered well crafted, interesting, entertaining, personal, and quirky (unique).

## outcome

After completing this course, the students are equipped with all the skills that are needed to work in the field, but more importantly they have, in a disc, a few fine examples of the way they understood the experiment of "designing in a new dimension" with this new digital palette.

COURSE TITLE: Senior Graphic Communications
TEACHER: Beckham Dossett
FREQUENCY: One Semester
LEVEL: Senior
CREDITS: 3
DEGREE: Bachelor of Fine Arts in Graphic Communications
SCHOOL: University of Houston, School of Art, Houston, TX

## summary and goals

This is an introductory course to motion graphics for senior-level graphic design majors who have a strong foundation in typography and print design. The course instructs students in the use of motion-effects software, the design of typography for motion applications, and the development of short narratives. The first three weeks of the semester integrate the fundamentals of motion software with the principles of kinematics, both of which are then applied to the animation of type. As students gain technical proficiency, they develop original content for two longer projects. First, they look inward and realize a personal narrative. Second, they work on a practical project in which they create a fictional broadcast channel and its animated identification.

Outcomes: Students will become familiar with motion-effects software and learn how to use typographic motion and short visual narrative as methods of communication.

Technology: After Effects, Photoshop, Illustrator, iMovie

## week by week

**WEEK 1.** During the first two class periods of the semester, project 1 is introduced and students work in class learning the After Effects interface. Homework assignments include reading "Electronic Typography: The New Visual Language" from pages 105–110 of Jessica Helfand's book *Essays on Graphic Design, New Media, and Visual Culture.*

**WEEK 2.** Project 1 is viewed and critiqued in class. Project 2 begins. Technical instruction in After Effects continues with a focus on controlling motion with keyframes.

**WEEK 3.** Project 2 is viewed and critiqued in class. Project 3 begins. Technical instruction continues with an introduction to sound in After Effects. *The Way Things Go* is viewed in class. This film, by Swiss artists Fischli and Weiss, portrays a bizarre Rube Goldbergian chain of events that employs some of the physics principles introduced in project 1.

**WEEK 4.** Project 3 is viewed and critiqued in class. Project 4 begins. Reading pages 28–37 and 112–126 from *The Body in the Mind* by Mark Johnson is assigned as homework and discussed in the following class. *La Jetée*, a film by Chris Marker, is viewed during class. The film is made entirely with still photographs, yet conveys a sense of filmic motion.

**WEEK 5.** Critique of project concepts and storyboards by each student. Read chapter 3, "Blood in the Gutter," on pages 60–93 and chapter 4, "Time Frames," on pages 94–117 from *Understanding Comics: The Invisible Art* by Scott McCloud.

**WEEK 6.** Critique of refined project storyboards by each student. Read chapter 6, "Show and Tell," on pages 138–161 from *Understanding Comics*.

**WEEK 7.** Critique of working video projects by each student. Students have photographs and sound placed in After Effects.

**WEEK 8.** Critique of working video projects by each student. Students have text placed in After Effects. The typographic motion is sketched out in the software.

**WEEK 9.** Critique of working video projects by each student. Videos are near completion.

**WEEK 10.** Project 4 is due and critiqued in class. Project 5 begins. Reading pages 1–8, 31–42, 73–99, and 101–131 from *The Brand Gap* by Marty Neumeier is assigned as homework.

**WEEK 11.** Students present ideas for their fictional channels. At the end of the week, each student has selected and named his channel.

**WEEK 12.** Students work on avatars (animated logos) for the channel.

**WEEK 13.** Students continue working on avatars and present storyboards for the videos.

**WEEK 14.** Students place all elements in After Effects.

**WEEK 15.** Students continue working in After Effects.

**WEEK 16.** Project 5 is due and critiqued in class.

# assignments and projects

## Project 1: Motion

Learning to create and control motion in video-effects software begins by understanding kinematics, the branch of physics that studies the effects of mass, force, and velocity on objects. Watch selected chapters from the DVD series *The Video Encyclopedia of Physics Demonstrations*, and make one sixty-second video that uses simple geometric shapes to demonstrate the following principles: constant acceleration; Atwood's Machine; angle, velocity, and distance; and collisions of equal and unequal mass.

## Project 2: Motion and Type

Carl Stalling composed and orchestrated music for Looney Tunes cartoons during the middle of the twentieth century. Select one of the tracks from the CD *The Carl Stalling Project: Music from Warner Bros. Cartoons 1936–1958* and list fifteen to twenty words that you think of while listening to it. Select one word from your list and animate it without sound according to the following principles of typographic contrast: size, case, weight, and letterspacing.

## Project 3: Motion, Type, and Sound

Return to the list of words you generated in project 2. Select three or four words and animate these using forty-five seconds of sound from your chosen musical track. Key typographic movement to sound, vary pacing, and instill your animations with a sense of the narrative suggested by Stalling's music.

## Project 4: Personal Narrative

In his book *The Body in the Mind: The Bodily Basis of Meaning, Imagination, and Reason*, Mark Johnson states that image schemata are recurring patterns with which we structure our experience of the world. Without them, our experiences would be chaotic and incomprehensible. He provides the following examples of the verticality schema up/down: We stand upright, we climb stairs, and we experience water rising in the bathtub.

Johnson goes on to show how we use the verticality schema to structure our understanding of quantity through metaphor. For example, "the price of fish goes up" and "the stock market falls." "More" is *up*, not *down*. Why? Johnson claims our everyday bodily experiences reinforce this interpretation of direction.

Johnson's theory of image schemata is simple—so simple, in fact, that we are unaware of ourselves actively engaging in image schemata. For example, everyone in the senior class is engaged in the path schema. Each of you started from point A, freshman year of college, and are metaphorically traveling to point B, a college diploma.

Choose one of the following examples of image schemata from Johnson's text: cycles, balance, or paths. Make a one-minute video that communicates how this image schema is realized in your life. The experience you choose to explore may be serious, banal, or humorous. Use still images, sound, and motion typography.

## Project 5: Broadcast ID

The proliferation of television channels demands that consumers quickly discern the difference among the visual identities of broadcast brands. Color, sound, and avatars (animated logos) are design elements that quickly alert viewers to their location as they surf the mediascape.

Define a specialty broadcast channel that you would like to watch. Name the channel, design an avatar for it, and design one, ten-second or two, five-second animations that incorporate the avatar and function as broadcast identifications.

## recommended readings

Helfand, Jessica, *Screen: Essays on Graphic Design, New Media, and Visual Culture*, Princeton Architectural Press, 2001.

Johnson, Mark, *The Body in the Mind: The Bodily Basis of Meaning, Imagination, and Reason*, University of Chicago Press, 1990.

McCloud, Scott, *Understanding Comics: The Invisible Art*, Harper, 1994.

Neumeier, Marty, *The Brand Gap*, New Riders, 2003.

## recommended viewings

Fischli, Peter, and David Weiss, *The Way Things Go*, VHS, First Run Features, 1987.

Marker, Chris, "La Jetée," in *Short Dreams*, DVD, Warner Home Video, 2000.

*The Video Encyclopedia of Physics Demonstrations*, DVD, The Education Group, 2000.

a process-oriented approach
to all types of designing,
which has met with much success
with both students and professionals,
and is particularly relevant to movement design

impetus    movement designers
all through the ages
have moved to express
on all types of "stages"

234

for movement design is
the whole potpourri
of subjects and objects
alive and quite free
expressing through movement
for all to see
the nature of being
the need to be "me"
to put in a phrase—
choreography

caution    the moment you begin
to think of yourself
as a choreographer—
your designs
will begin to dance

prerequisites    a willingness to move and be moved in a space with your
fellow students

some facility in the medium in which you will be working, or a
willingness to learn a simple animation program and/or simple
video recording

raison d'être    the movement designer's process
and the choreographer's process

have many similarities,
since both create movement-based design

to be a truly creative and effective movement designer,
movement has to be the primary expressive/communicative element

to design affective movement, you have to move,
and to feel the kinesthetic and emotional components
of that movement in your body

mimetic devices (from mirrors to motion capture) lead to mimicry
and demonstrations of technical prowess—
rather than emotionally compelling affective representation

transforming the felt experience into a physical movement,
which preserves the flow of body energy,
may lead toward abstraction

if the quality of movement feels alive with the flow of the creator's
body energy,
then the entire work will feel alive—and this feeling sense can
then become
a visceral, palpable body experience for the willing viewer/participant

through using your body to initiate and develop your ideas,
you will start sensing movement design as "performance"

focus      a process of designing
using the transformation of body energy
into feeling-motivated expressive movement,
in any medium capable of providing the illusion of movement

aim      to empower the movement designer
to create truly affective movement-based design
by adapting relevant attitudes and principles of
that other movement-based design known as choreography

method      the creative process of discovery-development-performance has
seven steps:
*becoming* (the character/object/environment/idea)
*moving* (as the character/object/environment/idea might—if it could)
*feeling* (the emotion provoked by moving as expressively as possible)
*transforming* (body energy and feeling into doodles/movement
sketches/concept)
*concepting* (based on body energy and feeling)
*developing* (based and dependent on maintaining the flow of body
energy and feeling)
*executing* (while maintaining the flow of body energy and feeling)

this design process is applied specifically to movement-based design

through an exploration of the fundamental principles and elements of movement

| teaching tools | lectures, demonstrations, discussions, crits,<br>body-awareness exercises, environmental-awareness exercises,<br>emotional-awareness exercises, insight-development exercises,<br>physical/kinesthetic floor-based movement exercises,<br>movement visualizations and improvisations,<br>film/video/photo/illustration/graphic design examples |
|---|---|
| result | emotionally compelling movement-based design<br>that provides the willing viewer/participant<br>with a visceral, palpable experience |
| notes | you may use any medium capable of creating the illusion of movement for your assignments (animation, live-action film/video, motion graphics, interactive multimedia, etc.)<br><br>all feeling-motivated movement studies may be based on any character, object, environment, or idea<br><br>if you wish, you will be taught a simple animation technique for movement sketching and/or a simple movement sketching technique with video<br><br>you can use "frame movement" as an expressive movement in any medium<br><br>if you are using any type of movement-recording device for movement sketching, it must be used as an extension of your body<br><br>all class sessions begin with a movement warmup and assignment crit, and end with relevant film/video screenings<br><br>movement sketches and movement studies are executed in black and white, without sound<br><br>students must wear loose, comfortable clothing—<br>which allows for complete freedom of movement—<br>to every class (women must wear pants)<br><br>shoes will be removed during all class sessions |
| week 1 | introduction (why move? what is movement/choreography?)<br>body-awareness exercises<br>movement floor exercises |

236

movement vs. motion
movement vs. mime
the creative process: discovery (*becoming/moving/feeling/transforming*)
sketching movement (on paper/in a movement medium)
historical antecedents (still/moving "sketches")

*assignment*: choose two different characters/objects/environments/
ideas, and then, using the creative process outlined in class, do a
series of movement sketches for each (both on paper and in at
least two different movement mediums)

week 2    discussion and review of creative process: discovery-development-
performance (focusing on *transforming/concepting/developing/
executing*)
discussion and review of movement sketching techniques
movement and the power of abstraction
movement and stillness
the moving shape/form
mass/weight
movement floor exercises
the movement study

*assignment*: two feeling-motivated movement studies, each of
which makes a statement or communicates an idea (one must be
abstract/nonrepresentational; one must emphasize stillness as a
positive element)

week 3    energy/force (internal/external) (active/passive)
energy/force exercises
momentum
single/multiple bodies/objects/environments/ideas
energy/force improvisations

*assignment*: a feeling-motivated movement study that makes a
statement or communicates an idea, emphasizing energy/force as
an expressive element

week 4    line (internal/spatial)
line exercises
dance
line improvisations

*assignment*: a feeling-motivated movement study that makes
a statement or communicates an idea, emphasizing line as an
expressive element

week 5     space (internal/external) (open/closed) (empty/full)
environmental-awareness exercises
scale
distance/depth
negative space
figure-ground ambiguity
space and line
animating/activating space
space improvisations

*assignment*: a feeling-motivated movement study that makes a statement or communicates an idea, where the moving forms interact with an undifferentiated, yet dynamic, space which has been animated/activated by the moving forms

week 6     moving compositions
group-movement floor exercises
structure
tension
counterpoint
moving composition improvisations

*assignment*: a feeling-motivated movement study that makes a statement or communicates an idea, made especially potent through the nature of its component and overall compositional structures

week 7     time/rhythm (internal/external)
body rhythms–awareness exercises
environmental rhythms–awareness exercises
tempo
momentum
continuity
structure
visualizing rhythm
time/rhythm improvisations

*assignment*: a feeling-motivated movement study that makes a statement or communicates an idea, made especially potent through the simultaneous use of at least two different visual rhythms

week 8     working with a partner (designer-mover/facilitator)
learning by facilitating
designer-mover/facilitator partnering exercises

*assignment*: with your partner, take turns facilitating each other in the discovery and development portions of the creative process we have been using, as you each create a movement study of your choice

| week 9 | movement design as "performance" |
|--------|----------------------------------|
| | "putting on a show" |
| | pacing |
| | dramatic ebb and flow |
| | climaxes |
| | "stage" presence |
| | personality/charisma |

*assignment*: create a movement design of your choice as a fully developed performance piece

| week 10 | the sound of movement |
|---------|----------------------|
| | sound creation exercises |
| | expressive movement from expressive sound |
| | movement/sound improvisations |

*assignment*: create an extended movement/sound interaction in the context of a performance piece, where the feeling and the communication come especially from the nature of the interaction (do not use any music)

| week 11 | putting it all together |
|---------|------------------------|
| | concepts |
| | clients |
| | audience |
| | choosing an appropriate medium/venue |

239

*final project*: a fully developed and executed piece inspired by and utilizing the processes and concepts explored in the class, produced in any format, on any subject you wish (due week 14)

*assignment*: complete the discovery process for your final project

| week 12 | evaluation of processes/concepts for final projects |
|---------|---------------------------------------------------|

*assignment*: complete the development process for your final project

| week 13 | evaluation of development of final projects |
|---------|---------------------------------------------|

*assignment*: complete the performance process for your final project

| week 14 | presentation and evaluation of final projects |
|---------|----------------------------------------------|

bravo!

| postscript | when in doubt |
|------------|---------------|
| | make a move |
| | from inside out |

# section5

## graduate

**COURSE TITLE:** Motion Graphics: A Workshop

**TEACHER:** Christopher Dooley

**FREQUENCY:** One Semester, once a week for three weeks

**LEVEL:** Senior/Graduate

**CREDITS:** 3

**DEGREE:** Bachelor of Fine Arts

**SCHOOL:** California Institute of the Arts, Valencia, CA

## summary and goal of class

Have you ever tried communicating with someone who doesn't speak the same language as you do? How do you get them to understand? Generally, you gesture and pantomime to act like the idea or thing you're trying to say. Down to the smallest nuanced piece of information, you become very animated. You are using denotative information to express meaning. Why, when we watch two desk lamps interact, are we able to figure out that one is the parent and the other the child? It's not only that there's a big one and a small one, it's also clear by watching the dynamics of their relationship and their behavior.

## class projects

When the significance of the word is removed and the letterform is treated as a character, it becomes the sole responsibility of the animation to communicate its meaning. The goal of this project is not to illustrate the emotion with the letter (i.e., the letter "F" in the shape of a smile) but rather to animate the letter or letters to express that emotion, as though it were auditioning for a part as a performer in a play. Ideally, this would be a one-person show, without props or other actors. Nothing else should detract from, or modify, the behavior your character is acting out.

It is also important that you have a good idea of how you plan to execute the final animation. How you choose to do it should be based on your individual skill sets or interests. Whatever you feel the most comfortable using is acceptable: After Effects, Maya, cell animation, photography, or film. The technique you use for your animation is not important, as long as it communicates.

The final animation will be no longer than twenty seconds and presented on DVD. The piece should stand alone and the emotion should be clear without any additional explanation from its author.

# object of class projects

The primary function of language is communication. But what happens when language fails you? Imagine your native tongue consists of only a single character from the alphabet and you need to convey an emotion to someone who doesn't speak the language. Using only animation, you must make him understand what feeling you are trying to communicate.

# week by week

**WEEK 1.** Present your letter/character and the emotion you plan to animate. In coming up with each of these, consider a back-story for your character. Why is it behaving the way it is? It will make finding ways to animate it easier and may lead to a more nuanced performance.

Ideally your presentation should be in the form of sequential storyboard frames, either digitally created or hand drawn. If not, please have a detailed written treatment prepared.

**WEEK 2.** Present work in progress during scheduled one-on-one reviews with the instructor. This should include animation as well as a clear vision of how the final project will be executed. During this review we will discuss design elements as well as animation and editorial decisions.

**WEEK 3.** Final presentation will take place at our studio in Hollywood, and the final pieces will be presented to my partners who will be expected to understand the emotion of your animation. Students will then be expected to discuss their projects both conceptually and formally. All materials should be burned to a viewable DVD for final presentation and archiving.

# recommended viewings

Oskar Fischinger: *www.oskarfischinger.org*
Any Pixar film or short
Harold Lloyd films

**COURSE TITLE:** Motion Graphic Design

**TEACHER:** Christian Hill

**FREQUENCY:** Spring Semester

**LEVEL:** Senior/Graduate

**CREDITS:** 3 (six studio hours)

**DEGREE:** Bachelor of Fine Arts

**SCHOOL:** California State University, Fullerton, CA

## course description

This course is an introduction to motion graphics and film editing for animation and for very short productions, such as movie trailers. The course focuses on convincing special effects, effective storytelling, and attractive visual communication.

**Objectives.** This course is an introduction to the history, logic, artistry, and production of motion graphics, special effects, and editing for short productions. It is foremost about storytelling through images over time with digital tools. This upper-level course should be an opportunity for students to become efficient creators of near-professional motion graphics and visual special effects and to become able editors. Three fronts will be emphasized: solid storytelling, compelling aesthetics, and technical proficiency.

**Prerequisites.** Digital Illustration (ART 363B), Computer Assisted Graphics (483E)

**Methods of Instruction.** Lectures, in-class exercises, critiques, videos

## grading

Semester projects (2): complex composited shot (20 pts.), movie trailer (40 pts.)
Week-to-week homework: 20 pts.
In-class work: 10 pts.
Participation and punctuality: 10 pts.

Factors observed for grading: effectiveness of storytelling (structure, sequence, mood, timing, etc.), aesthetics, technical skills, conceptual and technical daring

# projects

## Complex Composited Shot

Using film footage or recording your own, add and remove visual elements that will redefine and heighten the storytelling in the given shot (the integration of your work onto the footage must be elaborate and perfectly convincing, so plan and polish every aspect down to reflected lights and cast shadows).

## Movie Trailer

Using either of the last Golden Globe–award winners, create a movie trailer no longer than ninety seconds. It must express the film genre and tell enough of the story to excite the audience, but not so much that they will not be left wanting to see the full movie.

## Homework Projects

They include a variety of assignments such as, but not limited to, turning a drawn animation storyboard into an animatic, converting an existing song into a "remix," formatting video and audio content for playing in different formats (DVD, Web, etc.), and so on.

244

# week by week

**WEEK 1.** Lectures: Introduction to motion graphics design and SFX
In-class practice: review of important Photoshop and Illustrator skills for this course

**WEEK 2.** Lecture: Review of animation fundamentals
In-class demonstrations: introduction to After Effects for animating
Homework due: viewing of two movies for movie trailer (project 2); viewing of fifty or more movie trailers

**WEEK 3.** Lecture: Compositing techniques
In-class demonstrations: advanced After Effects animating
Homework due: animatic; composited shot (project 1) concepts in storyboard format

**WEEK 4.** Lecture: Film fundamentals (shots to lighting for storytelling)
In-class demonstrations: compositing and masking with After Effects
Homework due: creation and collection of visual assets for composited shot (project 1)

**WEEK 5.** Production work in class
In-class demonstrations: advanced After Effects
Homework due: rough version of composited shot (project 1)

**WEEK 6.** Lecture: Movie trailer design and structure
   In-class demonstrations: introduction to Final Cut Pro
   Homework due: final version of composited shot (project 1)

**WEEK 7.** Lecture: Sound fundamentals
   In-class demonstrations: sound editing and control in Final Cut Pro
   Homework due: concepts and structure descriptions (in writing) for movie
trailers (project 2)

**WEEK 8.** Lecture: Editing styles and fundamentals
   In-class demonstrations: editing with Final Cut Pro
   Homework due: song remix

**WEEK 9.** Lecture: Story structure
   Homework due: selecting music tracks and sounds for movie trailers (project 2)

**WEEK 10.** Production work in class

**WEEK 11.** Lecture: Marketing fundamentals
   Homework due: rough version of movie trailer (project 2)

**WEEK 12.** Production work in class

**WEEK 13.** Production work in class
   Homework due: improved version of movie trailer (project 2)

**WEEK 14.** Production work in class

**WEEK 15.** Production work in class (polishing the final version of the movie trailer)

**WEEK 16.** Turn in a DVD with all the semester's work and a MiniDV with projects
1 and 2
   Final critique

# health and safety

In the context of computer use:

- Give your eyes a break: gaze away from the computer frequently.
- Give your hands and arms a break: take them off the keyboard periodically and stretch.
- Give your body and mind a break: get up, stretch, step away from your work, and come back with a clear mind.

# recommended readings

Cotta Vaz, Mark, and Craig Barron, *The Invisible Art: The Legends of Movie Matte Painting*, Chronicle Books, 2004.
McKee, Robert, *Story: Substance, Structure, Style, and the Principles of Screenwriting*, Regan Books, 1997.

Meyer, Trish, and Chris Meyer, *Creating Motion Graphics with After Effects*, CMP
    Books, 2004.

Taylor, Angie, *Creative After Effects: Animation, Visual Effects, and Motion Graphics
    Production for TV and Video*, Focal Press, 2001.

## art materials/supplies

External storage (10 gigabytes or more)

One MiniDV tape

Five blank DVDs

Ten blank CD-ROMs

COURSE TITLE: Introduction to Motion Design

TEACHER: Karen Zimmermann

FREQUENCY: One Semester, once a year

LEVEL: Senior/Graduate

CREDITS: 3

DEGREE: Bachelor of Fine Arts/Master of Fine Arts in Studio Art

SCHOOL: University of Arizona, Tuscon, AZ

## summary and goals

This course is an introduction to motion design. Students work with text, image, audio, and motion to create communication pieces. Projects include research, historical, process, and technical components.

Outcomes: Understanding of the production and creation of time-based design.

Technology: After Effects and Flash are the motion programs used. Students also use programs such as Photoshop and Illustrator. Hardware varies from project to project.

## week by week

**WEEK 1.** During the first week, time is spent introducing the objectives and goals of the course. Examples of time-based design work are shown and discussed in terms of similarities and differences between time-based work and two-dimensional design. Introductions between students and faculty are made.

**WEEK 2.** This week is an overview of After Effects software and methods of working and an introduction to the first assignment, Place. This assignment bridges two-dimensional composition, in-camera work, and adding motion.

Screening of Chris Marker's film *La Jetée*.

**WEEKS 3–4.** Continue working in class on production. These weeks continue an overview of vocabulary and technical aspects of file management. Individual critiques of work in progress. Introduction to audio techniques.

**WEEK 5.** Critiques of project 1, Place. Quiz on vocabulary.

**WEEK 6.** Introduction of project 2, Exquisite Corpse, and student assignments into teams.

Screening of the surrealist film *Andalusian Dog* by Salvador Dali and Luis Bunuel.

**WEEK 7.** In-class production and individual critiques. Students develop rough sketches, mind maps, and strategies to working in teams.

Introduce research project.

**WEEK 8.** Groups present storyboards to the class, showing how they will develop the piece. Outline of responsibilities is due.

**WEEK 9.** Discuss readings. Revise storyboards. Work in teams in class.

**WEEK 10.** Critique of group projects. Each team presents work and describes process and methods. Feedback from class.

**WEEK 11.** Introduction to project 3, students choose either Poetry in Motion or Title Design. Some students can elect Title Design and work with a Media Arts, BFA candidate who has a film for his or her senior design project.

**WEEK 12.** Research presentations. Each student will present research and discuss.

**WEEK 13.** Present storyboards. Production time in class to develop poetry/film sequence.

**WEEK 14.** Production time in class to develop poetry/film sequence. Individual critiques with instructor. Revise storyboards with changes.

**FINAL EXAM.** Presentation of poetry/film sequence. Discussion in class of work. Final closing statements of class. Collect digital files from class.

# assignments and projects

## Project 1: Sense of Place, Photography and Motion

> *America is a country made of places; not just the places marked by road signs and maps, but also the less tangible but no less meaningful places forged in the crucible of memory, longing, and desire.*
>
> *—Thelma Golden*

Starting with a camera, please document a place. It could be about something that happened there, completely fictional, a feeling, or a metaphorical place. Your story will be developed from your photos. You may need to go back and reshoot if you are missing information.

You will want to sketch or write what the place is and what you will need to shoot. Sketches, notes, diagrams, whatever methods work best to help you develop your shot list.

After you have finished shooting, make $3 \times 5$ inch cards and attach them, end-to-end, in a horizontal strip with tape. Twenty-four frames only. Fold your story strip in accordion fashion and bring it to class for discussion.

Consider *La Jetée* and the use of still images.

Optional: Use of audio and/or titles.

Vocabulary: keyframe, frame count, in-between, stop-motion, rotoscoping, time code, aspect ratio, frame, shot/clip, scene, sequence, video compression (codec), frames per second (fps)

## Project 2: Exquisite Corpse (Surrealist-Informed Animation)

Surrealism is a cultural, artistic, and intellectual movement oriented toward the liberation of the mind by emphasizing the critical and imaginative faculties of the "unconscious mind" and the attainment of a state different from, "more than," and ultimately "truer" than everyday reality: the "sur-real," or "more than real." For many surrealists, this orientation toward transcending everyday reality to reach one that incorporates the imaginative and the unconscious has manifested itself in the intent to bring about personal, cultural, political, and social revolution, sometimes conceived or described as a complete transformation of life by freedom, poetry, love, and sexuality. In the words of André Breton, generally regarded as the founder of surrealism: "beauty will be convulsive or not at all." At various times individual surrealists aligned themselves with communism and anarchism to advance radical political and social change, arguing that only transformed institutions of work, the family, and education could make possible a general participation in the surreal. More recently some surrealists have participated in feminist and radical environmentalist activities for similar reasons.

*Exquisite corpse (also known as "exquisite cadaver" or "rotating corpse") is a method by which a collection of words or images are collectively assembled, the result being known as the exquisite corpse or* cadavre exquis *in French. . . . The technique was invented by surrealists in 1925 and is similar to an old parlor game called Consequences, in which players wrote in turn on a sheet of paper, folded it to conceal part of the writing, and then passed it to the next player for a further contribution.*

*The exquisite corpse game is played by a group of people who write a composition in sequence. Each person is only allowed to see the end of what the previous person wrote. The name is derived from a phrase that resulted when surrealists first played the game,* "Le cadavre exquis boira le vin nouveau." *("The exquisite corpse will drink the new wine.") While initially sentences were constructed using the method, poems and stories were later also written using it.*

*Later, perhaps inspired by children's books in which the pages were cut into thirds, the top third pages showing the head of a person or animal, the middle third the torso, and the bottom third the legs, with children having the ability to "mix and match" by turning pages, the game was adapted to drawing and collage. It has also been played by mailing a drawing or collage—in progressive stages of completion—to the players, and this variation is known as "exquisite corpse by airmail," or "mail art," whether the game travels by airmail or not.*

*Another theory on the name exquisite corpse is that this collaborative drawing version predates the writing version, and that the mismatched body parts produce what is referred to as the "exquisite corpse."*

*Some have played the (graphic) game with a more or less vague or general prior agreement about what the resulting picture will be, but this defeats the essentially surrealist nature of the game.*

*There have been variations on the original procedure, such as the exquisite corpse wang-dang-doodle—a type of very long, rearrangeable exquisite corpse invented by Ted Joans.*

*The game of exquisite corpse has been adapted to be played using computer graphics, the construction of surrealist objects, and even an adaptation to architecture has been proposed. The technique has also been used in making at least one Doom level, and at NYU in making films.*

*In music, the composers Virgil Thomson, John Cage, and Lou Harrison (among others) collaborated on Exquisite Corpse pieces, where each composer would only be privy to one measure of music.*

*"Totems Without Taboos," organized by the Chicago Surrealist Group at the Heartland Cafe in Chicago, Illinois, was the first exhibition of exquisite corpses in the United States.*

*The San Francisco Cacophony Society performed the exquisite corpse game using a theater full of people with banks of typewriters.*

250 Mysterious Object at Noon, *an experimental 2000 Thai feature film directed by Apichatpong Weerasethakul was inspired by the exquisite corpse game. The film, shot on 16 mm over three years in varied locations in Thailand, featured Weerasethakul (or assistants) soliciting improvised extensions to a scenario improvised by a woman appearing early in the film. Weerasethakul then assembled the results into a "feature film." ("exquisite corpse," Wikipedia)*

Team Assignments: Each group should have three students.

In Flash, or a combination of Flash and After Effects, create a piece that contains a nonsensical animation of the parts. (Each person participates.) Then at the end, as a team, compile the parts to a Shockwave file (SWF) movie.

Include in the beginning or end titles that explain the process of the surrealist game, the exquisite corpse. Use the premise of the game as a point of departure. The essence of this piece should leave the viewer with an idea of the game and the artistic movement. You are open to add examples of surrealist historical images and/or figures.

Images, type, and importing QuickTime movies all are OK.

Criteria and ideas to explore for this project:

- Teamwork (attendance, participation, effort)
- Documentation of ideas
- Storyboards
- Experimentation in animation

## Research Project: Motion Designer/Artist

Objectives: To define the motion design profession. To survey influential designers or artists and their work throughout history. To discover some of the philosophies, theories, and breakthroughs developed by these designers. To collect reference materials for future use.

Write a biographical essay about an influential motion designer or artist of your choice. The essay should cover specific innovations, breakthroughs, and/or discoveries made by this designer. Be sure to look at the designer's influences as well as whom this designer influenced. Compare and contrast this designer's style and philosophies with others of his/her time, as well as those that came before. You may give an overview of the time period in which this designer lived including influential historical and/or social events. You must include a bibliography for this essay that lists Web sites you researched, and at least one source must be a book or magazine article. This essay should be at least five pages, typed and double-spaced. The paper can include visuals; however, sources for the images must be cited.

Present your research to the class in a multimedia project to be designed as a PowerPoint presentation, Flash, or After Effects.

This presentation can include clips from movies or Web presentations of the subject's work. The presentation should be ten to forty minutes long.

Here are some possible artist/designer choices: Kyle Cooper, Pablo Ferro, Saul Bass, Hillman Curtis, Bill Viola, John Cage, John Maeda, Joshua Davis, Joel Baumann, Yugo Nakamura, Nam June Paik, RGA, Mathew Barney, or Gary Hill. Or you can make a suggestion—instructor's approval required.

Research books, periodicals, and the Internet for source material available for the above designers.

## Project 3a: Poetry in Motion

For this project you are to create an animation of a poem of your choice. Research a poet and pick a poem to use as your content. You may use images. Be prepared to talk about the poet and his/her work.

You must have an audio component for this piece.

Include the title, name of the poet, poem, and, at the end of the poem, a brief bio of the poet (this could be you).

Software is your choice.

## Project 3b: Title Design

For this project you are to create a title sequence working with a media arts student's project as discussed. You can work in teams if desired.

Objectives: Utilize what you have learned about timing, typography, audio, and time-based sequences to create an engaging animation.

Legibility is required.

Final format is a QuickTime movie turned in on a CD or DVD.

## recommended reading

Woolman, Matt, *Motion Design: Moving Graphics for Television, Music, Video, Cinema and Digital Interfaces*, Rotovision, 2004.

## recommended software technical guides

*Adobe After Effects Classroom in a Book*, Adobe Press, 2006.
Bolane, Anthony, *After Effects for Macintosh and Windows: Visual QuickPro Guide*, Peachpit Press, 2006.

## software

Flash, After Effects, and Photoshop

## useful web sites

*www.adobe.com/designcenter*
*www.adobe.com/flash*

COURSE TITLE: Type IV: Experimental Text for Screen

TEACHER: Tony Brock

FREQUENCY: Spring Semester, sixteen weeks, twice a week for
two hours

LEVEL: Graduate (Type I, II, III and permission of instructor prerequisite
for juniors and seniors)

CREDITS: 3

DEGREE: Master of Graphic Design, Bachelor of Graphic Design

SCHOOL: North Carolina State University, College of Design, Department
of Graphic Design, Raleigh, NC

## summary and goals

Type IV is an advanced typography course focusing on the range and role of time-based texts on screen. Screen-based typography is positioned as generally counter to the development of cinematic and televisual traditions in which both making and reading privilege image and spoken word. Students bridge narrative concepts of page and screen media by exploring distinctions between spatial text/image synthesis and time-based text/image mutability. The course makes distinctions among the use of words that label, list, and credit—as is the case in the majority of motion design—with experiences of reading a paragraph or page, or engaging in spoken dialog.

Temporal contrasts—continuity, modulation, and duration—are presented as a set of necessary fundamental concepts that draw from histories of the performing arts, literature, and perceptions of time passing in daily life. This study of temporal contrast does not begin with nor presume motion. From this perspective, students better understand how to exploit the nuances of duration before compounding their explorations with motion.

Continuity and modulation are discussed as the building blocks of temporal structure and narrative presentation. Experiences of sound, motion, gesture, and the interplay of projected light on the viewer in cinema are discussed in contrast to a range of experiences in graphic design, architecture, dance, music, and theater. Experimental practice is defined as generative, divergent, and challenging to established ways of reading, writing, and media use while relying on historical contexts, contemporary media studies, and collaborative speculation.

# week by week

**WEEKS 1–3.** Discussion focuses on a formal gradient of time and space for use by designers in a range of media. This helps students digest the vast possibilities of choreographing image, text, and sound in time and motion. Temporal contrasts are defined. Screenwriting methods are discussed and explored. *Understanding Comics* (Harper, 1994) and *The Language of New Media* (MIT Press, 2001) are reprised from prior courses in imaging and new media. Assignments one and two are developed simultaneously.

Questions:

- What is a "temporal sign"?
- How do we define when a "temporal sign" begins and ends?
- What are the shortest and longest durations of a film?
- What are the differences between simultaneous and sequenced presentation?
- What are the expectations of a filmic experience? How has this changed over the last hundred years?
- How have graphic design and film influenced each other?
- How has cross-media influence challenged approaches to typography and typographic design?

254

**WEEKS 4–6.** Experimental practice and modes of experimentation are defined while assignments one and two continue with additional iterations and approaches to process. Time and motion studies are translated into prints—books, maps, posters—which are, in turn, used as storyboards for additional movies. Moving between and synthesizing 2-, 3-, and 4-D media is encouraged. Pacing and larger temporal structures are discussed in terms of continuity and modulation. Graphic scores, musical notion, and sound are considered in detail.

Questions:

- What does it mean to experiment? How divergent is your design process?
- How do representations and experiences of time correspond with those of space?
- When do text and image become each other? How do we "read" text and image differently in time?
- How do text/image transitions alter experiences of reading and watching?
- How does music imply temporal structure? How do sounds function like text or image?

**WEEKS 7–10.** Students form working groups and begin assignment three. Projects one and two continue. Generating options collaboratively, improvisation, stage directing, acting, and capturing motion on video are the primary focus. *Mise-en-scene* is discussed and students further consider the conceptual differences between cinematic methods and practices with those of graphic design.

Questions:

- In contrast to animating with software in the box, what is it like to work on a physical set where motion, duration, and form can be manipulated "directly"?
- How does collaboration influence your range of considerations and production?
- What are the differences between painting with light in a dark space and inking a white page?
- How do 3-D environmental variables affect a filmic experience?

**WEEKS 11–12.** Students shift from generating and capturing motion with a broad range of environmental subtleties in front of the camera to digitally animating individual black or white pixels. Planer symmetries—rotation, translation, reflection—combined with qualities of motion are reviewed in detail at pixel scale. Anthropomorphic, mechanical, and an array of symbolic movement and gestures are considered. Change/mutation of individual letterforms in one word focuses attention on both multiple meanings of the word and nuance in individual definitions.

Questions:

- How do patterns build, maintain, and alter temporal and spatial structures?
- What are the differences between a cinemagraphic and a graphic image?
- What are the differences between spatial text/image synthesis and time-based text/image mutability?
- How can 2-D and 3-D spaces transition in and out of each other?

**WEEKS 13–16.** Assignments one through four are discussed as having primarily linear structures with prescribed durations in contrast to interactive texts with user-defined or user and designer–defined durations and primarily nonlinear structures. Interactive, CSS-formatted typography, and online reading environments are explored. Students conclude work on assignments one through five and reflect on the semester.

Questions:

- What general audience expectations and thresholds exist for reading online?
- What systems and conventions exist for reading online? How can they be exploited and/or subverted?
- How do we begin to collapse approaches to, and concepts of, print- and screen-based reading spaces?

- What distinctions remain among media types and the experiences one has with them?

# class projects

## Assignment One: Alternates in a System

Students design a range of base-seven bitmap typefaces and alternates for characters in each face. They test screen readability while further exploring italic, bold, expanded, and condensed variations in a range of base pixel counts. This assignment reminds students of the micro level and has them revisit many of their fundamental studies including form/counterform. A graphic system is underscored as one with set rules that include alternates and gradients of change. This assignment is further developed in the fourth assignment as students animate a conjunction set in their bitmap typeface(s). This further expands the notion of a typeface to one that is mutable over time and establishes a dialog about spatial and temporal modularity and patterning.

## Assignment Two: Constructing a Story

Students are given a dictionary page and a 3 × 5 inch index card with a window cut in it. The index card serves as a framing device and motion camera. Together the two pieces are used to sketch a range of stories and treatments. Several short films are designed with a focus on writing, syntax, reading speed, and the integration of sound. No additional texts or images are used as editing, cropping, degree of focus, and limited color controls are explored as ways of developing reading path and meaning. The integrity of the original dictionary page—its composition, intended use, "authority," and form—is maintained as much as possible. Students assess each other's work based on the original context of words on a dictionary page, the degree to which pixels have been modified, breadth of exploration/questioning, and the effect of the story and how it is told.

## Assignment Three: Analog to Digital, Digital to Analog

Working in groups, students generate a broad range of motion and light studies working back and forth from analog to digital means. Still and motion text are projected into, and onto, an array of surfaces, textures, and environments. Three-dimensional letterforms are constructed out of a range of materials—ice, paper, soil, liquid—and/or suspended in liquid. Sets are built, multiple light sources projected, and several hours of experimentation are recorded. In-camera and digital editing take place and the results are projected, mixed, and rerecorded. This cycle continues as control and synthesis of digital and analog approaches are refined. Students present group and individual edits.

## Assignment Four: Animating a Pixel

Using bitmap type designed in assignment one, students digitally animate a conjunction or correlative set of conjunctions. Several studies are designed in black and
white with and without sound. Scale change, transitions between black and white
grounds, and simulation of 3-D space via 2-D and 3-D means are considered.
Extended durations are encouraged to better explore the range of temporal modularity and patterning.

## Assignment Five: Interactive Page

Each student identifies a range of extended-length texts and considers their potential
treatment online. One text is selected and presented on one or more Web pages.
Typographic variables including motion and interactive properties are defined in CSS.
Students are required to work with browser conventions and "limitations," and to
exploit style sheets to the fullest. They are assessed on their ability to work efficiently
and creatively within these systems.

## Object of Class Projects

The assignments are meant to give students diverse, process-oriented entry points
into the subject. Once students address the outlined processes and/or approaches,
they are encouraged to combine and/or expand the scope of their projects. Many
projects run concurrently so contrasts can be identified and hybrid approaches
developed. Confidence working across a range of media is supported by healthy
discussion and exploration of technological, conceptual, and contextual issues. As
this is an experimental course, projects are both based on and assessed by the divergent range of results and questions they generate. To this end, and to better optimize a cross-media curriculum, each project integrates print design as both process
visualization and possible final artifact.

# conclusion

The course is designed to slow students down, have them reflect on their prior studies
in motion and time, expand their range of typographic exploration, and project the
future uses of text on screen.

# recommended works

## Books

Aitken, Doug, *Diamond Sea*, Book Works, 2000
Drucker, Johanna, *The Visible Word*, University of Chicago Press, 1997.

Friedel, Helmut, and Ulrich Wilmens, eds., *Moments in Time: On Narration and Slowness*, Hatje Cantz Publishers, 2000.

Hanson, Matt, and Shane Walter, *Motion Blur*, Laurence King, 2006.

Manovich, Lev, *The Language of New Media*, MIT Press, 2002.

McCloud, Scott, *Understanding Comics*, Harper, 1994.

Murch, Walter, *In the Blink of an Eye*, Silman-James Press, 2001.

Ruscha, Ed, *They Called Her Styrene, Etc.*, Phaidon Press, 2000.

Sim, Dave, and Gerhard, *Cerebus*, vols. 14, 15, 16, Aardvark-Vanheim, 2003–2004.

Triggs, Teal, *Experimental Type Design*, Thames and Hudson, 2003.

Wells, Paul, *Understanding Animation*, Routledge, 1998.

## Films

*Dogville*, Lars von Trier, 2003.

*Fast, Cheap, and Out of Control*, Errol Morris, 1997.

*Mirrormask*, Dave McKean, 2005.

## Music

Revueltas, Silvestre, *Sensemaya*, 1938.

258

COURSE TITLE: Design for Television: Graphic Design Using Time,
   Motion, and Sound
TEACHER: Bonnie Siegler
ASSOCIATE TEACHER: Andy Capelli
FREQUENCY: One Semester, once a week
LEVEL: First year MFA
CREDITS: 3
DEGREE: Master of Fine Arts, Design
SCHOOL: School of Visual Arts, New York, NY

The line between the still image and the moving one has blurred.
A good designer should be able to move seamlessly from one media to another.
Our class is designed to help you do just that.

# the work

The class is a semester-long project in which you, the students, are asked to create an identity for a new television channel of your own invention. This will be done through understanding the content of the channel, designing its logo, and ultimately producing three short image spots promoting the channel. This main assignment will be peppered with two smaller assignments (one to two weeks each) that will explore the different ways a designer is asked to solve problems using the moving image.

Show and tell: We will bring different work for you to see as often as possible. If there is something specific you are interested in, please tell us and we'll try to track it down.

# grades

Just so you know, grades are based on the quality and thoughtfulness of your work AND how hard you tried. This means: attendance, being prepared for every class, participating in the dialogue about the work of your fellow students, and making your work better from week to week. And it doesn't hurt if you are a teacher's assistant.

# teaching assistants

Who wants to be one?

# the main assignment

Make a few related things on videotape.

You are to conceive of a brand new network (unrestricted by its commercial value or viability). Whatever the content is (it can be as obtuse or as direct as you wish), it must be thought out thoroughly and realistically.

1. Conceptualize your channel. Be sure it is something you want to stay with for the entire semester.

2. Name your channel.

3. Write a comprehensive Mission Statement. This is a general description of the channel's purpose and personality. Start with a paragraph about the general goals and personality of the channel. Invent at least five programs that could air on the channel and are representative of the overall feel. Tell us about its scheduling (what happens when) and about the intended audience; essentially, who will watch it and why and when. This should all fit on one page. Keep in mind that we will refer back to this document throughout the semester, as though a client gave it to you.

4. Develop/design a logo for your channel. Consider its appearance in video (which is low resolution), the possibility for movement, and its flexibility for usage in your IDs. Most of all, consider how it communicates the personality of your channel.

5. Create three IDs/image spots (no shorter than ten seconds and no longer than twenty-five seconds each) for your network. These are like the business cards of your channel. They are designed to explain the personality of the channel and acquaint the viewer with the network's brand identity (the logo). You can and may use whatever medium best suits your idea (film, video, animation, stills, claymation, whatever). Music and sound design are a very important part of this kind of work. You will have to edit with music or sound design and voice-over as is appropriate.

6. There will be two critiques with people from the outside: one interim critique for input and opinions, and then the finished product will be presented to a group of critics at the final class. At this final critique, two DVDs with the work of the entire class on them must be delivered. This is a group project that will require everyone's cooperation. One of the DVDs goes to me and one goes to the department for the permanent archive.

There is no required reading, although we do recommend that you start watching television with an eye on station identifications (which usually take place at the top of the hour), the personalities of the channels, and how well (or badly) they communicate their message.

# small assignment number 1

(1 week)

Make something on videotape.

We are supplying you with twenty-one short tracks by They Might Be Giants. You are to choose one of these tracks and create a video piece with it. The content is completely up to you. You can illustrate the music or just use it for rhythm as a background to your visuals. You can use footage from anywhere or no footage at all. Shoot it yourself, rent it from a video store, download it, or tape it off of your television.

# small assignment number 2

(1 week)

Make something else on videotape. This time we are supplying you with the text: a fortune.

You will be given a fortune cookie and then you will create a video piece with it. You must incorporate the text from the fortune in some way, but you do not have to photograph or re-create the actual fortune cookie fortune on that little piece of paper. In other words, write it out yourself or use whatever typeface you like or have someone say it!

What you do next is completely up to you. It can be an all-typographic piece or a narrative piece with the fortune as the title or as the conclusion. You can use footage from anywhere or no footage at all. Shoot it yourself, rent from a video store, download it, or tape it off of your television. And don't forget about sound design.

261

COURSE TITLE: Film for Graphic Designers

TEACHER: Jeff Scher

FREQUENCY: One Semester, five consecutive Mondays

LEVEL: Graduate

CREDITS: 1

DEGREE: Master of Fine Arts in Design

SCHOOL: School of Visual Arts, MFA Designer as Author, New York, NY

## synopsis

We will screen a wide variety of films and discuss them in the context of graphic design, visual perception, and sense of invention. The mechanics of the medium will be explored and hopefully demystified. A sense of the historical evolution of motion graphics from the early days of cinema to the present will build a deeper appreciation of motion graphics' lesser sung heroes and the techniques of the media that preceded today's digital.

262

The primary assignment will be to create a flipbook and "film" it via iStopMotion. The short film will be composed of sequential frames in the style of animation and then filmed, edited, and, in the final class, presented on screen in a class "festival" of finished films.

## week by week

**WEEK 1.** A brief history of early film and an exploration of the nature of persistence of vision. Films screened will include films by George Méliès and the Lumière Brothers, also Hans Richter's *Ghosts Before Breakfast, Richter on Film* (a fourteen-minute video interview conducted by Cecile Starr), Oskar Fischinger's *Allegretto* and *Walking to Berlin*, Max Fleischer's *Bimbo's Initiation*, and more!

**WEEK 2.** Film as time travel; the screen as window. Screenings include Walter Ruttman's *Berlin: Symphony of a Big City*, Francis Thompson's *NYNY*, and Joris Iven's *Regen*. Additionally we will look at ten rolls (two and a half minutes each) of assorted home movies from the 1920s through the 1960s.

**WEEK 3.** Montage and the communication of ideas with picture vocabularies. Literature vs. music as models. Vertov's *Man with a Movie Camera*, Frank Mouris's *Frank Film*, and Warren Sonbert's *Friendly Witness* will be screened.

**WEEK 4.** Experimental film and the personal vision. One person; one film. Poems in celluloid. Films by Maya Deren, Mary Ellen Bute, Bruce Baillie, Kenneth Anger, Stan Brakhage, Harry Smith, Jonas Mekas, Robert Breer, Peter Kubelka, and Jeff Scher will be viewed.

**WEEK 5.** Our flipbook iStopMotion festival (presentation). Screening of Alexander Calder's *Circus*. (A reward and a surprise film.)

# recommended readings

Gregory, R. L., *Eye and Brain (The Psychology of Seeing)*, 5th ed., Princeton University Press, 1997.

Livingstone, Margaret, *Vision and Art (The Biology of Seeing)*, Harry N. Abrams, 2002.

**COURSE TITLE:** 2-D Computer Animation

**TEACHER:** Myra Margolin

**FREQUENCY:** Three times a week for ten hours per week

**LEVEL:** High school (mixed level)

**PROGRAM:** After School Matters, Chicago, IL

## introduction

This course is part of an apprenticeship program in which teenagers are paid to study with working artists in order to acquire professional arts skills.

The session will consist of six major exercises/projects, each of which is designed to teach apprentice artists a specific skill set:

**1. Create a story.** Working with several distinct, preexisting Photoshop elements, apprentices must alter the different elements over time (through change in position, rotation, scale, and/or transparency) to establish relationships between them or form a very basic narrative.

Real world application: This uses similar skills to those required of an entry-level digital animator and will serve as an introduction to After Effects.

Screenings: Introduction to After Effects through viewings of: *Blue's Clues*, film/TV titles (e.g., *Desperate Housewives*, *Intolerable Cruelty*), and a clip from Lotte Reiniger's cut-out animation

**2. Experimental Film.** Using color- and shape-based experimental animated films as models, apprentices will manipulate solid shapes in After Effects with the goal of evoking a specific tone or emotion.

Real world application: This will serve as an introduction to the creation of experimental or abstract work.

Screenings: Norman McLaren (*Begone Dull Care* or *Lines Horizontal*), Len Lye

Show examples of work by Rothko, Mondrian, Miro, etc., to prompt discussion on how emotion and tone are expressed through color and shape.

**3. Bouncing Ball.** A classic animation exercise, the bouncing ball task will expand apprentice artists' capabilities in After Effects and introduce them to fundamental animation concepts.

Real world application: An understanding of the principles of animation is vital to the creation of good animation. The biggest flaw in bad animation is motion that looks stiff, computerized, or unrealistic due to a lack of application of basic animation principles.

Screenings: Early animation, *Felix the Cat*, *Dumbo* (clip), *Duck Amuck* (to contrast Disney and Warner Bros.)

Handout: Preston Blair on animation timing from *Cartoon Animation* (Walter Foster, 1994)

**4. Documentary.** An audio documentary will be provided as a starting point (this will be created by teens in an After School Matters video program). Using the Oscar-winning animated film *Frank Film* as a model, apprentice artists will create a moving photo collage to illustrate the provided audio. Each apprentice will be responsible for a particular segment of the documentary. Two advanced apprentices will "produce" (coordinate) the project.

Real world application: Because animation as a medium is so time consuming, it is almost always a collaborative process requiring many people to complete a single project. This task will give apprentices experience with creating one element of a larger piece, reaching collective decisions regarding the look and tone of the piece, and remaining within predetermined aesthetic parameters.

Screenings: *Frank Film* by Frank Mouris

**5. Rube Goldberg.** Working in small groups, apprentices will conceptualize, draw, and animate a "Rube Goldberg" machine. (Rube Goldberg was a Pulitzer Prize–winning cartoonist who created inventions in his cartoons that made simple tasks amazingly complex, for example, a ten-step contraption for sharpening a pencil.)

Real world application: This project will provide an introduction to storyboarding and the production process. It will allow apprentice artists to strengthen and build upon their After Effects skills while requiring them to work closely as a team to take a project from conception through to implementation.

Screen: "The Cog" Honda commercial, clip from *Joe's Apartment* by John Payson (to accompany hand-out of storyboards from same clip)

**6. *Le Merle*.** Using animator Norman McLaren's short film *Le Merle* as a model, apprentice artists will create a collaborative "exquisite corpse" project.

The parameters for this project will be defined by *Le Merle*: a story told through the movement and combination of simple white shapes on a black background to create characters, settings, etc. Students will be given a few basic shapes to work with and will be required to create a picture from these shapes and then transform it into the picture of the person sitting next to them.

Real world application: This project will provide a first opportunity for apprentice artists to express themselves artistically through digital animation. It is similar to the work of an independent animator but also has relevance in the commercial world.

Screenings: *Le Merle*

*contributors*

**Frank Armstrong** earned his MFA in graphic design from Yale University. His professional work has been published in numerous journals and books, including *Baseline* magazine, Rob Carter's *American Typography Today*, Steven Heller's *The Education of a Typographer*, and *Meggs' History of Graphic Design* by Philip Meggs and Alston Purvis. Frank is a senior lecturer at California State University, Chico (*www.csuchico.edu/~farmstrong*), and a member of AIGA, ATypl, and the International Institute for Information Design.

**Danielle Aubert** earned a BA from the University of Virginia and an MFA from Yale University. She has worked in New York, Moscow, and Detroit. She teaches at the College for Creative Studies and is a freelance graphic designer for the Museum of Contemporary Art Detroit. Her book, *Sixteen Months Worth of Drawing Exercises in Microsoft Excel*, was published by Various Projects in 2006.

**John Barton**, creative director and client services manager of Sight Creative in Minneapolis, attended the Minneapolis College of Art and Design and the University of Minnesota, graduating with a BA in applied design and visual communications from the University of Minnesota. He then attended the University of St. Thomas where he earned his MBA. John teaches Principles of Usability at the College of Visual Arts in St. Paul as an adjunct faculty member. He spent ten years as a creative director at Internet Broadcasting, and in 2006 he also joined the creative team at Sight Creative, *www.sightcreative.com*.

**Ravinder Basra** has over seven years of teaching experience within art- and design-based courses in the United States; he is currently a coordinator/assistant professor of graphic design at the University of San Francisco. His specific areas of interest are design for the Web and motion graphics. Most of his teaching practice involves getting students motivated and developing ideas and concepts for a variety of projects through experimentation, sketchbook development, and critiques at various phases of a project.

**Carl F. (Skip) Battaglia** has been making personal animated films that are screened worldwide for thirty years. He is professor in the School of Film and Animation at Rochester Institute of Technology, where he teaches a variety of graduate and undergraduate production, animation, and historical courses.

**John Bowers** is an associate professor in graphic design at Oregon State University. He earned BFA, MA, and MFA degrees in design from the University of Iowa and studied at the Basel School of Design. He has taught at the Corcoran College of Art and Design and Stanford University, and worked professionally as a senior identity designer at Landor in San Francisco. His work has been published in the *AIGA Annual, Communication Arts, Graphis, I.D.*, and *Print*, and he is the author of *Introduction to Two-Dimensional Design: Understanding Form and Function* (Wiley, 1999).

**Tony Brock** joined the North Carolina State faculty in 1999 and has taught serial and sequential imaging, experimental typography, and interaction design. His interests include cross-media education and online information spaces for distance and face-to-face learning.

**Laurie Burruss** is a professor of design at Pasadena City College where she teaches Flash, Dreamweaver, Director, After Effects, and interactive multimedia design. She is also director of the Pasadena City College Digital Media Center (*http://www.pasadena.edu/dmc-pcc/*) and partner/collaborator in interactive multimedia with Warner Bros, Inc., Disney Imagineering, Industrial Light & Magic, Cinesite, Gnomon, Lynda.com, Macromedia, Apple, Corel, Siggraph, and Newmediacenters.org. She was the recipient of the 2005 Macromedia Innovation Education Award in Digital Communication, the Award for Excellence in New Media by the New Media Consortium, and the 2004/05 Board of Trustees Performance/Lecture Award for Outstanding Teacher.

**Peter Byrne** is an associate professor in the School of Design at the Rochester Institute of Technology in Rochester, New York. His teaching includes courses in interactive design, Web design, and time-based design.

**David Cabianca** teaches graphic design at York University in Toronto, Canada. He holds master's degrees from Princeton University, Cranbrook Academy of Art, and the University of Reading (UK), and has written for *Emigre*, *IDEA* magazine (Japan), and *Design Issues*.

**John Canemaker** is an animator/filmmaker whose twenty-eight-minute short *The Moon And The Son: An Imagined Conversation* won an Oscar for Best Animated Short of 2005. He is the author of ten acclaimed books on animation history (including *Winsor McCay: His Life and Art* published by Harry N. Abrams in 2005) and a full professor and the executive director of the animation program at New York University's Tisch School of the Arts Kanbar Institute of Film and Television.

**Jay Chapman** is an educator, creativity consultant, movement mentor, curriculum developer, graphic design historian, and film historian. He is principal of the Los Angeles–based creative consultancy *movementsoundspacetime*. Since 1978, he has been teaching at Art Center College of Design, where he created the seven-course foundation curriculum for the original Movement-Based Design track. (jchapman@artcenter.edu)

**Tracy Colby** has taught Drawing and Composition, and Color and Design, and is currently teaching Media in Motion classes in the Digital Media Department at Otis College of Art and Design. The Media in Motion classes are the introduction to the world of motion design for students who will work in various areas of the entertainment industry and advertising. With an MFA from Syracuse University, Tracy is a practicing digital printmaker, has studied and worked in Europe, and exhibits her digital prints internationally.

**Cliff Cramp**'s work in illustration includes background painting for animation, storyboard and visual development art for feature film and television, and editorial and book illustration. He is an associate professor in illustration and illustration area coordinator at California State University, Fullerton. He instructs classes in traditional and digital illustration, and painting with a focus on narrative illustration.

**Ferris Werbin Crane** is an associate professor in Media Arts at Robert Morris University. Her research focuses on perceptual and aesthetic choices in context of historical and contemporary technology and culture. Ms. Crane's interdisciplinary and transdisciplinary research has been funded by the National Institutes of Health. Her design work has appeared in design magazines, annuals, and exhibits in the United States, Europe, and Japan.

**Christopher Dooley** is cofounder and creative director of National Television (*www.natl.tv*). Building his reputation as a motion graphics director, he leads National's creative direction on commercial productions for Honda, Coca-Cola, and iTunes. As numerous awards celebrated his design work, the Art Center graduate expanded his creative reach by exploring storytelling, writing, and directing animated spots for British Airways, Orange UK, and Volvo. As an experienced live-action director, he has also helmed music videos for Hilary Duff, Jewel, and the Scissor Sisters, as well as many other artists.

**Beckham Dossett** is an associate professor of graphic communications at the University of Houston where she teaches print design and motion typography. In addition, she maintains Small Project Office, a design practice.

**Graham Elliott** graduated from the Royal College of Art, London. He was an art director at the advertising agency Saatchi and Saatchi, designed record sleeves and directed music videos for the rock band Living Colour, and illustrated for the *New York Times* op-ed page. He has directed commercials for Sprint, Coca-Cola, and Trinidad tourism and made pop promos in Japan for Ami/Yumi Puffy. His latest incarnation is as documentary director. He worked with Martin Scorsese on a Bravo special and completed a feature documentary, *Greyhound to Cuba*, shooting extensively on the island. He teaches music video at the School of Visual Arts, New York, and runs his production company, Optic Nerve (*www.opticnerveny.com*).

**Christian Hill** has freelanced as an illustrator and computer graphic artist for clients such as the Smithsonian and Disney since 1995. As an aficionado of comic art, he encourages its practice through courses, workshops, and events, and he promotes its appreciation through presentations and scholarly publishing. He is working on graphic novels for children and adults, and he is a pioneer in the field of gallery comics. Students in Hill's Motion Graphic Design class have won twelve nominations and four awards in the *Hollywood Reporter* Key Art Awards.

**Catherine Jo Ishino** is an Emmy and Peabody award–winning video graphic designer and art director who worked in the television news business from 1981 to 1994. She began her career at CNN in Atlanta, then moved to NBC and ABC News in New York, and was art director of The MacNeil/Lehrer NewsHour from 1983–1994, as well as creative director at Globalvision. In 1995, Ishino was recruited by Michigan State University with a "Distinguished Fellowship" to attain her MFA in graphic design. Afterward, she became a tenured associate professor at the University of Minnesota, Duluth, where she taught for nine years. Currently, Ms. Ishino is working toward her PhD in Communications and Culture at Ryerson University in Toronto. *www.catherineishino.org*.

**Wojtek E. Janczak** is an associate professor in the department of design at York University in Toronto (*www.yorku.ca/janczak/*). His multidisciplinary professional practice, research, and teaching include interactive media, exhibitions, and signage systems design. Since 1994 he has specialized in developing and evaluating information architecture, interface design, and interactive systems. His current research focuses on time-based visual communication, interactive environments, and information spaces.

**James Kenney** is the principal of InterStitch Films (*www.interstitch.com*), a motion graphics and design film studio, which produces films and designs titles and animated graphics for dramatic and documentary projects. Film projects to which

Jim has contributed have been honored by prominent international film festivals and organizations, including the Sundance Film Festival and the Academy of Motion Pictures. In addition, Jim is cofounder and codirector of SF Shorts: The San Francisco International Festival of Short Films and was a mentor at the 2006 and 2007 Cannes Film Festivals.

**Doug Kisor** is the chair of the Graphic Design Department at the College for Creative Studies. He has been a guest speaker at numerous conferences and educational programs. Professor Kisor is the past president of the AIGA Detroit Chapter and a past member of the Graphic Design Education Association National Board. Examples of his work have been published in numerous design publications including *AIGA Annual*, *Typography Now Two: Implosion* (Booth-Clibborn, 2001), *Print*, and *ACD 100*.

**Joel Lava** graduated from Northwestern University with degrees in film and anthropology. After several years in Chicago film production, he transitioned into graphics, which took him to Industrial Light & Magic and then down to Los Angeles's motion graphics industry where he is a design director.

**Sarah Lowe** is an associate professor of graphic design in the School of Art at the University of Tennessee. Her design interests focus on developing educational experiences using digital media. Prior to teaching, she worked for several years in the interactive department of WGBH, Boston's public television station.

**Brian Lucid** holds the positions of associate professor and Graphic Design Program Coordinator at the Massachusetts College of Art and Design where his teaching spans from traditional communications in static and dynamic media to computational design and physical/digital interfaces. He also serves as one of the core faculty members at the Dynamic Media Institute, a graduate program focused upon design research at the intersection of technology and communication. Brian sat on the steering committee for the AIGA Design Education Community of Interest from 2005–2007 and previously served on the board of directors of the fourth largest AIGA chapter in the United States.

**Myra Margolin** is a PhD student in community psychology at the University of Illinois, Champaign-Urbana, where she is studying youth media and participatory video practices.

**Phil McNagny** is a 3-D artist living in New York. He got started as an animator on Nickelodeon's *Blue's Clues* and moved on to work as an animator/rigger for the 3-D component of Disney's *Little Einsteins*. In 2006 he was the assistant director for Nickelodeon's *The Backyardigans*. He is a full-time instructor in the Maurice Kanbar Institute of Film and Television Animation Program at New York University, where he teaches introductory, intermediate, and advanced 3-D courses at the undergraduate level.

**Isabel Meirelles** is an assistant professor in graphic design at Northeastern University in Boston. Her scholarly work examines the fundamentals underlying how information is structured, represented, and communicated in different media. Her research has been disseminated in journals and conferences. Her professional experience includes working as an architect and urban designer, as a chair of museum departments, and as an art director in publication and interactive design.

**Jeffrey Metzner** is an art director, graphic designer, television commercial director, painter, creative director of Metzner Productions, head of the motion graphics department at the School of Visual Arts, and author and illustrator of *STICK: Great Moments in Art, History, Film and More . . .* (Clarkson Potter, 2006). His clients include: Prudential, Minute Maid, Nabisco, Coca-Cola, Citibank, Chrysler, McDonald's, Xerox, Loco Soda, New York State Lottery, and Dr. Pepper. He has been published in *Film Comment, Millimeter, Backstage, GQ, Pulse, Art Direction, New York* magazine, *Look, Women's Wear Daily, Travel & Leisure,* and the *Guardian Weekend.* Metzner has received a Gold Medal from the Art Directors Club, the Gertrude Romm Levy award at The New School University, and awards from CLIO, ANDY, Effie, The One Show, Graphis, and the Cannes Film Festival.

**Jeff Miller** is a multidisciplinary graphic designer. After receiving an MFA from Cranbrook Academy of Art he worked on print projects and interactive content at April Greiman's Los Angeles studio. Later, at Imaginary Forces he was responsible for concepts, art direction, and designing motion for feature films and television. In addition to his current full-time work on broadcast, packaging, promotion, environmental graphics, and motion design projects, he teaches Sound + Motion at the Kansas City Art Institute. He received an Emmy nomination for HBO's *Band of Brothers* main title design and was recently selected for inclusion in the Type Directors Club Annual and exhibit.

**Hajoe Moderegger** graduated from the Bauhaus University, Weimar and collaborates with Franziska Lamprecht as "eteam." Their videos have been featured in exhibitions and screenings at the P.S.1 and Eyebeam in New York City, Transmediale Berlin, MUMOK in Vienna, the Museo Nacional Centro de Arte Reina Sofia in Spain, and the 11th Biennale of Moving Images Geneva. He is an assistant professor at the art department of the City College of New York where he teaches video and new media.

**Mike Nguyen** has been involved in the field of feature animation productions since 1988 and primarily as an animator. He has also instructed Character Animation at the California Institute of the Arts since 1994. In 2000, he cofounded July Films and began his independent journey *My Little World*, a traditional animated feature soon to be released.

**Matthew Normand** is a former designer from Prologue Films and Organic Online. He taught at the College for Creative Studies in Detroit and Ringling College of Art and Design in Sarasota. He is currently at the University of South Florida in St. Petersburg. He has received awards from the Type Directors Club and Art Director's Club and has been featured internationally in "Earthquakes and Aftershocks," a traveling exhibition of California Institute of the Arts posters.

**James Pannafino** is an assistant professor at Mercy College within its computer arts and design program. He teaches courses in graphic design, interactive design, animation, and game design. Before teaching at the college level, James worked as both a graphic and interactive designer in the professional field. His research interests include design fundamentals, motion design, and narrative and visual storytelling.

**Chris Perry** is an educator and filmmaker currently living in Northampton, Massachusetts. He has worked as a programmer and technical director at Rhythm & Hues Studios in Los Angeles and Pixar Animation Studios in Emeryville, California. He is currently employed as an assistant professor of Media Arts and Sciences at Hampshire College. His primary interests are in computer graphics and visual storytelling—particularly the intersection of the two.

**Chad Reichert** is an assistant professor at the College for Creative Studies. He teaches time-based media, typography, and visual communications. Chad has lectured on typography and his work has been exhibited throughout the United States. He received his undergraduate degree in graphic design from Valparaiso University and his MFA in graphic design from the Minneapolis College of Art and Design.

**Liisa Salonen** is principal of multidisciplinary design firm Elevator and designs in a variety of applications from print to new media. She has directed projects for culture, architecture, education, entertainment, technology, and pharmaceutical markets. Salonen is concurrently adjunct professor of design at the College for Creative Studies in Detroit and writes about design and typography.

**Louise Sandhaus** is the former director of the graphic design program at California Institute of the Arts (CalArts) and has her own design office, LSD (Louise Sandhaus Design, *www.lsd-studio.net*), a multifaceted practice centered in graphic design that frequently collaborates with other disciplines to realize innovative projects. Louise's work is in the permanent collections of the San Francisco Museum of Modern Art and the Bibliothèque nationale de France, Paris. Her work and writing have appeared in numerous publications including *Step*, *Print*, *Eye*, *Metropolis*, and *Emigre*, and her work has been recognized by AIGA 365, the Art Directors Club, and the American Center for Design, among many others.

**Jeff Scher** is an experimental filmmaker and animator who has taught at Columbia University, New York University, SUNY Purchase, and Bard College, and currently at the School of Visual Art. His films were described by the *New York Times* as "optical joyrides." They are in the permanent collections of the Museum of Modern Art, the Academy Film Archives, and the Guggenheim Museum.

**Heather Shaw** is a full-time lecturer at the University of Massachusetts, Dartmouth; her emphasis is on teaching design for motion and dynamic media. She is the creative director for Nieshoff Design in Lexington, Massachusetts, and currently serves as education director for the Boston Chapter of AIGA.

**Bonnie Siegler**, who teaches in the MFA Designer as Author program at the School of Visual Arts, founded Number 17 in the summer of 1993 with her partner, Emily Oberman. The company is a multidisciplinary design firm working in television, film, and print, and on the Web. Some recent work includes the collateral for the National September 11 Memorial and Museum; the title sequence for *Saturday Night Live*, the identity and advertising for Air America Radio, and the ongoing advertising and design for New York's River to River Festival. Other clients include IAC, Condé Nast, Nickelodeon, NBC, MTV, HBO, Hyperion, The Mercer Hotel, and the MGM Grand in Las Vegas. *www.number17.com*

**Amy C. Smith** graduated with a BFA from the University of Wisconsin, Stout. After joining Alpha Video as a multimedia designer, she went on to help found Internet Broadcasting in 1996 where, as senior art director, she designed award-winning Web sites for NBC, Hearst Argyle Television, Cox Television, Post Newsweek Television, and the Web sites for NBC's online coverage of the Athens and Torino Olympics. She is an adjunct professor at the College of Visual Arts in St. Paul, Minnesota, teaching Principles of Usability.

**R. Brian Stone** teaches visual communication in the Department of Industrial, Interior, and Visual Communication Design at The Ohio State University. Professor Stone's research is concerned with the creation of screen-based forms that enable interaction. These forms are manifested into products such as kinetic typographic messages, Web sites, and interactive multimedia presentations. He is the author of several articles on the subject and has presented his research at a number of international venues.

**Barbara Sudick** earned her MFA in graphic design from Yale University. Her design work, as a principal in a Connecticut interdisciplinary design/photography firm, has received numerous national and international awards and has been published in several design journals, including *Graphis*, *AIGA Annual*, and *Print*. She has presented her research at AIGA and international arts and humanities conferences. Barbara is an associate professor at California State University, Chico (*www.csuchico.edu/~bsudick*), and a member of AIGA.

**Scott Townsend** is an associate professor in the department of graphic design at North Carolina State University where he teaches new media, photography, and graphic design. His work is divided between academically-based research and electronically-based installation art, and other hybrid projects between different media and disciplines. For additional information see *www4.ncsu.edu/~sttwn/*.

**Martin Venezky** is the founder of Appetite Engineers (*www.appetiteengineers.com*) and author of *It is Beautiful . . . Then Gone* (Princeton Architectural Press, 2005).

**Al Wasco** currently teaches visual communication and design/interactive media at Cuyahoga Community College in Cleveland, Ohio. Before falling in love with digital media, he worked as a designer/typesetter for twenty years. His recent work can be found at *www.TheViewFrom32.com*.

**Karen Zimmermann** is an associate professor at the University of Arizona and has specialized in the graphic design and digital arts since the mid 1980s. She has worked in design, art, and animation using a predominantly digital process and has published and lectured extensively about the combination of art and technology and new media. She is on the board of advisors for the Journal of Book Arts (JAB) and is currently serving as area director of the Visual Communications Program in the School of Art.

*index*

277

279

281

285

# Books from Allworth Press

Allworth Press is an imprint of Allworth Communications, Inc. Selected titles are listed below.